ENCINA LIBRARY

ALSO BY RICK RIDGEWAY

The Shadow of Kilimanjaro
Seven Summits
The Last Step
The Boldest Dream

BELOW

ANOTHER

SKY

AN OWL BOOK

HENRY HOLT AND COMPANY | NEW YORK

Rick Ridgeway

BELOW
ANOTHER
SKY

*A Mountain Adventure in
Search of a Lost Father*

Henry Holt and Company, LLC
Publishers since 1866
115 West 18th Street
New York, New York 10011

Henry Holt® is a registered trademark
of Henry Holt and Company, LLC.

Portions of this book have appeared in different
form in the *Los Angeles Times Magazine, Backpacker*,
Summit, and the Patagonia catalog.

Library of Congress Cataloging-in-Publication Data

Ridgeway, Rick.
    Below another sky : a mountain adventure in search of a lost
father / Rick Ridgeway.
        p.   cm.
    ISBN 0-8050-6927-5 (pbk.)
    1. Ridgeway, Rick—Journeys—China—Tibet.
2. Mountaineering—China—Tibet.   I. Title.
GV199.44T55 R53   2001
915.1'50458'092—dc21   00-063219
[B]

Henry Holt books are available for special promotions and
premiums. For details contact: Director, Special Markets.

First published in hardcover in 2001 by Henry Holt and Company

First Owl Books Edition 2002

Designed by Paula Russell Szafranski

Printed in the United States of America

1   3   5   7   9   10   8   6   4   2

For Jennifer

I promise never to go above 8,000 meters

Contents

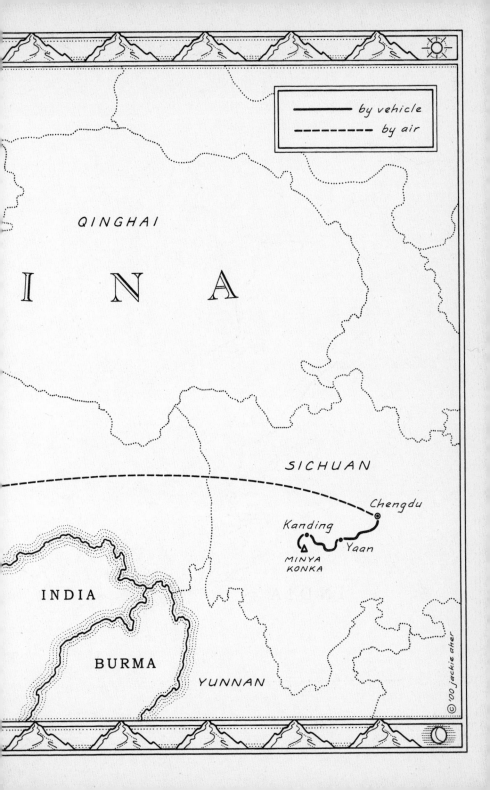

Prelude

*Journal Entries
October and November, 1980*

Minya Konka Base Camp

OCTOBER 14, 1980

I need to get this down while it's still fresh. It must have been nine-thirty by the time we got out of Camp 1 yesterday, but we all agreed that there should still be enough time to climb the fifteen hundred vertical feet to the next campsite, cache our loads, and get back before dark. I drew the first lead, postholing up the slope above camp. Then Kim took over, then Yvon. At noon we stopped next to a crevasse for lunch. Yvon bit off a piece of cheese, then turned to Jonathan. "Whenever you're on a glaciated section," he said, "always stop at the edge of a crevasse when you take a break. That way you'll know you haven't stopped on top of a hidden one. Same for setting up camps."

"Thanks," Jonathan replied.

Jonathan had asked us a few days earlier to give him pointers whenever we thought of anything, and Yvon is always obliging to anyone who wants to learn. We finished lunch and continued. Soon our options narrowed to a steep section of chest-deep snow, so we had no choice but to tackle it. I led and Kim followed. To get footing I had to pack the snow first by pressing my whole body into the slope, then my knee and finally

[3]

my boot. No matter how careful I was, I still knocked snow down on Kim.

"Sonofabitch. I'm getting buried."

"Sorry, I can't help it."

Kim looked up and grinned. "I wasn't cursing you. Just this snow flying down my collar."

I took another step and knocked down more snow.

"Sonofabitch."

I smiled to myself and kept going. In another hundred feet the snow firmed. In a clearing between clouds we could see just ahead an area of large seracs where the shifting glacier had cleaved into blocks. I stopped and studied our options.

"Two ways to go. Up the middle through the seracs, or off to the right."

"Looks a little better to the right," Yvon said.

While Kim moved up to take the lead, Jonathan stepped aside and took several photographs. I paid out rope, then followed Kim as he angled up the side of a serac that then turned into a long, steep slope. The heavy packs and thin air made the effort debilitating, but we maintained a steady pace. I tried not to look up but instead to focus on the steps in front of me, hoping I might achieve a kind of self-hypnosis.

"Heartbreak Hill," Yvon called out.

The rope on my waist went taut. I looked up, and Kim had stopped to wait patiently while I caught up. It was all I could do to match his speed, and he was the one punching the steps. I was tempted to unrope and go at my own pace, but there were still crevasses in the area. We had roped up earlier in the morning when we crossed the first crevasses above Camp 1. That was before we got into the soft snow, but footing had still been difficult, with about four inches of new snow over the older surface. Several times my boot skidded on the interior layer, leaving a streak through the new snow. In the back of my mind I knew this was avalanche potential. I wondered what Yvon and Kim thought, but if they were concerned they would have said something. Still, I noticed that whoever was leading stayed on the edges of crevasses, and close to the sides of seracs, avoiding whenever possible the wider slopes that might be dangerous.

Kim kept leading until the slope laid back, and I took over kicking steps for a long time. I was hypnotized: one foot up, breathe a few times, then move the next foot. I remember Jonathan yelling up, "Rick, you need relief?" Ahead I could see a flat spot on the edge of a crevasse, so I made that my goal.

"Thirty more yards."

When I reached the spot, I plopped down, leaned back on my pack, closed my eyes, and breathed heavily. The altitude was now over 20,000 feet, and I wasn't yet fully acclimatized. In a few moments Kim and Yvon arrived.

"Good effort," Yvon said.

Jonathan arrived. "Way to punch steps."

Kim just kept going, lifting his legs and pushing steps into the smooth snow. When the rope caught up, I had no choice but to peel off my shoulder straps so I could stand up, then saddle the heavy pack once more and start following. Ahead, in a glimpse between clouds, we sighted the top of the ridge only a hundred yards farther. The wind strengthened to thirty miles per hour, and the clouds now raced over the snow and again obscured our vision. Through another fleeting hole in the clouds I could see above that the best route was more to the side.

"Traverse left . . . to the crest . . . out of the wind."

In a few minutes we were on a flat bench sheltered in the lee of the ridge. We unshouldered our packs.

"Good place for the tents."

"Welcome to Camp 2."

We sat on our packs and had a second lunch, finishing our Fig Newtons and the last of our lemonade. Through brief windows in the occluding clouds we could see the ridge descending to a col and rising again to two higher summits.

"Must be Redomain and Dedomain," Yvon said. We had learned the names of these two peaks from reading an account of the 1932 expedition. The clouds opened further, and beyond we could see the yellow-green plateau, and once more I paused to consider our good fortune. The Chinese had just opened their doors to foreign mountaineers, and we were the first Westerners allowed into eastern Tibet since the 1932 expedition, fifty years earlier.

"Wuuwee" Jonathan said. It was his favorite expression, and even though he said it calmly—almost to himself—I knew it revealed his excitement because he had been saying it continuously since that day nearly a month before when we had first arrived in China. We turned and looked toward the summit ridge, now obscured in clouds. We had an idea what it looked like, though, from studying the 1932 photographs.

"Two more camps and we can make the summit," I said.

"Ten days, if we have luck with the weather," Yvon added.

We rested for a few more minutes, then, in the first clearing, picked up our empty packs and headed down toward Camp 1.

We made good time, slowing to test bridges over crevasses, or, as Kim preferred, to broad-jump them. In only a few minutes we were back at Heartbreak Hill. We down-climbed, belaying each other with our ice axes as anchors. When the angle eased, we decided to glissade. We slid down on our butts, one going faster than the other, laughing and yelling, the rope going taut, pulling one, then the other. I felt like a kid in a giant sandbox of snow. It seemed like only seconds and we were at the bottom and on our feet and continuing down in big jumping steps.

It went that way for another half hour. We were moving fast, and our spirits were high. We arrived at the hill above Camp 1. We could see below our three yellow tents, and on the trail through the snow leading into camp, three figures. We knew that would be Edgar, Peter, and Jack, moving up to camp. Harry was probably already there, in one of the tents. Everything was on schedule and according to plan.

We decided to make another glissade. Yvon went first, then me, then Jonathan, then Kim. I heard Kim give a whoop, and I answered with a yoo-hoo. I remember thinking that those guys coming up will get a kick out of watching us slide down.

Then it happened.

I was in Yvon's track, and I quickly gained speed. Snow built up around me and flew in my eyes. It was hard to see where I was going, but then I didn't need to see since Yvon was first and all I had to do was follow his track.

I remember my thoughts.

This is great, we'll be down in a few seconds. The rope is tugging on my waist, though. Yvon must be going awfully fast. But wait, he's first so he can't be going faster because he's making the track. That's funny. All this snow building up around me. There's too much snow. Something's wrong. We've got to be careful. Too much snow, and we'll load the slope. We have to stop glissading. Now, right now, stop! Stop! Oh my God, it's too late.

It was as if the snow all around me had started to boil.

Get off to the side. Quick. Stand up and run. Can't get up. You have to. Get up. Can't.

Then underneath me the snow seemed to explode.

No way to get out now. It will stop, just below the tents, has to. No, we're gaining speed. No, no. There's someone beside me. Jonathan? Kim? Can't tell. Someone yelling, "Oh, Christ, here we go!" Who was it? Kim? Jonathan? No, Kim. Start thinking. Think fast. We can't get out, but we still might stop. If we stop, I might be buried. Smothered. Remember what they say, "If you're in an avalanche, start swimming to stay on top." So try to backstroke. You're still on top, stay there. Backstroke, hard. It'll stop. Oh no, losing control. Can't, have to stay on top. No, I'm flipping.

I made a complete cartwheel, snow, sky, snow blurring across my vision.

Everything spinning. Tumble, up, down, up. Then in. Oh my God. I'm buried. Under the snow. Eyes open. White, everything still moving, moving fast. Curl up tight. Like you're supposed to do in a plane crash. Trap air in front, have an air pocket when it stops. That way I'll last long enough until those guys dig me out. Those guys in camp, they're watching. They'll know where we are and be right here. They'll dig. Air pocket, curl up. I'll make it. Look past my arms. Ice pulsing around me, like it's breathing. Must still be going fast, can't breathe. I need air. Spots in front of me, black and white. Am I still alive? I must be.

Then suddenly my face surfaced. I sucked air as fast as I could, then backstroked until my chest, then my knees, pulled out. Around me the snow was heaving and pulsing, as if it were alive and taking huge, deep breaths. To the side an outcrop sped by in a blur. Then in front, past my feet, I saw the slope steepen, then disappear over an edge. It was the cliff, the rock face below Camp 1, and it went several hundred feet down. Then I remember how suddenly everything slowed. I must have breathed deeply, and exhaled deeply, because I paused, and in that brief second I managed to calm my thoughts. I looked ahead and to the side as the whole slope of snow we were riding, the tons and tons of it, pitched into space, and I recall very clearly my next thought:

October 13, 1980. Thirty-one years old. Buried in Tibet.

*I*nside the snow again, curled up in the airplane-crash position. Something hits hard. Ice blocks punching my back, then my arm. Hard, hard on my arm. Am I dead? My arm hurts, pain. Am I being broken? I see myself as they dig me out, all rag doll. It's okay. Listen, mom, dad, brother, everybody. I know you love me and I love you but listen, it's okay, this isn't that bad.

Hit again. Still alive? Dead yet? Pain. I feel pain. Must be alive because I feel pain. I'm still buried. Open my eyes. Snow. Big ice blocks in front of my face, moving in and out, shifting ice blue shifting and moving. Any moment now, any second and that's it, one final blow.

Surface . . . I'm on top. Breathe, I can breathe. Suck in the air as fast as I can. Can I survive this? Maybe, so breathe fast, hard. If I go under again, I'll need it. Pull my arm out, good, now the other arm. Legs out. Pull hard, strain. Legs are out. Ice moving all around me, pulsing, breathing, moving fast. Roaring noise. To the side, rock cliffs whirring past. Must be in the gully, going down the rock face.

Think fast. On top, made it this far. I can make it. Maybe. Have to fight. Fight for everything, everything. Swim. Breathe fast, stay on top no matter what. Backstroke. Look, there's Yvon in front of me, right there. His head is up too. Stay on top, backstroke. Wait, it's slowing. The avalanche, it's stopping. It's stopped.

Get out. Can't move, the rope so tight on my waist, can't get out. Knife? My pack? Where is it? Oh my God, the snow, it's moving again. It's going to start again. No. Get out, quick, out, out. God no, here we go again. There's the lower cliff. We're heading toward it. God, I remember, it's a big one. We can't survive. Sliding slowly, toward the cliff. Pull, pull as hard as you can. This rope! Cliff getting closer, no, no! Not after we have stopped. No, no . . . wait . . . wait . . . it's slowing again. Slowing, slowing, slowing, it's going to stop, going to stop . . . it's stopped. Now get out, quick. Out of the rope. There, I can slip it off. Off my waist, slide the loop down my legs, over my boots. Okay, now go to the side, crawl if you have to, careful so the snow doesn't start sliding again. Probably have fractures, so go slow but quick. Slow and quick, like this. To the side, crawl, yes, keep going. To that rock. The rock is safe, off the snow. There, I made it. I'm safe. Okay breathe, breathe again, again. Alive. God, I'm alive . . . alive . . . alive. . . .

The strain on the rope as we each tumbled helter-skelter had widened the loop around my waist enough so I was able to slip it over my legs, then flee from the mass of ice blocks I was certain would start moving again, sliding toward the next cliff. When the avalanche had stopped the first time, then started again, I had lost hope. I felt cheated. I had accepted death, then had been given a reprieve, then was sentenced again, all in a minute or less. Now the ice had stopped a second time, and I feared it would again start moving, this time toward the cliff just in front of us, a cliff I knew would spell our end. I had struggled like a caged wild animal to remove the rope so I could crawl off the avalanche ice to the security of a rock I had spied a few feet away, at the edge of the jumbled ice.

Once on the rock I sat panting, unable to do anything until I caught my breath and the dizziness went away, anything except repeat to myself over and over that I was alive. I was certain to be injured, but where? I felt my legs, moving them carefully. Then my arms, my ribs, my back. Bruises, bad ones, but apparently no broken bones. I wasn't seriously injured.

What about the others? I looked over and saw Yvon, at an angle below me, thirty feet away. He was buried to the waist, but his arms were free and he was working slowly to free himself. There was blood running down his face. I looked up the narrow slope where we had stopped and saw Kim. He was staring back at me. Our eyes held, and I remember they were eyes like blue diamonds. At that moment he may have thought he was dead, or that maybe the ice was going to start moving again. His eyes had the look of an animal that knows it is about to be killed. There was blood on his face and blood trickling out of his mouth, staining his teeth. Then suddenly he screamed. It was an animal scream, and it made me look away.

Jonathan was closest, only a few feet from me, at the edge of the ice. He was head down, with the rope around his waist stretched tightly to where it disappeared into the snow that was now set hard as concrete. He was trying to say something, but I couldn't tell what it was. I didn't move, but continued to lie on the rock thinking that somehow we were all alive and we were all going to get out of this. When my breathing slowed, I realized I needed to think of what to do next. We were all alive, but the others seemed hurt. I wasn't hurt, and I needed to help them. Who first?

I looked again toward Yvon. He was still buried to the waist, and now he was leaning back on the snow as if he had given up trying to get out. Blood was running out the corner of his mouth. He still had his glacier glasses on. How could that be? Then I called to him, "Yvon, are you okay?" He turned and looked up at me but only stared, not saying anything.

"Yvon, are you hurt?"

"Where are we?" he said.

Kim screamed again, and I looked back at him. He was on one knee, struggling in a frenzy to stand up. Maybe he still thought the ice would move again. "I can't breathe," he yelled. Panic in his voice. "Get this rope off." He started pulling the rope where it disappeared into the ice. He pulled like a madman, screaming as he yanked on the rope. "I can't breathe!" Help Kim first, I thought.

I stood and made a few steps toward Kim, but then looked at Jonathan. He was moaning. "Jonathan, are you okay?" He mumbled something, but I couldn't understand him. Then I thought, Better help Jonathan first; his head's downhill, and he's having trouble breathing.

I bent down and looked in his eyes and said, "Jonathan, we're all alive. We all made it. Everything is going to be okay." Then I asked him where he was hurt, but he couldn't answer. Our eyes held for a moment, and I said, "Don't worry." I had to get him upright, but then I thought, Careful, he might have broken bones. Move him carefully. I reached under his head and tried to get my hand along his back in case it was broken. He was heavy, but lifting slowly I straightened him out. "Okay, buddy, that should be better." He still didn't answer, but we looked at each other and then I heard Kim scream again, "I can't breathe! The rope. Get the rope off." Kim was on his feet, charging against the rope like a wild animal against a leash, screaming. I looked at Jonathan and said, "Hang on, I've got to help Kim. He can't breathe. I'll be right back. Everything's okay."

When I reached Kim, I told him to stop pulling against the rope. "Can't breathe," he screamed in panic. "My back. I'm hurt. Can't breathe."

"Relax, relax. Take the strain off the rope so I can untie it."

Kim collapsed on his knees. I coaxed him to move a few inches, to relieve tension on the rope. But the knot was too tight to untie. I thought, Should I keep working on it, or help the others? How is Yvon?

I looked down. Yvon had nearly dug himself out, but he was again leaning back against the snow. He seemed dazed.

"Yvon, are you hurt?"

"What happened?" he said, looking up.

"Are you okay?"

"Where are we? What happened?"

I couldn't tell if he was seriously injured. I managed to untie the knot in the rope around Kim's waist.

"Okay," I told him, "now I've got to help the others."

I stepped across the avalanche debris to Yvon.

"Are you hurt?"

"I don't think so. What happened?"

"We were in an avalanche. Stay right here. I've got to help Jonathan."

When I got to Jonathan, I bent down to ask how he was doing. I looked in his face and felt my stomach tighten. His eyes had rolled back in his head. I thought, No, it can't end this way. We're all going to come out of this okay. I knelt close to his mouth. He wasn't breathing. I put my hand on his neck and felt his pulse. It was quick and strong. I thought, He's still alive. Have to get him breathing, fast. I held his head in my lap and placed my finger on his tongue and breathed into his mouth. Once, twice, three times. Nothing. Again, once, twice. Nothing. Then I saw his chest rise and fall. He started to breathe again. He's going to make it, I thought. Things will turn out okay. We're all going to get out of this alive.

Then the breathing stopped. I waited, but he had stopped breathing. I breathed into his mouth once, twice, and again he started breathing on his own. But there was a sound from inside his chest. I thought, No, no, this isn't going to happen. We've all got to come out of this okay. We're all still alive. It has to stay that way.

He breathed three times, and stopped, and I breathed again into his mouth. He breathed, stopped, I breathed into him, he started. His pulse was still strong. I had to keep him going until the others arrived. The others. Where were they? Edgar, Peter, Jack? They saw us go down, so surely they were right behind, coming down to help. They should have been here by now, though. Wait. Maybe the avalanche was so wide they had been swept away, too. They could be buried in this snow.

I stood up and looked around. Yvon was below, now on his feet, standing and staring at me. Kim was crawling off the ice, still crying in pain, blood trickling from his mouth. Our red rope wove in and out of the jumbled blocks of snow and ice like a string of intestine from a gutted animal. But no sign of anything else. I thought, If the others were in here, they're all buried. No, that couldn't be, because the debris isn't that thick. If they were here, I'd see some sign. So they must still be coming down.

I turned back to Jonathan and saw that he had stopped breathing again, and once more I started mouth-to-mouth. His chest would rise, fall, I would breathe in his mouth and his chest would rise, hold, fall, not move, then rise again on its own, fall, rise, fall . . . stop. I would watch, wait, then put my mouth again to his and start over. I kept my finger on his neck and his heart still beat. He stayed alive, and I kept hoping.

I looked up and saw that Yvon had walked over and was standing a few feet away, watching me administer to Jonathan. He was stiff and not moving, standing like a scarecrow. There was blood on his face.

"Are you sure you're not hurt?"

"What happened?"

"We were in a big avalanche, Yvon. We just fell fifteen hundred, maybe two thousand feet. I don't know, a long ways. We're all alive. But Jonathan is hurt bad."

"What mountain is this?"

"Yvon, go help Kim."

Yvon looked toward Kim who was now off the ice, lying on his side, doubled up and moaning.

"What mountain did you say this was?"

Yvon then started toward the place where he had been buried. I was afraid he would walk off the cliff that was only a few yards away.

"Yvon, don't walk around. Come over here; help Kim."

Yvon turned and started back my way, still in a daze. I needed more help. Where were the others?

"Help!" I shouted. "Down here. Help!" There was no reply, and I called again. Yvon was now standing nearby.

"Where are we?"

"Minya Konka, Yvon."

"Where?"

"Minya Konka, in Tibet, in China."

"What are we doing in China?"

I turned back to Jonathan. He had stopped breathing, so I resumed mouth-to-mouth, but each time I breathed into him there was that sound in his chest. I waited. His head rested on my knee. I moved my fingers through his hair and watched his face. His lips had lost color. All of a sudden his face paled, as though some part of his being suddenly evaporated. In less than a second he was different. I held him in my lap as I continued to slowly stroke his hair. I bent down and gently kissed him on the forehead, then set his head down and folded his arms on his stomach so he looked comfortable. Yvon stood watching. He didn't say anything, and I didn't think he understood.

"Yvon," I said, looking up at him, "Jonathan just died."

Konka Gompa Monastery
OCTOBER 16, 1980

We're back at the camp just below the ruins of the monastery. It's hard to believe we were here two weeks ago. It feels like two years, even longer. This morning it was clear, and I hiked up the hill above the ruins, through the rhododendron forest to a clearing where I sat alone and looked at the mountain. The scar from the avalanche was visible, and I could see we must have fallen at least fifteen hundred vertical feet, maybe two thousand. I could see the cliff we flew over, when I knew I was dead, and the place where the snow finally stopped. I could see the area where we piled the rocks over Jonathan's frozen body.

After Jonathan died, I knew I had to get help for Yvon and especially Kim. There was still no sign of the others from Camp 1. I knew they must be coming, but I couldn't wait for them. It made more sense to descend as fast as I could to alert Al and Dick in Base Camp.

I told Yvon one more time to stop wandering around and wait for me to get help. I took off, running as fast as I could, jumping from rock to rock. I stumbled once and skidded down scree. I lay at the bottom breathing hard, telling myself to slow down or I'd sprain an ankle. I was close to my limit, but whenever I thought I had to stop, I said out loud, "Kim needs help more than I need rest. Run." I must have said that ten times.

I reached the last scree above camp. Clouds had obscured the valley, and through the mist I yelled, "Help!" I descended farther, yelled again, and this time heard someone call back. I fell to my knees, strained to catch my breath, and looked up to see Dick and Al coming out of the mist.

"Avalanche," I said. "Just above Camp 1. Carried us down. Kim, Yvon . . . they're injured. Jonathan . . . Jonathan's dead."

"Slow down," Dick said. "What about Jonathan?"

"He just died."

"Are you sure?"

"Yeah, I'm sure."

Al arrived, and Dick said, "Sounds like we lost Jonathan."

"Oh God."

Dick and Al helped me back to camp, and then with calm thoroughness that must have come from his years in Vietnam as a field doctor, Dick questioned me about Yvon and Kim while he got his first-aid kit ready. In a few minutes they were gone, and I was alone in camp, standing outside one of the tents staring at the mountain through an opening in the building storm clouds, not certain if I was dreaming or if it all had really happened.

The others told me later that help arrived from two directions. Everyone in Camp 1 had witnessed the avalanche. They heard us and, looking out, saw us sweep by, looking like cork floats in river rapids as the snow slid past with a whooshing sound, then fell over the cliff below camp. Harry said the avalanche missed his tent by five feet.

At first, no one in Camp 1 believed any of us could have survived because below the cliff the avalanche had funneled into the gully and the angle didn't ease until nearly a thousand feet below. Still, they descended as fast as they could. They must have been close when I made my final call for help. It probably took them thirty minutes to get down, but to me it seemed as if hours had passed. Harry arrived first and found Yvon sitting and Kim curled up, just as I had left them. He examined Jonathan and found he was dead. Harry asked Yvon where I was, and when Yvon pointed over the cliff just below where the avalanche had stopped, Harry assumed I had been swept over the edge and was dead for sure. He didn't investigate because he judged it more important to attend to Kim and Yvon.

It wasn't much longer until those I had notified in Base Camp arrived. They placed Jonathan in a bivouac sack. Because the weather was building, they decided to send Yvon, who was regaining his senses, down to Base Camp with Harry as escort. Meanwhile the others pitched a tent on a nearby ledge and carried Kim inside. They planned to spend the night there, then get Kim down in the morning. As Yvon and Harry set out, the first thunder rolled down the valley, and through rifts in the cumulus they could see lightning illuminating the summit ridge on Minya Konka.

At Base Camp I stood alone outside the tents, watching the electrical storm. The undulating texture of the gray layer of quilted clouds that covered the sky lit with each flash. Thunder rolled down the glacier, and more lightning followed, then again the percussion of thunder. One of us was gone.

I crawled inside a tent, and I was lying down, curled up like a fetus, expecting to spend the night alone when Yvon arrived. I was immensely relieved to see him. With short, painful breaths he crawled inside the tent. He was out of his daze, and except for a few broken ribs, he wasn't injured. I put my arm around him and helped him to lie down. Harry brought tea and then left, and Yvon and I sat quietly sipping our brew. It was impossible to digest how quickly things had changed. It felt like somehow the nightmare would be shaken off, that we would wake up and again be the happy foursome that only hours ago had been descending the mountain, glissading and laughing at the end of a good day. We finished our tea and crawled inside our sleeping bags.

"Yvon, are you asleep?"

"No . . . not yet." His voice came from his throat, his words punctuated by painful breaths.

"Have you ever been with somebody who died? In your arms, in front of your eyes? So you could see them go?"

"I've seen dead people . . . never seen . . . anybody die in front of me . . . like that."

"I knew the second it happened. I was holding him, breathing in his mouth, checking his pulse from time to time. It stayed strong, about eighty a minute. Then this change, all of a sudden. It's hard to explain, but it was like an aura about him—I guess it was an aura—but whatever you call it, it disappeared. I knew the second he died. The split second. Then when this change overcame him, when he died, it wasn't like I was holding Jonathan anymore. It was like, it was . . . just like something that was dead."

It was difficult to talk this way. It felt as if I was making a cold analysis in place of the grieving I should be feeling. Yet I could not purge from my mind the image of that change I saw the second he died. I also had the thought that next morning, when everything started to sink in—when the grieving really did take hold—that this image of his dead body would wash away. So I needed to tell Yvon.

"Yvon, the second Jonathan died, something left him. I saw it."

Yvon didn't answer, but I knew he had heard me.

They brought Kim down in the morning on a jury-rigged litter. He was semicoherent and full of morphine. His skin was sallow, and the blood had dried on his lips and chin. His eyes were cloudy, like a milky glacial stream, and it was hard to believe that only hours earlier those same eyes had been blue diamonds. I bent down to say, "We made it, Kim," and he said, "We'll get out of this." Dick's field diagnosis was torn ligaments in the knee, injury and possible fracture to the back.

As soon as Kim was stable, we would begin the evacuation. There was no helicopter to call; we would have to go out the way we had come

in. Al sent word to have the porters come up and bring two poles to con-
struct a more substantial litter for Kim. Al also asked the healthy members of the team to dismantle Camp 1. As it was unrealistic to carry
Jonathan's body any distance, we all agreed that he should be buried at
the base of Minya Konka. Edgar and I would perform the burial the
next day.

Next morning at first light I left to bury Jonathan. The others would follow after breakfast. It was too early to have an appetite, so I took a small
sack of nuts and raisins. The sun was bright through a few scattered
clouds. I retraced the route I had made a few days before with Jonathan
behind me, remembering how we had exchanged smiles, acknowledging
without words our happiness to be in the high mountains.

I absorbed the colors of the rocks, the whiteness of the snow, the
blueness of the sky; everything was vivid. I stopped to snack on my nuts
and raisins. Sitting alone, I ate the food, one kernel at a time, tasting
each one I chewed, feeling each one as I swallowed, thinking how those
inert pieces were then being digested to nourish my moving, functioning
body. I imagined the chemicals breaking down the food, the energized
blood coursing through my body to the muscles. They were muscles that
I then commanded to cause my body to stand and continue climbing to
the site where my friend lay, his muscles now lifeless.

I arrived about an hour before the others. Jonathan was as I had left
him, but now covered with a blue nylon bivouac sack. I could see that his
knees were bent and his arms crossed over his chest, and he looked comfortable. I folded back the opening of the sack to touch his head, and
when I felt his hair, it took me back to that moment he died.

His pack lay partially under him where I had placed it to keep him as
warm as possible in those last moments. I opened it, looking for something to take back to his wife. I thought about her, wondering how long it
was going to take to send the news, and when it arrived, how it would
affect her and the little girl, too small to understand. I found his camera,

damaged but with the film intact, and put it in my pack. Then I saw his baseball cap. It had somehow stayed with us the distance of the avalanche. I remembered how he had worn that cap every day of the trip. I picked it from the avalanche debris, fingered it, looked inside. Sweat stains discolored the rim where he had marked with an ink pen his initials, a stylized monogram derived from a Buddhist mantra. There were also bloodstains from his wounds, so I wasn't sure I would ever give it to her, but I put it in my pack anyway, next to the camera.

Looking around, I noticed a rock promontory that stood out in relief from the slope, a sentinel over the plateau of Tibet. It was sloped, but I could see the slate stones were well suited for constructing a platform, so I began the task of building the grave. A short time later Edgar arrived, and in silence we worked together. When we broke out the flat stones from the slope, they had an earthy smell. When we set them in place, they struck with the sound of breaking pottery. Sweat beaded on my nose and dropped on my lips, and I could taste the salt. I stripped to my long underwear. Some of the others arrived on their way to dismantle Camp 1, but they stayed only a moment before moving on. As his closest friends, Edgar and I wished to build the platform ourselves. We were silently thankful to them for their sensitivity.

Al and Dick offered to help us place Jonathan's body on the platform. We lined up two to each side. His body was frozen through, and he was heavy. The footing was difficult up the steep slope to the platform. I had to ask the others to stop so I could switch sides. My left bicep was badly bruised, and no matter how hard I tried, it wouldn't agree to carry the weight. On the downhill side, I was able to get my shoulder under him. There was no wind, and I could feel sweat bead on my forehead.

As we stepped closer to the platform, I tasted salt on my lips, listened to the flat stones clink under my boots, felt the cold of Jonathan's body through the nylon resting on my shoulder. There was bright heat from the sun on one cheek of my face, and on the other shadow cool from the morning mountain air.

We laid him on the platform. His bent knees fit perfectly inside the slight curve of the tumulus. We began to cover him with more flat stones. That morning I had brought up two bamboo wands originally intended to mark our climbing route, and I also had the Buddhist prayer flags that had fluttered between the poles of my Tibetan-style tent. We planted the wands at the head of the grave, and then strung the prayer flags. Each flag was printed dozens of times with the mantra, "Om Mani Padme Hum," "The Jewel in the Heart of the Lotus." A slight wind set in from the west, and the flags fluttered gently. The breeze blew across the grave, carrying aloft, as the Tibetans believe, our prayers. We covered him, except for one small area on top, at his head, where we could see a swatch of the blue nylon.

We were silent. Then Edgar said, "Jonathan would have laughed at us standing here trying to say something." He paused, then added, "It's such an irony he died in the land that for so long had filled his dreams."

I stood across from Edgar, with Jonathan between us. I looked up and saw the great west-face glacier tumbling to the moraine valley, its meltwater beginning the journey to the Yalung, the Yangtze, the China Sea. The grave stood to the west, toward the valley's opening and the distant and mysterious peaks of Konkaling.

I said, "Each of us who knew him are in some ways improved. In his quiet way he always taught something to those who came close to him."

The swatch of nylon was still exposed. I looked across to see the scene of the avalanche, the hundreds of tons of snow blocks and littered here and there the remnants of our gear: broken packs, shredded parkas, crampons, an ice axe, a single mitten. And the red rope, weaving in and out of the avalanche debris.

Al and Dick left, and Edgar and I stood over the grave. We were silent. The only sound was the slight flutter of the prayer flags. Edgar reached down and touched the swatch of nylon, and I did the same. He then picked up a last stone and set it in place, and we both turned and descended to Base Camp.

Faria Beach, California

I drove Geri and her daughter, Asia, back to the airport today. During their three days here, I told Geri about the details of the avalanche, Kim's broken back and carrying him out on the jury-rigged litter, Yvon's concussion and broken ribs, and how I somehow got off with a few bad bruises. I told her about burying Jonathan on the promontory near the place where the avalanche stopped, and I gave her a photograph of the grave, with the prayer flags between the two bamboo wands.

I told her that the day of the burial I arrived before the others and sat next to Jonathan and rested my hand on him, and after a while I noticed his billed cap in the snow. I asked her if she would like to have it, and she said she would. I warned her about the bloodstains on the brim.

She held the cap, fingering the dried blood, and wiped her tears. She told me she had been upstairs in their home when she received the news. She had heard someone pull up, and, looking out the window, she saw a close friend get out of her car. Geri was on her way downstairs when the friend walked in. Geri knew immediately something was wrong; a second later her friend cried out, "Jonathan's been killed." Geri slowly backed up the stairs and said, "Don't tell me that." Her friend was sobbing, and Geri said again, "No. Don't tell me that." Her friend followed her upstairs and tried to comfort her, but Geri kept pacing the room. She told me she felt like a dog she had once seen hit by a car, and how—not knowing it was fatally injured—it had kept walking in circles. Her friend left, and later that evening Geri went to her closet and began sorting through Jonathan's clothes. Everything had just come back from the cleaners so it would be fresh when he returned. Then she saw a jacket she had missed. She removed it from the hanger and raised it to her face. It still held his smell, and finally she was able to start crying.

Geri looked gaunt and frail, but I suppose that is to be expected. She seemed to be out of the initial shock but still in a state of confusion. She told me she had a dream while she was at my house in which the world had somehow spun off its axis and people were flying around as though in a tornado, trying to hang on to anything they could grab.

She was thoughtful enough to ask me how I was doing. I told her my situation didn't compare to hers—to losing a husband and facing the challenge of raising a sixteen-month-old child on her own. But I confessed that it was hard, that frequently I saw the image of Jonathan's face as he died while I was holding him in my arms. I explained how I was trying to keep busy writing magazine articles and proposals for film projects, but most days I bounced between a pervasive sadness and a sudden euphoria that I was still alive. I would be doing fine, and then a seemingly ordinary thing like smelling tea as it brewed or hearing a favorite song on the radio or even seeing the glint of sunlight on the ocean would bring me to tears.

I didn't tell her that for now, anyway, I am giving up mountaineering; she had come out to visit so I could be there for her, not the other way around. It would have been good to talk to her about it, though. Between these feelings of thankfulness that I am still alive, I'm left wondering what I am going to do.

All I know for sure is that every day I must remember to cherish the small things, like the smell of brewing tea and the glint of sunlight on the ocean. Which is more than Jonathan can do. I owe it to him never to lose sight of that, never to waste a day. It's the only way I know to acknowledge the fact that he died while I lived, that for some small shift in our trajectories as we flew down the mountain, I would be there, under that pile of rocks on that remote peak in Tibet, and he would be here, with his wife and young daughter.

It was a delight to have Asia in the house for three days. She wore blue denim overalls, and her black hair was in a cute Dutch boy cut. She was just learning to walk, and after she took a few steps she would turn to make sure you were watching. I realized right away that the house wasn't set up for toddlers, so I had to pull the food from the bottom shelves of the open cupboards in the kitchen, and pick up the mousetraps in the corners.

So I have the house kid-proofed, but now there is no kid . . . just me and the sound of the waves hitting the bulkhead. I admit I'm feeling lonely. Much more than I did before the avalanche. I don't know where things are going for me. Not just me, either, but for little Asia, growing up without a father. What will her life be like?

Part 1

*Khumbu and the
Everest Region
May 1999*

1

Asia and I are on the second day of our trek through the Khumbu district of Nepal. Our goal is Tengboche Monastery—about halfway to Everest Base Camp—and at the moment the trail traverses a steep hillside covered by a mature forest of blue pine and silver fir. The dense trees muffle the roar of the Dudh Kosi a hundred or so yards downslope. Nima, our Sherpa guide, is ahead of me, and Asia is a minute or so behind. I stop at a lateral creek cascading in ribbons into a small pool alongside the trail. On both sides of the falling water, ferns grow in emerald swatches out of sharp cracks in the wet black rock. Long wisps of moss—Old Man's Beard—hang from the lower branches of the conifers. At the corner of my eye something moves, and, turning, I spot a small, energetic bird near the water. It has iridescent black wings and shoulders, a chestnut-red tail and rump, and a snow-white cap. It's called the white-capped river chat, and it's common alongside streams and rivers throughout the Himalayas.

It will be a few moments before Asia catches up. Taking advantage of the solitude, I pause and watch the river chat forage at the edge of the pool water. I breathe in the ionized air, listen to the spill of the water, feel the cool of the shadows. Then, with only the small bird as audience,

I give voice to my thoughts and say out loud, "Pause." The bird doesn't seem to notice, so I say it again, "Pause." I say it because that's one of the reasons I am on this journey. To pause, and to remind myself what I have tended to forget since that afternoon long ago when I crawled to the side of the avalanche saying, "Alive, alive, alive." To remind myself that I am living on probation.

The river chat hops to a rock illuminated by a shaft of direct sun reaching through the pine and fir canopy. The light makes its dark body scintillate. As I watch the bird, I begin to have a sense of déjà vu. Then I remember the past event that connects to this present moment with a symmetry so uncannily parallel it leaves me dizzy. The memory is of the first time I saw a river chat. It was somewhere near here, no more than an hour's walk either up or down the trail. It was 1976—four years before the fateful trip to Minya Konka—and I was a member of a climbing team ponderously called the American Bicentennial Everest Expedition. We were on our way to becoming only the second American team to scale the mountain, and Jonathan was part of the film crew documenting the ascent for a television special. It was the first time the two of us had been together on an expedition, and it was the beginning of our friendship. I was stooped alongside a rushing stream, watching a black and chestnut bird, trying to find it in my bird guide, when Jonathan came along. Together we thumbed through the book until we identified it as the same one I was now looking at.

That is not what leaves me dizzy, however. Rather it is the feeling that I know what is going to happen next. In another moment Asia comes up the trail, and seeing me squatting next to the pool, she stops and says, "What are you looking at?"

"That little bird," I reply, feeling as though I'm reading from a script written long ago. "See it, next to the water?"

"Oh, yeah. What is it?"

"It's called a white-capped river chat."

"It's really pretty."

"It's one of my favorite birds."

I decide to leave it at that. I want neither to add to nor take away from this moment next to this pool, looking at this little bird. It's not that Asia wouldn't understand. Even though we have been together only a few days, I can tell she has an ability to empathize with others, and I suspect she would understand how I feel, were I to tell her that nearly twenty-five years ago I was squatting next to a small stream just like this one—maybe it *was* this one—looking at this same type of bird when her father walked up behind me in the same way she just did, and asked me, as she just did, what I was looking at.

I decided to start this journey with Asia in the Everest region for several reasons. It was a place her father had visited on his first trip to the Himalayas, when he was about the same age she is now, and he came back to it nearly every year after that, until he died in the avalanche. He wrote about those journeys and expeditions in his journals, copies of which we have brought with us to refer to in our travels, as Asia sees for the first time the places he was describing, and has some of the same experiences.

At noon we stop for lunch at a trailside teahouse that belongs to Nima's aunt. In 1976 Jonathan, Nima, and I also stopped here to rest. Nima was one of the Sherpas we had retained to help us carry supplies up Everest. The three of us hit it off, and we often walked together during the month it took to trek from just outside Kathmandu to Base Camp. On that particular day, after the three of us had finished our tea, I noticed up a steep hillside a deep alcove at the base of an overhanging rock wall that protected a small hut built on stilts and festooned with prayer flags. Nima told Jonathan and me the hut was the refuge of an old lama who lived there by himself. We asked if we could visit, and Nima told us, "No problem. The lama is my uncle."

Now Nima, Asia, and I hike up the same path toward the alcove. The hut is still there, but the old lama has long since died. We all three stoop to enter the low doorway. Inside I am astonished to see the walls still painted with intricate scenes of Buddhist parables, and in the corner the small table behind which the old lama had sat cross-legged. My surprise isn't that these things have survived through the years, but that I now recognize them with a clarity that once more causes the present to melt into the past.

"Remember how the old lama sat right here?" I say to Nima. "He had a red robe over his shoulders, and old-fashioned glasses that rested on his nose, and a large conical red hat. I'll never forget that hat."

"He lived here by himself for twenty years," Nima explains to Asia. "He was very happy. Every morning and night the kids brought him his food, and he prayed here all day. That's not such a bad life."

"The old lama did a chant for us," I tell Asia, "so we would have good luck on the mountain. Then he picked up a pair of dice and held them to his forehead. Do you remember, Nima? He rolled the dice on this small table, and we stood waiting for the verdict. It was like the Middle Ages, the old lama with the conical red hat looking like Merlin the magician. Finally he mumbled something, and Nima looked at your dad and me and told us the lama had said, "Things don't look so good." Jonathan and I raised our eyebrows, and then the old lama rolled the dice again. He studied them; then he told Nima it looked better the second time, so maybe we'd have good luck after all."

We remain in the abandoned hut for a few more minutes. I watch Asia as she examines the paintings on the walls, now covered with dust and spiderwebs. She has her mother's dark hair, Japanese eyes, and high cheekbones; but she has her father's long legs and his fair skin. She has on sage trekking pants and a complementary maroon hiking shirt, and her trekking shoes have a swatch of green the same color as her pants. She wears a Tibetan necklace of turquoise and coral that was given to her by a friend for good luck on our journey. Her hair was cut short the day before we left by my oldest daughter—who at sixteen is three years younger than Asia—and the two of them sat on the veranda of our house and giggled as the long locks of black hair fell to the tile floor.

I think of the sense of completeness Jonathan would feel to be here at this moment, with his daughter, reliving the adventures of his youth.

Then for the second time in as many hours, I feel his presence. Not his ghost, but his spirit.

After Geri and Asia visited me in California in November 1980—a little more than a month after Jonathan died—I made a vow to stay in touch, and also, in reverence to Jonathan, to be there for Asia if she needed me. In the years that followed, however, I didn't see much of Asia. It wasn't that I considered my vow unimportant, but since it wasn't urgent, seeing her unfortunately seemed always to fall behind the other things that quickly began to fill my life. Eighteen months after the avalanche I married a woman who had suffered a tragedy in a sailing accident that nearly killed her, and did kill her first husband; our two experiences, so uncommonly parallel, were an important part of our bond. Less than a year later we had the first of three children, and soon after I began again to go on expeditions, climbing mountains and running rivers and exploring jungles. I decided I would never return to extremely high altitudes, and also that I would avoid mountains with potentially dangerous snow or rockfall conditions. Even then, my wife and I both knew I was only reducing the risk, not eliminating it. But we also knew the adventures in large measure had made me who I was. With my wife's understanding, I made a decision to keep adventuring, even though I now had a family and had to weigh the benefit of sharing with the kids the stories I would bring home against the possibility of not coming home at all.

Jonathan had been struggling with the same decision; I had wondered at the time he died what price Asia would pay in her life for his choice. As she grew up, I did check in with her mother from time to time. She told me that Asia was a good student, that she loved skiing and hiking in the Colorado Rockies, where they lived. Geri did not remarry, and they remained a household of two. When Asia was nine, she came out to the Tetons to stay at Yvon and Malinda's summerhouse while I was there with my family; she went rock climbing with all our kids. After that,

I didn't see her until she was nearly out of high school. She told me then during a brief visit how, starting at age thirteen, she had discovered snowboarding, and had gone on to make the U.S. junior team. That evening Geri took me aside. She wanted me to know that Asia knew I had been one of her father's close friends, and had been with him in the avalanche on the mountain in Tibet, and that he had died in my arms.

Although the visit was too short for anything but a quick chat with Asia, I sensed an unspoken expectation that at some point in our lives we would get together again, and I would tell her about her father, about the climb and the avalanche, and about how he died. Toward the end of her freshman year in college she called to say she hoped to come to California for the summer, and wondered if she could stay with us. It was with nervous anticipation that I looked forward to her visit.

Asia's ambition was to follow in her father's footsteps and become a professional photographer. By then I had developed an agency representing outdoor photographers, so she worked half-time for me that summer, filing and editing images. She also had an interest in design, so she worked the rest of the day at Yvon's company, Patagonia (which manufactures outdoor clothing), helping to develop a new line of snowboarding clothes for kids.

After she had been with us a couple of weeks, I took her to a small café for lunch. I told her about the avalanche, how I assumed for perhaps one minute—sixty long, long seconds—that we were all dead. I told her how her father had died, and how we had buried him.

"Mom's shown me the picture you gave her of the grave."

"Everyone who knew your father held him in such a high regard," I said. "He was so quiet and polite and respectful. But what everyone noticed more than anything was his incredible equanimity. I never once saw him angry."

"I've heard that from everybody who knew him," she said. "But I don't know, somehow it still seems like a story. All my life, when people first get to know me, they've asked, 'What does your father do?' and I've answered, 'He was a *National Geographic* photographer, but he was killed in an avalanche on a remote mountain in China when I was a baby,' and they answer, "Wow, that's incredible.' It doesn't sound real to them, and in a way it's never been real to me."

"Have you read his journals?"

"I've read parts of them, but somehow they've been abstract, too. The only physical connection I ever had were his photographs. They hung on the walls of our house, and I grew up with them. They were mostly pictures of Nepal and the Himalayas. I knew that was his favorite place, and that's why he gave me my name. When I was about eight, I had this idea that if I could somehow go there, I would be able to figure out who he was. I asked my mom how much the trip would cost, and she said about two thousand dollars. We didn't have a lot of money, and I knew it probably wouldn't happen, but I couldn't let the idea go. So, beginning in the eighth grade, I decided I would earn the money and go by myself. I started working odd jobs after school, and saving. But it took forever, and finally I realized I'd never be able to get that much money."

"So you gave up?"

"Not exactly. I still want to go, but now I want to do something else."

"What's that?"

"Well, it's something that would involve you."

I assumed she was going to ask me to help her get to Nepal. I was already forming my answer—that I could contribute half but she would have to work for the other half—when she told me what she had in mind. It was not what I was expecting.

"Would you take me to Tibet?" she said. "To Minya Konka? To climb up the mountain and help me find my father's grave?"

The evening after Asia asked me to take her to Minya Konka, I asked my wife what she thought.

"You have to go," she replied.

"It wouldn't be easy, reliving the avalanche."

"But Asia needs you."

"I know. She needs to learn who her father was."

"More than that, she needs to have a father."

My wife was right. But how could I be a father for Asia, even for a short time? Then I realized a more precise question was how could I be a father for Asia if we *had* only a short time. Perhaps the answer was to extend the trip, so Asia and I would have sufficient time not only to get to know each other but also to have the larger number of shared experiences that I knew, from my relationships with my own two daughters, was essential to building a bond.

I knew that it took only two or three days to walk from the road head to the base of Minya Konka, and only another day to climb from there to the promontory where we buried Jonathan. Then I remembered a plan Jonathan and I had developed before the avalanche so suddenly changed everything. At that time the two of us had an assignment from *National Geographic* to do a story on the newly chartered Mount Everest National Park. We had planned, once the Minya Konka climb was over, to go to Lhasa, then continue overland to Kathmandu and on to the Khumbu, the Sherpa homeland on the south side of Everest. What if I did the same trip with Asia, only in reverse?

I was attracted to the idea of starting our journey in the Khumbu, one of her father's favorite places. In addition, I thought it would be interesting for her to see firsthand how much the Khumbu had changed since her father first saw it nearly thirty years earlier. More specifically, I wanted her to get a sense of what was happening on Everest, where hundreds of climbers crowded Base Camp, many paying fifty thousand dollars and more to be guided to the top of the world. I wanted her to understand that what motivated these climbers—and by extension what the popular press assumed was what motivated most climbers—had little to do with what drew her father to the mountains and to mountaineering.

I also knew that to understand this difference on a visceral level, it would be helpful for the two of us to climb a mountain, preferably one that, as counterpoint to Everest, was in a location as remote and little known as possible. But I didn't know if Asia would be interested in doing that, and even if she were, I didn't know if I could find a mountain that would be safe. All the peaks in eastern Tibet, in the region around Minya Konka, would have avalanche hazards because the area is exposed to monsoon weather that creates wet and heavy snow. On the other hand, I had heard that western Tibet was a high-altitude desert, and in a place called the Chang Tang Plateau the mountains were said to have snow conditions that were dry and cold, with little potential for avalanche.

I knew that the famed wildlife biologist George Schaller for many years had been conducting a survey of the mammals of this region. I located a book he had recently written on his project, and read in the preface that "the Chang Tang is a wild and bleak land where humankind has barely intruded, and animals live as if becalmed in time and space." That matched my criteria for being remote and little known. I called Schaller, and he invited me to meet him in his office at the Bronx Zoo. He unfolded his creased and worn maps of the area, the margins penciled with numerous notes, and suggested Asia and I go to the remote northwestern corner of the Chang Tang, to a place called the Aru Basin and to the mountains above them, a range of peaks 20,000 feet high that had never been touched by mountaineers.

It seemed fantastical to hear, one year short of the twenty-first century, that there was still on Earth an entire range of mountains that remained unclimbed. That they were mountains apparently safe to climb seemed even better. But I still had no idea if Asia would be interested. I had a rule I followed with my own daughters concerning climbing. The older of the two is a committed rock climber, and the younger an enthusiastic hiker and mountaineer, but I decided early on that if they wanted to try climbing mountains, the motivation had to come from them. Intuition told me I should follow the same strategy with Asia. I wasn't concerned about her capability. I knew she had done some rock climbing, and because she seemed to be a good athlete, I assumed she would also be a quick study if I gave her some on-the-job training in the use of crampons and ice axe.

I phoned to tell her about the idea of reversing the trip her father and I had wanted to do twenty years before, starting in the Everest Park, returning to Kathmandu, going north and west to the Chang Tang, then east to Minya Konka. I also told her another idea I had: to make, as we drove toward the Chang Tang, an interlude stop at a peak called Mount Kailas. There we would join the pilgrims who gather each year to make a devotional *khora*, a three-day trek around this sacred mountain. Then we would continue for another week or so, driving for two or three days completely off-road, until we reached the Aru Basin.

"There's one more thing," I said. "Above the Aru there is a range of twenty-thousand-foot peaks that George Schaller calls the Crystal Mountains. They've never been climbed or even explored. In fact, it sounds like no one has ever even set foot on them. I thought maybe while we're there we could try and climb one. But only if it's something you would really want to do."

Her reply was instant. "Yeessss!" she said with the same enthusiasm her father had used when saying "Wuuwee!"

By midafternoon of the second day of our trek in the Khumbu, Asia and I arrive at the confluence of the Dudh Kosi and the tributary Imja Khola, whose headwaters begin at the terminus of the glacier that descends off the south side of Everest. We cross the Imja Khola on a cable bridge and begin the ascent to the trading center of Namche Bazaar on a trail that switchbacks nearly three thousand vertical feet up a steep hill. A sixteen-year-old Sherpa boy named Kami, whom Nima has retained to carry our duffel of extra gear, steps around us, nodding and smiling as he passes. Hiking at a pace much faster than ours, he disappears in less than a minute around a hairpin in the trail.

The altitude is about 10,000 feet, and Asia has started to slow. Although she has grown up at 8,500 feet, she revealed to me yesterday that she has always had trouble breathing at higher elevations—and she learned only a month ago that she has mild asthma. This is a concern because if she is having trouble here, she will have even more trouble on our climb in the Chang Tang, where we will be above 20,000 feet. She stops and fishes out of her pack one of those small inhalers, takes in the spray with a deep breath, and says, "That's better."

With the spray she indeed does much better, and we are able to maintain a slow but steady pace. The sky has become overcast, which keeps the air at a comfortable temperature but also obscures the surrounding mountains. I remember that from an elbow on one of these switchbacks it is possible to see Everest, and also Ama Dablam, a smaller but more impressively shaped peak sometimes called the Matterhorn of the Himalayas. I hope it will clear enough so Asia can at least get a glimpse of it, because Jonathan was part of a team that in 1979 made the second ascent. We will be in this area for several more days, however, and it is early May—the middle of the premonsoon—a time of year when clear days predominate.

We hike for another half hour when I look up and see Kami now coming back down the trail but without his pack. "He has already reached Namche and left his load there," Nima explains. "Now he is back to help one of you with your pack."

Even though Kami has carried much of our stuff, Asia and I still have day packs—filled with cameras, lenses, books, and journals—that each weigh about fifteen or twenty pounds.

"Go ahead and give him yours," I suggest to Asia. "You can take a break."

"I don't need a break," she says firmly.

"You've got asthma."

"I'm doing fine."

"I'm just trying to make it easier for you."

"If you want to make me happy," Asia says, "give *your* pack to him and then take that load from that little girl."

Asia points to a small girl perhaps ten years old coming up the trail. She carries by tumpline a large basket filled with bamboo shoots. The girl has stopped on the trail just below us and is looking at us with a broad smile. I can see that Asia is moved by the inverse proportion of the size of her load to the number of her years.

"Okay," I reply.

I give my pack to Kami, then ask Nima to tell the young girl I want to carry her basket.

"She is very shy," Nima says. "She won't understand if you take her load."

I turn back to Asia and say, "I can't take her basket without embarrassing Nima." Meanwhile Kami has left with my pack.

"So give me your pack," I say to Asia, "and I'll carry it."

"I'm carrying my own pack," she says with finality, then stands and leaves.

I take a deep breath and follow her, thinking that she is certainly a young woman who doesn't hesitate to state her opinions. I noticed this yesterday when, after a short flight from Kathmandu, we arrived in Lukla, a small dirt airstrip that services the Khumbu, and Nima introduced us to Kami. When Nima explained that the Sherpa boy was going to carry our duffel, Asia was affronted by the idea of hiring someone even younger than she is to carry her stuff. She was only partially mollified when I explained that this was the tradition in the Himalayas, and that, furthermore, these people appreciated the work. She then asked Nima how much Kami was getting paid, and when he told her about 150 rupees a day, she exclaimed, "That's only three dollars! Not even."

"We also pay for his food," Nima added, "and that would cost one hundred, or even one hundred thirty rupees."

"That's still not fair," Asia replied. "We have to pay him more."

I didn't want Nima to be in the position of having to refute Asia, so I said to her, "If we pay him more, Nima will have a more difficult time hiring porters next time, because they'll want more."

"They should want more," she said indignantly.

"Maybe," I said, "but that's not a topic we can resolve in one conversation."

"They should organize."

"They probably should, Asia, but that still doesn't mean Nima's in a position to pay them more now."

She let it drop, and we started our trek. Now a day later, as we continue up the hill toward Namche Bazaar, I am wondering if perhaps Asia's willfulness is somehow tied to growing up without the mandatory accommodations you learn to make when you have siblings. Whether that's true or not, I remind myself I need to make my own accommodations to avoid getting frustrated with her. I would do well, for example, to balance her willfulness against her good cheer, her enthusiasm, and, perhaps above all, her sincere appreciation for the opportunity to make this journey.

I would also do well to remember Jonathan's remarkable ability on journeys and expeditions to avoid frustration with his fellow travelers and teammates by viewing small differences and minor conflicts with a kind of bemusement. Asia's father was one of the most accommodating people I have known, self-effacing to the point that when people spent any time around him most would become conscious—if for no other reason than contrast—of their own egoism. Jonathan once told me, however, that he wasn't born with his equanimity but had acquired it over the years by self-discipline. He said, in fact, that as a teenager he had a reputation for owning a quick temper. One day, on his first trip to the Himalayas, he was in a Sherpa house when he stood and smacked his head on a beam and nearly knocked himself out. He cursed the beam with a string of expletives until he noticed the Sherpas looking at him as though he had lost his mind. Even though his head still hurt, he started to laugh. Soon the Sherpas were laughing with him, and then they began to stand up and pretend to smack their heads on the beam, pointing to it and cursing. That made all of them laugh even more. Jonathan told me from that day on, whenever he realized he was getting angry, he just reminded himself of the beam.

Now I tell myself that if Jonathan was able to sweeten his temper, Asia should be able to soften her tendency to be a little overly assertive. I make a mental note to talk to her about it, when the time is right, anticipating that the topic may be tricky but also realizing that I need to overcome my own propensity to let things like this go unresolved. My wife thinks I do this because I tend to avoid conflict, and she says that's probably because I come from a broken family. So dealing with this issue could be good for both Asia and me.

In the weeks before departure, as I worked on the logistics of our journey, I continued to ponder the challenge of using the trip to teach Asia about her father. Jonathan and I were by several measures different and even opposite in temperament and character. I was commonly frenetic while he was typically serene; my innate skepticism countered his devout Buddhist belief; his consistent equanimity contrasted with my occasional indignation. But we shared an overreaching passion for adventure that had given us by other measures considerable common ground. We dreamed equally of remote ranges and wild jungles and vast ice caps. We both were willing to work hard to get to those places, and were willing to continue to work hard once we were there. We were both tenacious. He was committed to being a successful adventure photographer and cameraman, and I was equally committed to being a successful adventure writer and film producer.

We decided we would be a team, and the *National Geographic* assignment to do the story on Everest National Park was only one of several proposals we had submitted. We also had an idea to make a coast-to-coast traverse of Borneo, directly through the middle of the island, descending a river no one had ever navigated; the magazine was interested. We knew of a mysterious unclimbed granite spire in the most remote part of the Amazon that would require, in order to find our way through the jungle, retaining people from the primitive Yanomami tribe; network television said it would consider it.

I knew that if Jonathan had lived, he would have been with me on those and many of the other adventures I did have in the years that followed the avalanche. He would have brought home stories from these trips and shared them with Asia. So perhaps I could do this in his stead— tell Asia stories from my adventures, just as I had told them to my children. Perhaps that would at least fill one of the gaps in her life that started that day Jonathan died.

Then, as the date for our departure approached, telling Asia these stories began to take on an additional purpose. In a few months I would turn fifty, and I was feeling a growing need for a midlife pause, a chance to take a break and look back over the decisions I had made, the roads I had taken, the experiences I had lived. I had the intuition that although I had learned a lot from my travels and adventures, and without doubt they had shaped my life, there were a few more things I could take from them, and there were no doubt a few more things that, if I used to know them, I had forgotten as my life filled with deadlines, checklists, obligations, and commitments.

As our journey progressed over its two-and-and-a-half-month course, I wanted to start at the beginning, with the sailing trip I made to French Polynesia with five buddies on a small sloop when I was eighteen. In some ways I knew my life had been a long search to recapture the magic I had felt on the morning we first sighted a small tropical island off the bow. I would follow the thread of stories through the next thirty years, up to my last adventure, the first big-wall climb ever done in Antarctica. I was there with five other buddies, and from our porta-ledge bivouac high on the wall, I looked to the distant ranges, the vertical line of rock on one side of my view meeting the horizontal line of the ice cap on the other. It was a landscape that imprinted on my consciousness, and approached the magic I felt on that first trip.

Images of distant lands were one thing, but I also wanted to revisit the comrades whom I had accompanied on those adventures, to remember the friendships, the shared adversities, the triumphs, and the disappointments. Most important, I wanted to look back at the avalanche and make sure I had taken from that experience everything it had to offer.

So the trip with Asia promised to be not merely a long journey, but a pilgrimage; and like any pilgrimage, it also promised to have not only physical but emotional challenges. When Asia first asked me to take her back to find the grave, I knew it would be difficult to relive those sixty long seconds when I thought I was dead, and the even longer twenty minutes or so before Jonathan died. It would also be a challenge to find the grave. The promontory where we laid his body and covered it with stones was in the middle of a complex series of rock and ice buttresses on a long ridge descending from the 25,000-foot summit. I had taken photographs, though, that showed its location, and I felt they would serve as maps to get us back to the spot. Of more concern, I didn't know what condition the grave would be in, or if it would even be there at all— another avalanche or a rockfall could have swept it away.

I didn't say anything to Asia about this possibility, but I knew at some point I would have to bring it up. But even if the grave were gone, I knew returning to that location would be enough to trigger the emotions that had coursed through me when I crawled to the side of the rocks, saying, "Alive, alive, alive." As the date for our departure approached, I realized that the journey, coinciding as it did with this midpoint passage in my life, had the potential to be a turning point, one of those places you look back to when you are approaching the end of your life and see as a kind of marker buoy around which your course had taken a change.

Asia is just ahead of me, stepping up the trail slowly but still keeping a consistent pace. I notice that she has hitched her thumbs through the shoulder straps of her pack, and she's bent forward slightly as she hikes. She lowers her arms and continues walking with her palms turned slightly outward. Throughout the day I have noticed a few similarities she shares with her father, such as the length of her legs compared to her torso, but now I see them in every nuance: the carry of her shoulders, the length of her stride, the athletic bounce in her step, even this turn of her wrists.

Once again on this day, as I did this morning when I stopped to watch the river chat, and later when we were in the old lama's hut in the mouth of the cave, I have this sensation of the past melting into the present. Now the sight of Asia hiking in front of me carries me back in time just as a certain smell can carry you to a memory long forgotten. And there he is, hiking in front of me on a day long ago on a mountain far away.

2

Asia and I gain the top of the steep hill, traverse through a grove of blue pine, then round a bend that reveals the two-story houses of Namche Bazaar. The town is a horseshoe wrapped around a level point in a gully that otherwise drops steeply into the deep valley. Asia and I stop for a moment to catch our breath and admire the view of this fabled Sherpa trading center. The little girl with the oversize basket of bamboo shoots and the irrepressible smile has kept pace with us, and Asia motions her to sit next to us, then shares her energy bar with her. These children of the high mountain tribes, who all seem to radiate a perpetual sunniness, were an endless delight to Jonathan, and I see his daughter takes the same joy in their company.

"The first time I saw Namche was in the same spot, in 1976," I tell Asia. "By then we'd been on the approach march for nearly three weeks."

In those years to get to Everest we had to walk from just outside Kathmandu all the way to Base Camp, a distance of 175 miles. Ours was one of the last of the old-style expeditions, rooted in the time of the British Raj at the end of the last century. We had over twenty tons of supplies—including about two hundred bottles of oxygen—and to carry it all we had to hire 625 porters. They were a ragtag assortment from the low hill tribes, bandy-legged and barefoot men wearing dog-eared vests, ragged shirts, and jodhpur shorts. Every morning they would squat with their backs against the large cardboard boxes they were charged to carry, adjust the tumpline across their foreheads, then leg-press to a stand and begin the day's stage. Once all of them were under way, they created a line of human figures that stretched as far as we could see.

"For a lot of us on the expedition, this view was like seeing the city of our dreams," I tell Asia. "When I was in my early teens, I read adventure books about expeditions to Everest in the early fifties, when Nepal first opened and the mountain was still unclimbed. And I always remembered the name Namche Bazaar."

"I'm pretty excited myself," she replies.

As Asia and I enter the village, we walk up narrow cobble streets that have the intimacy of corridors designed for people and animals instead of cars. I am relieved to see the place looks much the same as it did twenty-five years ago. There are some changes, however. Back then Nima ran a hostel called the International Footrest Hotel—a single room with tiered platforms where everyone spread their sleeping bags around a central fire pit. Now he owns the Danphe Bar and Lodge, which indeed has a bar with an assortment of international liquors, and a pool table that was disassembled in Kathmandu and flown in pieces to Namche by helicopter.

Past the bar and down a long hallway are a dozen guest rooms, and Asia and I carry our packs to the one farthest from the pool table, to avoid the noise. The bar is packed, but our room is far enough away that we have no trouble falling quickly asleep. In the morning a diffused light illuminates the single window of our room, and looking out I see the sky is still overcast. From up the street a resounding bell rings six times to announce the hour. I know from previous visits that this bell is actually a spent oxygen cylinder, collected off Everest, that hangs from the rafters of the village bank. The night watchman, striking it each morning with a metal bar, heralds the beginning of the day and the end of his shift. As the last ring diminishes, we hear the hauntingly deep voices of chanting monks.

"What's that?" Asia asks.

"A *puja* ceremony," I tell her, "where Buddhist monks chant."

"Where's it coming from?"

"Somewhere across town. We'll ask Nima about it."

I get out of my sleeping bag and pull on my pants and shirt. Asia gets up, and I see she is in her pile pants and fleece jacket. I ask her how she slept, and she says she is still a little cold. In the bar Asia and I join Nima in front of the wood-burning stove. The air is filled with the yeasty smell of spilled beer, and cigarette butts are scattered on the floor like fall leaves. A young boy with long black hair sweeps the floor around the pool table in a desultory slow motion.

"The *puja* is for an old Sherpa man who died last week," Nima says. "His wife has hired many monks who come from all around, and they chant every day for maybe two weeks, to guide the old man into his next life."

Nima asks if we would like to see the *puja,* and we accept enthusiastically. We have decided to spend a layover day in Namche, to acclimatize before continuing up to Tengboche Monastery, and I realize this will be a chance for Asia to glimpse an otherwise private side of Sherpa life. We follow Nima, coffee cup in one hand and cigarette in the other, up a narrow street to the widow's house. About thirty Sherpas gathered in front are helping distribute plates of *tsampa,* a paste made from roasted barley flour and yak-milk tea. The widow is paying for this, and the food will be handed out to the entire village every day of the two-week vigil.

"She feeds the monks and pays them for chanting," Nima explains. "It is all very expensive, but it is the way she shows her respect for her husband."

Nima escorts us inside the house to the second floor, where more than a dozen monks line the walls. The room is packed with Sherpa women carrying plates of food downstairs. Two of them bring small benches for Asia and me, and the widow crosses the room to greet us, clasping our hands in hers. When the chanting reaches a crescendo, some of the monks blow long bass horns called *gangdungs*, others smaller clarinet-like horns called *gyalings*, while one beats a drum and another clashes two cymbals. The music and the chanting suddenly stop, except for the drum, which continues beating like a heart; and then one monk begins to chant, and then another, and then another—one deep voice layered on the next—until all of them once more repeat the mantric cycle.

We stay for an hour, thanking the widow before we leave, and again she clasps our hands and smiles. As we walk back to our lodge, Asia says she is amazed that the widow is spending what Nima told us will be most of the money she has on this ceremony. I explain that most cultures in the world organized at a tribal level have some sort of potlatch tradition that functions to redistribute wealth.

"We need something like that in our culture," she says.

"We have something like that. It's called the inheritance tax."

"Yeah, but it's not the same. It's too impersonal."

I am pleased that Asia is having a chance to see directly some of the Buddhist traditions of Himalayan culture that so moved her father. Buddhism was one aspect of Jonathan's life that I feel ill-prepared to explain, because I have only a layman's knowledge of the subject. But it was an important part of Jonathan's life. On his first trip to the Himalayas, when he was the same age Asia is now, he stayed for twenty days in a Buddhist monastery. His sister, who had stayed in the same monastery a year or two earlier, once told me that his time there, more than any of his other experiences, set the course of his life.

The only way I knew to expose Asia to this part of her father was to weave into our itinerary visits to places where we might encounter aspects of Buddhist culture. That is the main reason I want to include the stop at Mount Kailas to join the pilgrims circumambulating a mountain held by both Buddhists and Hindus to be the most sacred on Earth. And why I'm pleased Asia has had the chance to experience this *puja*.

In the afternoon Asia and I decide to hike to the neighboring village of Khumjung. We climb the steep path above town, past a hilltop that in clear weather offers a superb view of Everest, Ama Dablam, and other surrounding peaks.

"I hope it clears so you can see the mountains," I say once again.

"If it does, fine, and if it doesn't, that'll be fine, too," she replies.

While I take heart knowing that was the answer her father would likely have given me, I also remember reading in his journal how excited he was when he saw these mountains for the first time, and I remember it was from this exact vantage point.

> March 16, 1973. I made it, Namche Bazaar! It was a long day, then finally the white houses wrapped around the hillside, just as I imagined it. I wanted to look around but it was late so I busted ass to get to the top of the hill above town to photograph the mountains. I couldn't believe it. Everest, Lhotse, Nuptse, Taweche, Ama Dablam, Kangtega, Khumbila, Kwangde. Wow!

As we pass the same hilltop my mind's eye sees Jonathan with his manual Olympus camera as he turns one way and then the other, carefully composing each frame, working efficiently but never frenetically. His face is lean and angular, his light brown hair in curls over his ears. He moves in long strides with legs that are overlong for his torso, like the legs of a young colt. He is over six feet tall, and his large hands hold the camera firmly, his elbows braced like a tripod against his chest, and as he takes pictures, he grins. It's a knowing grin, like the immutable grin on the statues of Buddhas he has seen in the monasteries, although he would be chagrined to hear the comparison. Now he turns and sees that the moon is rising over Kangtega, and he says, "Wuuwee!" with the same infectious enthusiasm he'll have when I meet him five years later, at age twenty-four, and the same enthusiasm he will still have until the moment he dies, at age twenty-eight.

I like the idea of Asia seeing this place at the same age her father was when he first saw it. Nineteen is a good age to begin traveling. In Europe it's the *Wanderjahr,* the year between high school and college that you spend vagabonding. I turned nineteen when I was in the middle of my first big adventure—that sailing trip with five buddies in a small sloop to the South Pacific. I had been attending the University of Hawaii, and summer was approaching. On a whim I scrawled "Crew position wanted to the South Pacific" on an index card and posted it on the bulletin board at the yacht club. Within a week I was signed on to a thirty-six-foot sloop with five other crew members, all between eighteen and twenty-two. We set sail in June for Tahiti and the Leeward Islands of French Polynesia. We had been to sea for twenty-four days when the skipper said he thought we should have seen Tahiti by now. Two days later I lay in the quarter berth waiting for my watch to be called, reassuring myself that food wasn't a problem because we had a tackle box full of feathered jigs and there was plenty of tuna in the waters. Fresh water was another matter. We had eight one-gallon jugs left in the fo'c'sle, and we were going through two a day. Then I heard a fly buzzing somewhere inside the cabin. I listened to it for a few seconds before my thoughts connected; then I bolted from the berth, grabbed the binoculars, and climbed on deck to see on the horizon a small mountain rising out of the sea.

As we approached the island, we could see a single peak carpeted with verdant jungle. A white sand beach lined with coconut palms circled the hill, and a turquoise lagoon lay between the beach and a concentric outer reef. As we sailed around the island, a gathering of trade-wind clouds formed against the windward side, and the bottoms of the clouds picked up the turquoise of the lagoon. We got out the binoculars. On the beach we could see, above the tide line, huts with roofs of palm thatch.

There were a few people walking on the beach, and although we could not tell for sure, the women appeared to be topless. Except for the skipper, who was busy with charts and calculations, we all agreed that this looked like paradise. But there were two shortcomings. First, we couldn't find a pass through the barrier reef that would allow us entrance to the lagoon. Second, the island wasn't Tahiti. The skipper confessed he had no idea where we were.

One of my crewmates was a radio buff, and he fashioned a directional antenna out of a coat hanger, attached it to our portable transistor, and tuned in Radio Tahiti. He rotated the receiver until the signal was strongest, pointed across the open ocean, and said, "That way." Then he pointed in the opposite direction and added, "Or that way."

We chose the direction we thought most likely, and two days later we watched the dawn fill the shadows of the deep valleys of Tahiti's central peak. A small pilot boat came out to escort us through the pass in the outer reef to the harbor where the yachts were moored stern-to at the waterfront of old Papeete. It was midmorning. We watched transfixed as couples arm in arm wove drunkenly down the streets littered with empty beer bottles and confetti. A small pickup drove slowly by, several locals in its bed beating on log drums while a beautiful young woman in a flower-print cotton wrap stood dancing. All of us lined up at the rail to stare at the dancer, ignoring the efforts of the skipper to get us to ready the anchor. We assumed this was a typical day, and for the second time in as many days were convinced we had found paradise. But it turned out to be Bastille Day, the French equivalent of the Fourth of July, and in French Polynesia the biggest celebration of the year.

We cruised among the islands for two more months, and when we departed, sailing from the back of a deep bay fringed with coconut palms, I bid farewell to one of the crew who was by then a close friend. He waved good-bye with one hand while the other held by the waist a young French-Tahitian woman he had fallen in love with. By the time I returned to Honolulu, I was nearly a month late for the start of the fall semester, but I made up for it by going to night school. I switched my major to anthropology and enrolled in beginning French. I figured both would serve me well once I figured out how to get back to the South Pacific.

After dinner in Nima's lodge I suggest to Asia we go to bed so we can get an early start in the morning to Tengboche Monastery. She complains that it feels colder than it did the previous night, and I answer that the temperature seems about the same. Our room isn't heated, but last night I had to sleep with my bag, rated at twenty degrees *above* zero, zipped open and spread like a comforter, while Asia, sleeping in her bag rated at fifteen degrees *below* zero, and wearing her fleece pants and jacket, was still cold. Now I go to the kitchen and fill a drinking bottle with hot water, then come back and give it to her.

"Put this in the bottom of your bag."

"Thanks," she says as she crawls in, wearing her fleece pants and jacket and this time her down jacket as well. I assume that she sees my raised eyebrows because she adds, "I've got low blood pressure."

"But I thought you were a snowboarder?"

"I am, and I'm okay when I'm moving, but I freeze when I ride the chair lifts."

"The water bottle will help."

"It already does. Thanks again."

"You're welcome."

I don't say anything more, but my mind skips ahead to the Chang Tang. I picture the open, snow-swept alpine steppe where temperatures dip frequently below zero and the wind is said to be so incessant it sometimes drove the early explorers crazy. Hiking and climbing in the Chang Tang, I tell myself, is going to make a ride in a chair lift seem like, well, like a ride in a chair lift.

In the morning, however, Asia gets out of her bag at first light without complaining, and, joined by Nima, we are soon on our way. It's a five-hour walk to Tengboche, on the well-traveled route to Everest Base

Camp. The sky is still overcast, and the leaden clouds have formed an inverted mantle that obscures the glacial peaks. The trail crosses a hillside corrugated with drainage runnels, and the only sound other than the padding of my feet is the murmur of the Imja Khola about a thousand vertical feet below.

Asia is hiking a few steps in front of me, Nima in front of her. We come up behind a line of yaks loaded with mountaineering supplies—most likely consigned to one or more of the various teams headquartered at Everest Base Camp—and when the trail widens, we pass the caravan. The effort has Asia breathing hard, however, and we stop for a moment while she takes a whiff from her inhaler. Then we continue and soon round a bend that allows a view upvalley where we can see, perched like a jewel atop a promontory on the other side of the river, the Tengboche Monastery.

At midday we stop at a trailside teahouse owned by Tibetan refugees and enjoy a bowl of Chinese steamed vegetables, a recipe I assume they brought when they crossed the Himalayas trying to escape the Chinese. Ironies of world politics aside, it's welcome fare for Asia who usually has to settle for rice and potatoes in order to maintain her vegetarian regimen. The day has warmed enough that we take turns going behind the teahouse to change from long pants to shorts. Being warm enough leads my thoughts back to Asia's experience as a snowboarder, and I ask her to tell me more.

"I started when I was about thirteen, and I really got into it because it was my thing. Up to then I had depended on my mom and friends' parents when I wanted to do something. But I could do snowboarding on my own; I didn't need a father to teach me. I started to ride competitively, and I was out every weekend. I even arranged to get PE credit so I could train after school. I made the junior national team and qualified for the world championships in Japan. That was my first time out of the country, and I loved it, but I realized I loved the travel more than the competition. Later I was in a training camp back East, and I looked around at my teammates and I could see they had a competitive edge that I was missing. They were ready to commit their lives to competition, but that just wasn't me."

"So you quit?"

"I quit competing, but I continued to snowboard for fun. I still do, and I love it. My mom is competitive, you know, but I always heard my dad wasn't. So maybe I got that from him."

"Your dad wasn't that competitive," I tell her, "but he was ambitious. There's a difference, you know."

She nods, Nima pays the bill, and we continue.

The trail begins to drop toward the Imja Khola, and we pass first through a forest of mixed silver birch and tree rhododendron—the latter with red, pink, and white blossoms—then a zone of blue pine and silver fir. From the treetops we hear the songbird melodies of warblers and tits. "I rest and let the others go ahead," I read yesterday in Jonathan's journal when he was describing this same section of trail. "I need the smell of pine, the sight of blooming rhododendron, the distant sound of the river. Down the trail I hear the tinkling of yak bells, and closer the songs of the birds. I leave a *mani* wall on my right as I pass, chanting, 'Om Mani Padme Hum,' and I feel part of the Grand Design."

If it is true, as many say it is, that for all of us there is one place on Earth that, when we see it, we know it immediately as where we belong—as though we recognize it across some distant, ancestral memory—then that place for Jonathan was the Himalayas. When I was reading his journal, I could hear his enthusiasm as though he were reading the words aloud: "the rhododendrons, red, white, pink, splashing whole hillsides with color, like they were decorated for Christmas" and "another crystal morning, the white peaks piercing the blue sky, and I feel *alive*." At the end he wrote, "I will come back," and he did, every year but one, until he died eight years later.

I don't know whether or not Jonathan's parents worried about him when he was away on his climbing expeditions, but I suspect they did.

They knew that on our Everest climb in 1976, in the great ice valley above Camp 1 known as the Western Cwm, Jonathan one day had stepped on a hidden crevasse and fallen fifty feet into the blue-white chasm before the rope stopped him. He was uninjured, but it easily could have been otherwise.

My wife and I have already had a small taste of what it feels like to have your kids out adventuring in the world. Our oldest daughter spent her junior year of high school studying in France, and during spring break she left with four buddies—all of them no older than sixteen—to travel by bus and train through Spain for two weeks. That is a long way from knowing your child is on some distant glacial mountain on the other side of the Earth, but I am steeling myself for that, or its equivalent. I know they are not to be discouraged in this, either; in fact, I know I must do the opposite.

My underlying anxiety about my kids vagabonding into the world is probably exacerbated remembering some of my own experiences. My most frightening encounter—and the one I consider my coming-of-age as an adventure traveler—happened three years after that first voyage to the South Seas. I was finishing my senior year at the University of Hawaii when I was offered a position crewing aboard a ninety-eight-foot ketch leaving for the Society, Tuamotu, and Marquesas Islands. The boat belonged to a wealthy businessman, and the pay was four hundred dollars a month, in hundred-dollar notes, all cash, no deductions. The owner visited the boat only a week or two here and there, and in between the captain and crew could do with the vessel as they pleased.

We spent two months in the Societies, sailed to the Marquesas, made a long windward passage to Mexico, then gunkholed down the coast of Central America. In Panama I met two rascals with an eighty-two-foot Alden schooner who told me they knew of a remote tribe in central Colombia that had a large supply of emeralds but needed .22 shells for hunting birds and small game. These two had befriended an employee at a rifle range who said he could get the .22 shells. I had been saving all my hundred-dollar bills, so I left the ninety-eight-foot ketch, signed on to the eighty-two-foot schooner, and added my money to the grubstake. We ordered fifty thousand rounds. Our plan was to smuggle the ammunition into Colombia (surely we were safe trying to smuggle contraband *into* Colombia), trade the shells for emeralds, and then sail to Fiji where we had been told the Hindu community ran a robust market in gemstones. There we would convert the emeralds to cash, and use the money to market a charter service sailing tourists around the islands in the schooner.

We failed to consider that in a small place like Panama it is hard to order fifty thousand rounds of shells without people hearing about it. We were arrested, and the first night I was thrown in a large holding tank with thirty other prisoners, including a drunk who cursed the guards abusively. We tried to quiet him because the guards, walking by every few minutes, glared at him from under the low rim of their billed hats. He finally passed out, and I was lying on a small piece of cardboard offered by another prisoner when, in the predawn hours, the guards came and hauled the drunk away. He was no longer cursing but pleading. They brought him back an hour later. Two of the other prisoners who helped me aid him said the expansive black and red marks on his sides and back were from rubber cudgels. We tried to keep him alive, but by dawn he was dead.

I was moved to a small cell with several other prisoners, and each day I was taken for interrogation by police who were convinced that my partners and I had planned to trade the .22 shells for marijuana. When I was arrested, I had been allowed to keep a small stuffsack with a few personal items: toothbrush and paste, small notepad and paper, and, most valuable, a pouch of tobacco and a pipe. After the fifth day of my interrogation, when I was returned to my cell, I discovered my stuffsack was gone. My cell mates shrugged their shoulders when I confronted them. I didn't know how long I was going to remain in prison, but I did know that whatever the length of time, if I didn't do something then to recover my stolen belongings, I would only be abused more by the other prisoners. In high school I had never been in a fight, and I had on occasion wondered, If I were ever put in a corner where there was no choice, would I have the resolve both to throw and to take the punches? I realized I was then in just such a corner, and there was only one way out. My stomach was in a knot as I considered what it was I had to do, but I told myself I had no choice.

Of my cell mates there was one who I was almost certain was the thief, the one others seemed to defer to. When I had asked them about my stuffsack, he was the one who most adamantly denied knowing anything about it. I watched him out of the corner of my eye, and when I saw him shift to a position apart from the others, I sprang with as much force as I could muster and landed a punch to the side of his head. As he fell, I cocked my arm for the next blow, but another prisoner grabbed me and in a second they were all pummeling my back and head in a hail of punches. I heard the guards' whistles blowing, and as fast as my assailants were on me, they were off. But as we got up, the one I had punched said to me in a snarl, "As soon as you go to sleep," and made the motion of sticking a knife between my ribs.

My only hope was with the guards. I told the overweight and aquiline-eyed sergeant in charge of our floor that I had started the fight, and I told him why. He asked my cell mates if they had stolen my stuffsack. They all denied it. He looked at me and said, "They don't have your things." I was about to tell him they were going to kill me as soon as I was asleep when a prisoner from across the hall called to the sergeant. I recognized him. Everybody knew he was in for murder and that he was not a man to fool with. The sergeant walked over and spoke to him, then unlocked his cell door. The murderer, maybe forty years old, was slightly built, but his eyes moved unceasingly, missing nothing. He stepped into my cell and looked at the others.

"Where is the gringo's things?" he said with a kind of disarming ease.

The others shrugged their shoulders. He looked at each of them, giving them time to consider their answers. Then suddenly, with a voice like a knife, he said, "I want the gringo's things. Now!"

The one whom I had punched reached in a cheap plastic case that held his belongings and produced my stuffsack. He gave it to the murderer, who then handed it to me. The murderer looked at the sergeant and said, "I want the gringo in my cell." The sergeant nodded, and I followed the murderer across the hall into my new home. He introduced me to my new cell mates, all of whom had been in the prison for many years.

"That took some guts, what you did," the murderer said.

"It was kind of stupid."

"You got your tobacco back."

"All I got was lucky."

He looked at me hard in the eye, then, after a pause, said, "There's no such thing as luck."

Asia, Nima, and I cross the Imja Khola River over a swinging cable bridge, start the long climb up the promontory toward Tengboche, and by midafternoon enter the grounds of the monastery. Tengboche was built using traditional Buddhist *gompa* design, but it is not old. First constructed in 1923, it burned down and was rebuilt in 1933, then burned down again in 1991. Many of the trekkers who had listened to and admired the monks' chanting sent funds to rebuild Tengboche and to hire Bhutanese artisans to paint its new walls with large frescoes depicting Buddhist parables.

We check into a small trekker's lodge owned and operated by the brother of the reincarnate lama. In the dining room Asia and I sit on benches covered with colorful Tibetan saddle blankets and sip tea while Nima goes to arrange an audience with the lama. A trekker tells us he has heard on his shortwave that NATO forces have bombed the Chinese embassy in Yugoslavia. Even though NATO claims it was a mistake, the Chinese are outraged. There is anti-American rioting in Beijing and also in Chengdu, where Asia and I must pass on the last leg of our journey. The news is disquieting, but I try not to dwell on it until we return to Kathmandu and receive better information.

In the late afternoon Nima takes us down a narrow passage alongside the monastery, through a gate, and into a courtyard. We stop at a low door and, following Nima's lead, take off our shoes. Nima removes from his day pack three silk *kata* scarves and gives one to Asia, one to me, and keeps the third. Again following Nima's lead, we each fold our *kata* around a Nepalese banknote and enter a small room where the lama, in a burgundy robe draped over a saffron shirt, sits cross-legged in the light of a small window. Nima greets him, and the lama motions us to approach. We each lay our donation on a small table in front of him, then clasp our hands and bow our heads as he drapes the *katas* around our necks and invites us by hand gesture to sit. He claps his hands, and when an attendant monk appears, orders tea.

He looks much the same as when I first saw him in 1976, when he performed a *puja* ceremony to bless our Everest expedition against "bad luck on the mountain." Following the climb, Jonathan and I remained in Tengboche for a few days, and in the mornings we used to walk with the lama through his flower garden grown from seeds brought as gifts by visiting trekkers. On one of these walks I had asked him if he could be granted any wish in the world, what would he want.

"I would like to live alone in a cave high in the mountains and meditate," he had replied.

Now I ask Nima to see if the lama remembers our walks in the garden and my question about being granted any wish. The lama listens and shakes his head, telling Nima he doesn't remember, but adds that if it weren't for his responsibilities to the monastery and to the Sherpa people, he *would* like to live in a cave.

"Please explain to the lama," I ask Nima, "that Jonathan was killed four years later in an avalanche on a mountain in Kham, and that Asia is Jonathan's daughter."

Nima translates, and the lama nods to Asia, and she smiles and nods back. "Then please explain that she and I are at the beginning of a long journey that will end on the mountain in Kham where we hope to find her father's grave."

The lama nods to Asia, and again he claps his hands. The attendant appears, the lama speaks to him, then the attendant leaves and returns in a moment with a square of parchment folded into a small envelope. The lama holds the square to his forehead as his lips move to an unspoken mantra. Then he passes the envelope to Asia, explaining to Nima that it contains a powder she is to dissolve in warm water and drink if during our journey she misses her father and becomes sad. Asia clasps her hands, bows, and thanks him.

"Can you please ask the lama if he has any other advice for Asia and me to consider during our pilgrimage," I say to Nima.

Nima translates. The lama listens, then looks at me, looks at Asia, and says to Nima, "Tell them to watch out for the Chinese."

In late afternoon, in the last hour of daylight, Asia, Nima, and I walk the grounds of the monastery. We can hear from inside the *gompa* the basso voices of chanting monks. The mantle of clouds has lowered to a misting fog that shrouds the monastery and, around it, the birch and rhododendron forest where long wisps of moss hang from the branches. The chanting, the forest, the mist, the moss . . . together they create a kind of drear enchantment.

We walk to the open commons in front of the *gompa*. When the weather is clear, there is a good view from here of the Lhotse-Nuptse wall, and above that the tip of Everest. In 1976 our expedition camped here on grass cropped by visiting yaks to a stubble lawn. It was toward the end of the monsoon, and the clouds had closed over the monastery, as they have now. In the morning there was a brief clearing, however, and I stood apart from the tents, looking at the mountain and wondering what story I would have to tell in a month or two, when I was on my way home. Then I paused and thought about what story I would have to tell *if* I came through here again on my way home.

Three days later we passed a row of six chorten monuments, made of stacked stones, commemorating six Sherpas who had died three years earlier in a single, massive collapse in the icefall. Nearby was a large granite boulder with inscriptions of other climbers who had died on Everest: Jake Brittenbach, 1963; Mick Burke, 1975.

By then I knew I wasn't immune. I knew there was a chance that a month or two hence my name might be carved on that rock alongside Jake's and Mick's. Before leaving on our expedition all of us on the team had read a report that one in ten climbers who attempted Everest did not come back. Even though I was skeptical and thought the real number closer to one in twenty, two things had occurred in the previous three years to make me worry about having my name carved on rock.

It is said that in warfare soldiers go through three stages of accommodating danger. The first is to convince themselves that death *won't* happen to them. The second develops when they see the first one or two of their buddies die, and know it *could* happen to them. The third stage is when so many have died around them, they know that it is only a matter of time before it *will* happen to them.

By the time I got to Everest, I was at the second stage. After I was released from prison in Panama, I hitchhiked to Peru and found a job working for an anthropologist in a Quechua village in the Andes. My task was to complete a survey for a study of how much the Indian people articulated with the national economy. In fact, I spent most of my time convincing the locals I wasn't the tax collector, and by the time I finished, I was feeling the need for a rejuvenative sojourn in the wild world. I met a climber living in Lima who sold me some used gear, and following his suggestion I hitchhiked to the Cordillera Blanca. I arrived at night and slept on the dirt floor of a hut that belonged to the driver of the small truck who had given me my last ride. The next day I walked outside to see sunlight reflecting in dazzling brilliance off the summits of a line of mountains over twenty thousand feet above sea level. Looking up at Huascaran, the highest peak, I felt a yearning to know what the opposite view was like, standing on top looking down.

Separating me from my dream, however, was an assortment of very used mountaineering equipment. My funds had been insufficient to pay for a rope. The flimsiness of my boots was matched by the tattered condition of my lightweight sleeping bag. My climbing knickers were made of cheap cotton. And whatever I knew about mountaineering technique had been largely self-taught.

My interest in the sport had started as a teenager. I grew up in the orange groves of southern California, making money trapping gophers for a buck a tail. The Santa Ana River still flowed in its natural channel, and it was a good place to stalk rabbits with my single-shot .22. Then, in a period of only three years, the groves were bulldozed and burned to make room for row after row of cookie-cutter houses along freshly paved streets with names like Elmwood, Briarwood, and Maplewood. To find solace I fled to the local San Gabriel Mountains, and with a copy of the mountaineering manual *Freedom of the Hills,* I taught myself how to walk on snow slopes with crampons and self-arrest with an ice axe.

By the time I reached the Cordillera Blanca, I was still inexperienced. Not only was my gear inadequate and my clothing inappropriate, but even more glaring, I had no one to climb with. But I had the name of a hotel where all the climbers stayed, so I went there. Expecting a hovel, I was surprised to find it the most elegant lodging in the valley. I was told that the owner, an eccentric Peruvian known as Don Carlos, liked climbers and had converted a changing room next to the thermal pool into a bunk-bed dormitory with cheap rates. There I found two experienced climbers, a woman from New Zealand and a Dutchman, who were looking for another partner. I introduced myself, but they were reluctant to consider me. I was trying to talk them into taking me on an easy climb up a smaller peak when an American named Ron Fear arrived. The Dutchman whispered that he was one of the better climbers in the world. He had been in the Cordillera Blanca for over a month, and now he was back from Huascaran, where he had successfully guided a group of clients to the summit.

The others had already met him, and they introduced me. He was in his late twenties, lean, with a black beard that filled out his equally lean face. He stood about five feet ten, but seemed to fill a larger space because his enthusiasm was so contagious everyone drew to him. When he spoke he smiled, and when he listened he smiled. Even more memorable was the way he dressed. When I met him, he was wearing green ski pants with red knee and seat patches, a yellow shirt with red stripes, and a rainbow-hued knit cap. During the next fourteen months, I never saw him in anything other than some harlequin combination of clothes made for him by his girlfriend, Jan (who had a fledgling line of backpacks called JanSport).

Ron announced that his clients had been so exhausted coming down Huascaran they had abandoned most of their equipment at high camp, and had told him he could have it if he wanted to go back for it.

"That's not all," Ron told us. "Don Carlos wants to start a rental service for climbers, and he told me he'd trade the gear for credit at the bar! Who wants to go up Huascaran!"

We left the next day. The New Zealander and the Dutchman also volunteered. The gear was cached at the 20,000-foot level. On the way up Ron took time to show me how to scout a route through a crevasse field, and how to belay the rope on my ice axe while he crossed a snow bridge. On the side of an ice block he showed me how to ascend the rope to complete a self-rescue if I were to fall into a hidden crevasse. He gave me tips on breathing evenly in time to my steps, and on varying my crampon placement to minimize fatigue in my leg muscles.

At the cache we set up camp. Ron said it was an easy day from there to the top. He suggested that in the morning the New Zealander, the Dutchman, and I continue to the summit while he carried down a load of the abandoned equipment, then came back for more. The top of Huascaran was over 22,000 feet, an altitude that only a week before I had considered an impossible dream. The next day the weather held, and by noon we made the summit. There was a bamboo marker wand on top, and next to it an empty champagne bottle with an inscription on the label that said, "Fear Was Here." Three days later we were back at the hotel. We traded the gear to Don Carlos for a credit line at the bar of $450. A Pisco sour cost the same as a night in the dormitory, about sixty-five cents.

We climbed two more peaks that season, including a first ascent of a steep face. We bivouacked on the summit, and my cotton knickers were so wet that when I bent down, plates of ice broke off my legs. In the last hours before dawn, when we were all shaking uncontrollably, Ron told me the only qualification to be a mountaineer was a short memory for pain.

By then I had been traveling continuously for two years. I returned to Hawaii to work in the boatyard of a yacht harbor, but my thoughts were still in the mountains. Ron was planning an expedition to the Himalayas with a team that was already complete, but he said he could meet me afterward back in Peru, to attempt what he said was the best unclimbed ridge in the country. He asked another of his climbing partners, Chris Chandler, an emergency-room physician, to join us, along with three others who would stay in Base Camp.

We planned to ascend the peak alpine-style, carrying what we needed on our backs and climbing the route in one push. In our second camp, however, we were penned down by a storm, and as our small food supply dwindled, we knew we would have to retreat. Chris said he had to return to his job in the United States. I tried to talk Ron into making another attempt, but he confessed he was worn out from his previous climb in the Himalayas, and he wanted to go someplace warm.

"Don Carlos has a rubber raft." Ron suggested. "I bet we've got enough left on our line of credit to rent it and go down to the jungle and float a river."

We had heard it was possible to float the Urubamba River below Machu Picchu, putting in at the end of the railway. There was said to be one major rapid, however, and Ron was the only one of us who had experience running white water.

"Don't worry," he said. "I'll give everybody a lesson before we get to that part."

The others disembarked at Machu Picchu, which they hadn't seen, while I continued downriver to the end of the railway. There I intended to buy supplies and meet them when the next day's train arrived. But when it pulled in they weren't on board. Ron was always running late, so I assumed he had missed the departure. When the next day's train arrived, I saw Ron's girlfriend and another friend step down from the old wooden railway car.

"Where's Ron?" I asked.

"That's what I was going to ask you," she replied.

"What do you mean?"

"We missed the train yesterday, so he blew up the raft and said he was going to float down the river from Machu Picchu. But he should have been here by now."

"That section's got huge rapids."

"He was mad he missed the train. I'm not sure he was thinking clearly."

"Oh Christ."

"You think he's in trouble?"

"Listen," I said, "I've got to get on this train right now, go back to Machu Picchu and start scouting the river back this way. You stay here until you hear from me, okay?"

The train was leaving, and I hopped aboard. In two hours I disembarked at the Machu Picchu station. Just below the tracks, the water of the Urubamba was fast but smooth. As I walked downriver, I heard the roar of approaching white water. The canyon narrowed, and the river gained speed as it flowed around large granite boulders fallen from the surrounding walls. Even though I knew nothing of rafting, I could tell that if Ron and his other friend had still been in the river at this point, they would have had a very hard time escaping from the flow. I continued downriver, climbing over the boulders, and at each turn, as the roar of the water increased, my hope for their survival decreased. I scrambled up smaller rocks to gain a large, smooth boulder, and when I reached the top, my stomach tightened. The roaring river dropped in a fifteen-foot waterfall, then disappeared completely under a knot of boulders that choked the canyon one side to the other.

There was no sign of the raft or their bodies. I was sure all three were pinned by the water under the rocks. I sat on the boulder for an hour staring at the river. At first I was angry, wondering how Ron could have been so impetuous, not only getting himself killed but his friend, too. I climbed back to the railway tracks and started walking toward the end of the line, where Ron's girlfriend was waiting. She would be the first one I would have to tell. Then I would call Ron's parents.

I walked alongside the tracks, double-stepping the ties, considering how in one more week I would be twenty-three years old. I thought I knew about death because I had seen the prisoner in the Panama jail die. But this felt different. I continued along the rail line until I saw a tarantula next to the tracks. There was a large wasp on its back that I knew was the species known as the tarantula hawk. It looked like it was stinging the spider, but it was actually laying its eggs inside the host's abdomen. I sat on the rail and watched, knowing that when the young wasps hatched they would begin slowly to consume the spider until it died. Then the wasps would rise into the world and start the cycle again. The tarantula twisted and spun, trying to shake off the wasp. The effort, I knew, was futile.

I sat on the rail wondering if the spider had any sense of its doom. And what about Ron? Hadn't I known he was doomed when I first saw that green champagne bottle sitting on the windswept summit of Huascaran? Had he known? And what about me? Staying in this game of adventure, could I continue to ignore the possibility that my fate, like the tarantula's—like Ron's—was already sealed?

By that fall, however, I had renewed my conviction that people make their own fate. I told myself that Ron was headlong, that he had never recognized, much less heeded, his limits, and that imprudence had cost him his life. Sometimes I missed him with an ache I could feel in my heart. I told myself, however, that as long as I remembered always to exercise caution, I could avoid what in those days of adventure all of us referred to, with graphic crudeness, as "the chop."

For the next two years I climbed everywhere in the Western states, rendezvousing in the Cascades with Chris Chandler, and in California with a new partner named Mike Blake. Mike and I made the rock climber's circuit: Yosemite in the spring and fall, Tuolomne Meadows in the summer, Joshua Tree in the winter. He was twenty years old, a handsome blond-haired beach kid smitten with the mountains. Between climbs we worked together painting houses, saving enough for our next junket. He was like a younger brother, and it was a new role for me to be the older partner making most of the decisions.

I wanted to return to Peru, but Mike didn't want to spend the money, and Chris couldn't get off work, so I left with some other friends. I was in the dormitory in Don Carlos's hotel, talking to a group of climbers I had met previously in Yosemite, when one of them said, "That was really too bad about Mike."

"What about Mike?"

"Oh man, I just assumed you had heard."

"Heard what?"

"He was on the last pitch of The Nose (on El Capitan, in Yosemite), doing that traverse just below the top. It sounds like his jumars popped and he hadn't tied in short. He went the whole hundred and fifty feet, and then the rope snapped."

Later that summer, when I returned to California, I talked to another friend who had been halfway up El Capitan on the same route when she heard an odd whooshing noise and looked up to see Mike sailing through the air, the rope trailing behind him. He had fallen twenty feet below the summit rim, and after the rope paid out the force of his fall snapped it at the anchor, and he then free-fell another fifteen hundred feet. My friend said that as he flew by her he was still yelling, until he caromed off the rock where the foot of the wall is a little less than vertical.

I had left some of my gear stored in Mike's room at his father's house. I was hesitant to ask for it. Finally I called Mike's father, and he said to come over. He escorted me to Mike's bedroom behind the garage. My gear was in the corner where I had left it, and Mike's belongings where he had left them: his dirty laundry in another corner, his high-school trophies on the dresser, climbing pictures on the wall, bed unmade. I picked up my duffel, and as I passed the dresser I made a sudden pause. Mike's wallet was sitting next to the lamp. It was covered in crusty blood and pieces of dried flesh. I looked away and kept walking, but his father knew that I had seen it.

"They sent it with his belongings," he said when we got to the door. "I guess I should do something with it, but . . . but I can't."

A week later I was in Yosemite, standing at the base of El Capitan, staring up at the three-thousand-foot monolith. Near the top of The Nose there is a horizontal series of bolts that requires the leader to clip his ladder slings from one hanger to the next. From there it is only a few feet to the top, where the leader then ties the rope to an anchor, and the second man, who has the other end of the rope tied to his waist harness, ascends the rope using camming clamps called jumars. When you get to the bolt ladder, it's necessary to weight the jumars with care because they are clamped on rope that at that point is strung horizontally, and they can twist off. The standard precaution is to pause every twenty or thirty feet and retie the rope to your waist so if a jumar does twist off you don't have as far to fall.

Mike had forgotten to do that. He was only a few feet from the summit of a climb that had taken him four days, and he was excited. As I stood at the base of the rock wall, looking up at the path of Mike's fall, I knew that I also had been in situations where I had forgotten to tie in short before making a sideways jumar.

After Ron died I had convinced myself that if I were careful it *wouldn't* happen to me. Now there was a subtle but significant shift. *Wouldn't* was changing to *could*.

Asia and I have a tiny corner room in the trekker's lodge where we have spread our sleeping bags and inflatable pads on two wood benches that serve as beds. I am propped against the wall reading by headlamp Jonathan's journal from his ascent of Ama Dablam. There is a little nightstand between us, and sitting on it is the sacred *kata* the lama gave Asia, the parchment envelope of powder to protect her against sadness, and a string of prayer beads Asia has brought along that belonged to her father; they are familiar to me because they are the same beads he had when I was with him on Everest and later on Minya Konka.

Even though the window is open, Asia hasn't complained. But she does have her sleeping bag pulled over her head while she writes in her journal, so that the light of her headlamp is a dim glow through the yellow fabric. I read Jonathan's description of getting to the summit of Ama Dablam, then down-climbing in the dark and finally reaching High Camp at midnight. When he filmed a team of very strong climbers ascending this peak in 1979, it had been climbed only once before. Today Ama Dablam attracts dozens of climbers every season. As the filmmaker, Jonathan was not a lead climber, and in fact he was one of the least experienced mountaineers on the team. He worked as hard as anyone, however, and contributed his share to the team's success. He earned his right to be proud of their accomplishment, but he was careful not to let it boost his own ego.

"Asia, let me read you something from your dad's journal."

I see her face peer out from under the hood of her sleeping bag.

"He's finished the climb, and he's back here in Tengboche, looking up at the mountain.

"I know every feature of Ama Dablam. I know the campsites. I know the Yellow Tower, the Second Rockstep, the Ice Headwall. I know the summit. I also know memories of these places will only whet instead of quench my thirst to be part of another expedition. Soon the desire will return, to experience the cold and the altitude, to see sunset above the clouds, to climb again in order to expand my abilities and my awareness. But are these the only motivations of my desire? Isn't part of it also ego? And if it is a mix of awareness and ego, is this dual desire at once the wings as well as the chains of freedom?"

We are both quiet for a moment. Then Asia says, "He was always questioning his motives, wasn't he?"

"It was one of the most remarkable things about him. It's a habit I've decided I want to take up myself, to make sure I'm doing things for the right reason."

Asia goes back to her writing, and I return to my reading. Soon I see her other hand appear in the small opening of her sleeping bag, put the cap on her pen, and then turn off her headlamp.

"Good night, Rick."

"Good night," I say. I can see only one eye protruding from her bag, so I add, "Are you warm enough?"

"Well, I know you like the window open."

"What if I close it when I go to sleep?"

"That'd be great."

She rolls over and curls into the folds of her sleeping bag, and in a few minutes she is asleep, breathing steadily. I consider that we are now a little over a week into this journey, and while things are going according to plan, I have these concerns about her asthma, her sensitivity to cold, and what I suspect is a corresponding need to be comfortable. There are aspects of her that are delicate. She has a bug phobia, for example, that extends even to gnats flying around her head. I worry whether she will be able to accommodate the rigors of the Chang Tang. I also wonder if I will be able to accommodate her willfulness. I suspect she is picking up on these concerns, too, and that is contributing to what is, if not an awkwardness, then a kind of cautious formality between us.

We still have nine weeks to go, however, and I am confident we will have enough time to get comfortable with each other. Simply learning more about each other's backgrounds will help. She seems to be genuinely interested in my stories, which is a relief. When I told her about the sailing adventure to Tahiti, she responded most to the part about my friend falling in love with the French-Tahitian woman. What captivated her wasn't the romance, but that the couple had married and they were still living together, in France.

"His first adventure," Asia said, "and his life went in a totally different direction."

"I guess you never know," I replied.

I'm not sure what she took from my Panama jail story, but if it's only to be careful and not do anything stupid when you're traveling in the Third World, that will be lesson enough. And the other stories—Ron Fear and Mike Blake—maybe they're a prelude to whatever she will take from this journey about facing the specter of death.

While we are still in the Khumbu I want to tell her more about the Everest expedition in 1976, because it involves her father. I'm still hoping the weather clears—I have the intuition that seeing the mountain will provide Asia one more tangible connection to Jonathan. For the same reason, I would have also liked to have hiked with her the rest of the way to Base Camp, but we had only so much time between Asia getting out of school and the onset of the monsoon season. But I have received word that a friend named Peter Pilafian, who was with us on Everest in 1976, and also with Jonathan on Ama Dablam in 1979 and on our expedition to Minya Konka in 1980, will be in Namche tomorrow. Peter has been at Base Camp for several weeks directing a film, so maybe he can tell her what it's like there these days, so she can get a sense of how it's changed since her father was there.

When I consider it further, then, I'm still confident that all the pieces of this journey will, when fitted together, create for Asia a clear picture of the life and times of her father. More, I know the adventures the two of us will share—even if they are ones that try her abilities—will also be the ones that Jonathan would be having with her if he were still alive.

I glance over and see only a swatch of Asia's knit cap showing from the hood of her sleeping bag. She looks warm even though the window is still open. Outside I can hear the neck-bells of grazing yaks making a wind-chime tinkle. Out the window it is black, and no stars shine, but I know the sword-summit of Ama Dablam towers above us. I pick up Jonathan's journal from his climb of this same mountain, and continue reading. He is now walking back to Namche Bazaar, following the trail his daughter and I have hiked today, the one we will hike tomorrow when we head back. For him, the climb is over, he is going home. He stops and turns and in the distance sees the tip of Everest rising above the great Lhotse-Nuptse wall. He reaches Namche that day, and he goes to sleep that night in his tent, thinking about his wife who is pregnant with their first child.

"Someday I will bring this child to these mountains," he writes, completing his entry for the day, "to experience the truths of life, the truths that I am learning."

3

The next day Asia, Nima, and I hike back to Namche and check back into the Danphe Bar and Lodge. Again, Asia and I take a room as far as possible from the pool table. That evening a team of about a half-dozen Sherpas, who look to be in their late teens, challenge an opposing group of youthful trekkers, who look to be a mix of Americans and Europeans. Everyone is drinking Star beer, the Nepalese standard. There is a small stack of banknotes on the pool table in front of the Sherpas, and a corresponding stack in front of the trekkers.

Nima, Asia, and I leave the bar and walk up the street to the house of Pasang Kami, who in 1976 was the *sirdar*, or leader, of the Sherpas working on our expedition. P.K. is one of the most successful climbing and trekking leaders in Nepal, and the walls of his house are filled with pictures of him standing with luminaries he has guided: Dianne Feinstein, Jimmy Carter, Robert Redford. P.K.'s daughter and Nima's son, who are married and have a baby daughter, join us for dinner, and afterward P.K. offers to show Asia the video of our 1976 climb, which she has never seen. Nima tells me that nearly every house in Namche now has a TV and VCR, then adds that several also have satellite telephones and PCs.

"I am finishing a business plan," Nima tells me, "to open an Internet connection here in Namche. Maybe you know some investors?"

In 1976 the small hydroelectric generator that powers all this was still under construction, and I am realizing my initial impression that Namche hasn't changed may be superficial. P.K. pours Nima and me each a glass of whiskey, then starts the movie. We are all three amused to see ourselves as young men only a few years older than Asia is today. Because he was one of the cameramen, Jonathan is not in the film, but whenever I see a scene I remember was one he shot, I mention it to Asia.

It's nearly midnight when we get back to Nima's hotel. The Sherpas and the trekkers are still playing pool and drinking beer, and the stack of banknotes in front of the Sherpas is now noticeably higher than the one in front of the trekkers. They invite Asia to join them, and when she accepts I tell her I'll see her in the morning.

"I'll be quiet when I come in the room," she says.

"I doubt you'll be able to wake me," I assure her.

In our room I turn out the bare electric bulb that hangs from the ceiling, strip down to a T-shirt and boxer shorts, and crawl into my twenty-degree-above-zero bag. Before I drift to sleep I go back to the movie of the Everest climb. Seeing yourself in a documentary film has the odd effect of inducing, in an almost extrasensorial way, that perception we all have on occasions of stepping outside the confines of our bodies and seeing and hearing ourselves as others do. Watching yourself as you acted and sounded twenty-five years ago adds to that effect the sense that you are viewing your life from almost an afterlife position, as though you are in your next life looking back at a previous one.

What I see of my previous life, as I watch in my mind my climbing partner Chris Chandler and myself leading the route through the notoriously dangerous Khumbu icefall, is a young man in his mid-twenties who is outwardly convivial and even boisterous, who cultivates the impression of being carefree but feels at a deep level the anxiety that he won't live to see thirty. Later during the ascent I see the young man leading up the giant expanse of ice called the Lhotse Face, and on his own face I can see the desire to succeed in this huge endeavor to stand on top of the highest point on earth. Then I watch at the end of the expedition as circumstance and luck split him from his climbing partner, whom he has roped not only on this climb but on many many previous ascents over the years. His partner Chris goes on to make the summit, and he does not.

I see the young man and his other teammates as they leave the mountain, successful as a team, but returning to a culture—like most cultures—interested less in the management of successful teams than the achievements of heroic individuals. People want to know what it feels like to be on top of Everest. It's not that the young man doesn't understand this, either: he wants to know what it feels like, too. And therein is the poignant irony, because what I see lying in my sleeping bag looking backward is a man who is not unlike the modern Everesters, both those who hire guides and those who are self-guided, who all seem to be driven to climb the mountain for the wrong reasons.

I open my eyes, see a bright glow through the window, and immediately get up to have a closer look.

"Asia, wake up. It's clear."

"Huh?"

"No clouds."

"Oh . . . good."

"We can hike up the hill and see Everest. Come on."

She gets out of her sleeping bag, eyes sleepy and arms folded against the cold. With a cloudless sky the temperature has dropped, and I have to wipe my condensed breath from the single-pane glass. Looking out, I can see a snow-covered peak above the steep ridge opposite town. The summit, brilliant white against sapphire blue, rises to a height that I know, to someone who has never been close to a Himalayan peak, must seem mythical.

"Look at this."

Asia peers out the window. I see her eyes widen as she says, "Oh *wow!*"

Since she's slept in her clothes, she has only to put on her shoes and she's ready. We each stuff our daypacks with camera gear and leave. Outside the sky is cloudless. Between the houses the pathways paved with river-rounded cobble are empty. In the cool morning air we smell the wafting incense of burning juniper, and we hear, drifting to us across the rooftops, the Buddhist monks as they begin their chant to carry the old Sherpa to his next life. In a few minutes we see walking down the path an old woman spinning her prayer wheel. She is the only passerby at this early hour, and I suspect she's up because, unlike the young men whom Asia played pool with last night, her internal clock is still adjusted to the rise and set of the sun.

As we near the top of the hill, the tips of the peaks emerge above the foreground ridges. The snow-fluted face of Tamserku is bright white against blue sky. The features on the southwest face of Ama Dablam are lost in the backlight shadows of the rising sun, but the shape of its sword-summit is in dramatic silhouette. At the head of the valley the transverse wall of the Lhotse-Nuptse ridge looks like the rampart of Valhalla, and above it, as though rising from the inner sanctum, we can see the tip of Everest.

"Whoa," Asia says, 'I *am* glad it cleared. This is incredible."

"There's something different about an eight-thousand-meter peak," I say, looking upvalley to Everest. "It goes so high that no matter how clear the air, it looks like it's in a distant haze, like it's more mythical than real."

"How many eight-thousand-meter peaks are there?"

"Fourteen. They're all in the Himalayas."

"Have they all been climbed?"

"A long time ago. Annapurna was the first, in 1950. Everest and K2 were in '53 and '54. The last one I think was Shishapangma, in Tibet, in the mid-sixties."

"Has anybody climbed all of them?"

"A few people. Reinhold Messner was the first."

"I've heard of him, but who is he?"

"Most people think he's the best high-altitude mountaineer of our time."

I'm surprised Asia doesn't know anything about Messner's accomplishments. After all, she has done a little rock climbing, and she lives in Boulder, arguably the climbing center of the United States. Then I realize that these days being a rock climber doesn't imply, as it used to, that you would know anything about mountaineering. Now the sport continues to get more specialized, with many people focused only on subcategories such as bouldering, so-called sport climbing, and even gym climbing. I also realize that Asia *would* in all likelihood know more about mountaineering history if her father were alive, so I take a moment to tell her about Messner and how he also was the first to climb Everest without oxygen.

"It's hard from down here," she says, looking at Everest, "to imagine what it must really be like up there."

"It's exhausting, with or without oxygen. But on Everest, anyway, from what I've heard, there's no mystery left, with the route fixed top to bottom."

"So you don't have any desire to go back?"

"Less than zero."

I've arranged to meet my old friend Peter Pilafian at the Mt. Everest Bakery. It has a light and airy ambience, with two walls made almost entirely of glass panes that I assume, like Nima's pool table, were flown in by helicopter. It also has croissants and cappuccino that Asia and I enjoy while we wait for Peter. It's startling to me to have such things in a town that only twenty years ago was closer to the thirteenth than to the twentieth century, but my appreciation for these amenities is not shared by a group of trekkers who complain to the Sherpa girl serving us that the chocolate cake is stale.

"They should be more appreciative," Asia says.

"They probably don't realize that everything here, including flour, has to be carried in over a hundred miles by porters."

"I feel like telling them to shut up."

"Don't do that; you'll start a fight."

My mind quickly goes through the scenario of one of them slapping Asia, of me in turn punching one of them, of that starting a melee that results in someone going through one of these windows, and then of the bill arriving for the helicopter to fly in more glass.

"If they expect things to be like they are at home," she says, "they should stay at home."

The Sherpa girl replaces the chocolate cake with apple pie, and the trekkers are grudgingly pacified. A few minutes later Peter arrives, and I introduce him to Asia.

"I was with your father on all his major climbs," he says. "Peru, Everest, Ama Dablam. I was standing in Camp 1 on Minya Konka when Rick and Jonathan and the others swept past in the avalanche, and as they disappeared over the edge I just assumed they were all dead. Your father was a wonderful man."

"That must be true," Asia tells him, "because everyone I've ever met who knew him, they've all said the same thing."

Like most of my climbing friends, Peter has led a freelance life, starting in the sixties as the manager and electric violinist for the Mamas and Papas, in the seventies a documentary soundman, in the eighties a cameraman, and now in the nineties as a director and producer. He has been filming the placement of a satellite receiver on the summit of Everest so scientists can obtain an exact measure of the mountain's altitude.

"It's unbelievable what's happened on the mountain since we were there in '76," he tells us. "It used to be a team effort. As soon as we got two people to the top, our expedition was pronounced a success. Now it's the reverse of that. There are only individual climbers now, and their only concern is getting themselves to the top. A lot of them are clients, paying twenty-five to forty-five grand apiece to their guides."

"I thought it was sixty to a hundred grand," I say.

"It was, but since the big tragedy a few years ago the guides have low-ered their fees. That way they don't see themselves as responsible as they would be if each person paid more. But they make up for it in numbers, up to nineteen clients. The entire route is a highway. Hundreds of people going up and down, up and down, every day. There is absolutely nothing on the mountain that isn't fixed or set up in advance. The route through the icefall is put in and maintained by a climbing team that contracts with all the expeditions, who pay a fee. If there's something in the icefall you don't like, like a loose ladder, you complain and it gets fixed. And the Sher-pas now contract with the expeditions to stockpile the camps with food, equipment, and oxygen so the climbers don't have to carry anything.

"I saw an image on the mountain I'll never forget. I was at Camp 2, looking at the Lhotse Face, and I counted sixty-five people at one time on the fixed ropes. It looked like that famous old photograph of the long string of miners crossing to the gold fields in the Klondike. Then when there's a good summit day, it's the same thing high on the mountain, with twenty-five people stacked up at the Hillary Step. An absolute traffic jam. If you're stuck behind twenty-five people, it doesn't matter how good a climber you are, you're stuck."

"Let them have Everest," I say, remembering how much being there once meant to me, and to any climber. Then looking to Asia, I add, "There's other places to go."

"Like the Chang Tang?" she replies.

"Mountains nobody's been to or even heard of. And best of all, if you climb them, nobody's impressed."

I am sure Peter is right when he says one of the big differences between climbing Everest now and twenty-five years ago is that then it was a team effort. If I pause to look back carefully, however, and really see things as they were, I recognize that in 1976 the experience of climbing Everest was already beginning its shift to what it would eventually become. The change started in 1973 when an Italian expedition led by a wealthy industrialist hired two thousand porters to carry supplies that included heaters and carpets for their tents. Even that wasn't enough manpower, and two helicopters made a dozen round-trips a day ferrying fresh vegetables, meats, and even more supplies. That expedition happened to coincide with Jonathan's first trip to the Himalayas, and in his journal he complained about the incessant *tat-tat-tat-tat* of the helicopters as they flew over Namche on their way back and forth to Base Camp.

Although in 1976 we had forty-three Sherpas to help us freight our food and equipment from Base to the upper camps, we still had to engineer our own route through the Khumbu icefall, the labyrinth of ice blocks and crevasses where the glacier that inches off the south side of Everest passes over steep bedrock. Chris Chandler and I were selected to alternate each day with another team to scout the route. Chris was a natural athlete, six feet tall, solidly built, and, with Nordic features and long blond hair, uncommonly handsome. After Ron Fear had died in the rafting accident, Chris had taken over as my mentor, guiding my climbing skills to the next level, and we were a strong rope team. He had a regular job—as a doctor in a hospital emergency room—that allowed him time off for climbing. He always favored the harder routes, and preferred not to waste time researching them in advance. He was a complex mix, attracted to challenge but wary of responsibility.

I was still painting houses to make money to pay for my climbs and expeditions, and whenever I rendezvoused with Chris, I was conscious that he had a profession and I did not. Not that he ever emphasized it; in fact, he prided himself on wearing secondhand clothing, driving old cars, and living in low-rent apartments. He encouraged me to think twice about trading the liberty of my odd-job life for what he considered the chains of responsibility inevitable with any professional career. I couldn't imagine spending the rest of my life as a handyman, however, so I decided to go back to school.

I had managed to receive graduate-school credit for the anthropology work I did in Peru, and I considered what it might be like to be a college or university professor, getting away every few years to work in the field, perhaps with a remote group of people in the Amazon or in Borneo. I made an appointment with the cultural geography department at U.C. Berkeley, and with their encouragement I followed up with an application. I was surprised two months later when I received notice that I had been accepted into a five-year Ph.D. program. Two weeks before school started, however, Chris called.

"I got us on an expedition to the Himalayas," he said.

"The Himalayas?"

"By total blind luck I ran into somebody who has a permit and needs two more lead climbers. I told them about you, and they said they would consider us both."

"What's the peak?"

Chris made a little chuckle, as he often did when he was amused. He paused, and then said, "It's Everest."

Even on the approach march I was still second-guessing my decision, but by the time Chris and I woke at two-thirty A.M. on the morning of our first foray into the icefall, my thoughts were no longer on whether or not I should be a college professor. I was instead focused on the climb. We had breakfast and coffee, and then, with Jonathan, another cameraman, and a few Sherpas to carry ladder sections and rope, we left Base Camp under a nightsky electric with high-altitude stars.

Remembering an expedition is like remembering a film. You may recall the narrative spine, but what you remember most are a few scenes that, for whatever reason, resonate vividly. As we left Base Camp, we paused before the Buddhist altar the Sherpas had constructed, and breathed the smoke of smoldering juniper to cleanse our bodies. The goddess of Chomolungma—Everest—was less likely to strike someone who had been cleansed. The headlamps on each man in our small party were like torches in the hands of a procession of cabalists weaving through icy towers on their way to some secret rite. It was clear and cold, and the Sherpas chanted sotto voce as we climbed. In two hours we reached the high point of the previous team's effort. We unshouldered our packs and sat on them, waiting for first light. The cigarettes in the hands of the Sherpas were small orange points that brightened when they breathed in the tobacco. The starlight was enough to give shape to the labyrinth of ice towers behind and to our sides. In front of us the icefall dropped away to the rubble floor of the glacier. Across the valley we could see the cone shape of Pumori, and beyond, the massif of Cho Oyo, the ninth highest peak in the world, glowing dimly in the first faint light of dawn.

"Much view coming now," one of the Sherpas said.

When there was sufficient light, Chris led the first section, trailing the fixed rope that he fastened to aluminum stakes every thirty or forty feet while Jonathan, off to the side, filmed. I led the next section, descending into a crevasse and ascending the opposite side as the Sherpas bolted together two ladder sections they then lowered to me. We moved on to the next crevasse while another team came up and secured the ladders to anchors.

We made good progress until we encountered a difficult offset crevasse whose opposite wall was thirty feet high. The only way up was a thin rib of snow connecting the two walls. Chris and I paused to see who would lead it; we were both tired from several hours each of pushing through fresh snow. One of the Sherpas, the oldest on the team and a veteran of many expeditions, smiled and said he would do it. He climbed the rib and set up a belay. Then Chris followed, taking care as he was uncertain the rib could hold his extra weight.

He was halfway up when suddenly the crevasse gave a rifle crack and the ground around us shook. The glacier was moving. There were seracs on both sides of us, and they might topple any second.

"Up or down?" Chris yelled.

"Up!" I shouted, and in seconds I was on his heels. Jonathan and the other Sherpas backtracked as fast as they could. Chris and I reached the lead Sherpa and the three of us ran another fifty feet to get away from the seracs. We lowered to our knees, gasping in the rarified air to recover our breath. None of the seracs had collapsed, but the noise was surely a harbinger that something would soon topple.

"This road no good," the Sherpa said. "We leave now, okay?"

We nodded agreement, deciding to go down another way and scout for a more secure passage. As we left, the Sherpa paused and reached in his pack for a small cloth sack of sacred rice.

"May I have some?" I asked.

He nodded, and we both threw a handful of rice at the serac that this time had remained standing.

It took one week to establish a route to the top of the Khumbu icefall, good time considering most teams in those days took two weeks. The next stage of the climb was to scout a route through a labyrinth of crevasses that cross the floor of the high ice valley known as the Western Cwm. A new team of lead climbers took over, bolting together ladder sections they lowered across the wide crevasses, like soldiers of a medieval army crossing a moat. Jonathan was with them to film this stage of the ascent. Until then his experience traveling on glaciers had been limited to a relatively easy peak in Peru. He was thrilled to be out in front with the lead climbers. He was roped to a team of Sherpas, crossing the flat snow at the top of the icefall, when suddenly he disappeared as though swept down a trapdoor.

"I was walking in bright sunlight," Jonathan wrote in his journal, "and the next moment I was tumbling in a blue-black dream. Then boom, I hit a small ledge. After I took stock of my body and realized I only had a few cuts, I looked around and saw the bottom of the crevasse about thirty feet below. I was wedged in the narrowest part, and another thirty feet overhead the rope disappeared through a gray hole. My first thought was 'Welcome to Everest.' My next thought was, 'I hope this crevasse doesn't shift now, because if it does I will be crushed.' Then I realized the real danger was that I was wearing only a T-shirt, and if I didn't get rescued, I'd freeze to death."

The lead climbers heard the Sherpas' shouts, quickly rigged a ladder span across the hidden crevasse, and using a pulley system winched Jonathan out in only a few minutes. He was shaken but unhurt, and returned to Base Camp while the others continued their effort to advance the route.

It took another week to gain the back of the valley, where at 21,000 feet the other lead team established Camp 2, the Advanced Base Camp, or ABC, as we referred to it. A storm delayed us for over a week, but when it cleared Chris and I left the lower Base Camp to position for the next stage of the ascent up the steep expanse of ice known as the Lhotse Face. Jonathan, chastened but otherwise recovered from his fall, came with us to film and photograph master shots of us traversing the Western Cwm. We departed early, to beat the midday sun that can reflect off the snow-fluted walls and raise the air above the ice to oven-hot temperatures. At dawn we stopped to rest, and Chris lit his hash pipe and passed it to me. I didn't offer it to Jonathan because I knew he would abstain.

We sat looking out over the high ice valley, watching the wind plumes blow in long banners off the snowy summits of the neighboring peaks. Backlight illuminated these tailing clouds so that they were in stark contrast to the shadow shapes of the peaks. Jonathan pulled his still camera from his pack and steadied it on his knee. No one said anything. Protected as we were in the lee of the high walls, we were out of the wind, and in the calm, cold air I heard the camera click. Jonathan slowly advanced the film, adjusted the aperture, and took another shot. He lowered the camera and said, "I think that is the best mountain photograph I have ever taken."

Jonathan said he would send me a print of the shot, and I was confident he would follow through. He had already established a high level of credibility with everyone on the expedition, always doing what he was asked to do and never complaining. I was sure he and I would become good friends. I also suspected it would be a friendship different from the one I had with Chris, which was based more on doing things, whereas

my relationship with Jonathan was developing around our mutual plea-
sure in talking about things.

Chris's girlfriend had accompanied us on the approach march as far
as Base Camp, and since he had hiked most days with her, I spent much
of my time hiking with Jonathan and Nima, who was the Sherpa assistant
for the film crew. The expedition had spent an extra day in Namche
Bazaar acclimatizing, and Jonathan and I passed most of it sitting in
Nima's lodge talking about Buddhism, about Sherpa culture, about the
challenge of maintaining relationships with girlfriends we tended not to
see for months at a time.

Chris and I tended to avoid discussions about our deeper feelings. He
seemed more comfortable confiding to the women in his life, which I
accepted and never questioned. My friendships with most of my male
buddies was that way. But with Jonathan I sensed I had a new friend with
whom I could talk about anything.

In another week the leader of the expedition announced the summit
teams, and Chris and I were selected for the second bid. Chris was disappointed because he believed there wouldn't be sufficient oxygen for a
second attempt. I thought there would be, and because Chris had a sore
throat and cough, I felt an extra two or three days would give him time to
recover.

There were additional supplies to carry to the upper camps, and feeling guilty leaving this task only to the Sherpas, I decided to help ferry
two bottles of oxygen. Chris stayed in ABC to rest. When I returned later
in the day, one of the other climbers met me at the edge of camp.

"There's been a last-minute change in the summit teams," he said.

I went to the cook tent and saw Chris in a corner, looking down. At
first I thought he was still sick. Then I learned that one of the climbers
on the first team had become ill, and Chris, feeling better, had been
asked to take his place. He looked at me, and our eyes held.

"It's kind of tough," he said, "after being together on the whole climb."

"I guess it just didn't work out," I replied.

Early the next morning Chris and his new partner left camp. Those of us on the second team would follow two days later. I was still confident I had a good shot at the top, but it was hard to believe I would be making it without Chris. I gave him a good-luck hug as he departed ABC.

"See you up there," he said.

The next day my two new rope partners and I left for the intermediate camp halfway up the Lhotse Face. As we climbed the fixed ropes, we could see Chris and his partner—two red dots—halfway up the summit pyramid. Where we were it was calm, but higher on the mountain we could hear the jet stream as it blew across the summit, sounding like surf on a distant reef. One of my partners said, "I doubt they even try for the top tomorrow if the wind doesn't let up."

That night at our camp the windstorm lowered and began to buffet our tent. In the morning we decided to wait an extra day to see if it abated. We were surprised to learn in a radio call from Base Camp that Chris and his partner had been seen through binoculars leaving their high camp halfway up the summit pyramid, apparently headed for the top.

"In this wind they're risking frostbite," I said.

We waited patiently through the day, and finally, a little before three in the afternoon, Base Camp radioed they could see two dots scaling the Hillary Step. At four-fifteen the radio crackled again.

"We can see them. They're on top. They're on the summit of Everest."

The three of us slapped one another's backs, then realized that in less than two hours it would be dark. Would they have enough time to get back to their tent? Our teammates near Base Camp lost sight of them as they left the South Summit and disappeared behind the ridge. At our camp the wind came in strong gusts that buffeted the tent, and in occasional calms the only sound was the distant and steady roar of the jet stream. Daylight faded, and in the dark the wind gusts made the walls of our tent flap so violently that our condensed breath, illuminated in the beams of our headlamps, vibrated sympathetically. There was a rising moon, but I knew the spindrift blowing off the summit ridge would make it difficult for them to find their way. If they failed to reach their tent, the combined wind, cold, and altitude could make a bivouac fatal.

Sometime during the night I woke from a dream. It was a vision of Chris, old and hunchbacked, his face and beard sheathed in ice, emerging from a storm cloud, hobbling toward me with one arm extended, as though asking for help. I couldn't go back to sleep, and as I lay in my bag I could still hear in the calms between gusts the jet stream roaring over the summit. I was warm, but I wished I was able somehow to share the warmth with my buddy.

At first light I started the stove to brew tea, and an hour later we left camp to climb to the South Col. Far above we could see a red speck that marked the single tent at high camp. Were Chris and his partner in that tent, or were they still above it, stirring from a bivouac? And if they had bivouacked, were they even able to stir?

An hour later we arrived at a rock outcrop called the Yellow Band. We paused to study the tent at high camp. There was no sign of Chris or his partner. As we continued our own ascent, I was having difficulty breathing. I adjusted the oxygen flow on my regulator, but that didn't help. As I climbed my vision tunneled, and I was forced to my knees, breathing in quick gasps until my vision returned. Then I stood, made a few more steps, but again my vision narrowed and my own breathing seemed to echo in my head. I had pain in my lungs and congestion in my windpipe. Maybe I was getting pulmonary edema, a condition that at this altitude often ends when you drown in your own fluids. Should I go down? What about Chris? If he had bivouacked, he would need help.

It was now past eleven. If they had reached the tent last night, they would have begun their descent by now, and we would have seen them. I looked in the other direction, over the Western Cwm where I could see far below the tents at ABC, small colored dots on the white floor of the glacier. We were high enough to look across the sharp-edged ridge of the

Lhotse-Nuptse wall where the wind blew feathering fingers of spindrift high in the air that sparkled in rainbow hues before they dissipated. Such grandeur. But was my buddy in a condition to be able to admire it?

"Look, there."

One of my climbing companions was pointing toward high camp. I looked up and saw two red dots: Chris and his partner. They had reached the tent last night. We watched as they descended slowly but steadily. Maybe they were okay. I turned to continue my own task of climbing slowly. My companions were sympathetic to my plight but impatient with my pace. I was moving so slowly that Chris and his partner met us before we even reached the South Col. I gave Chris a tight hug. He told us they had found their way down from the summit by moonlight. In the morning they had been so exhausted they didn't leave the tent until nearly noon. Chris asked what we were going to do, and I admitted I was so exhausted I thought I should go down with him. With the wind continuing to increase, my two companions also decided to retreat.

As it turned out, that was the end of the expedition. A week later we were all hiking to a luxury tourist hotel above Namche Bazaar to have a celebratory feast when a group of trekkers stopped Chris to congratulate him. They pressed around to get his autograph. Jonathan and the director filmed the scene while the rest of us watched. I could see Chris was uncomfortable with the attention, but that didn't help my own disappointment. I tried to overcome it, telling myself it had been a team effort, that I had worked hard to scout the route through the icefall, that I had led a good part of the Lhotse Face. Then I recalled the extra work I had done to get the extra load carried to the higher camp, and how that extra effort had resulted in Chris and me being split between the first and the second team.

My self-pity must have shown on my face. When the filming was finished, Jonathan walked over and smiled.

"How are you doing?" he asked.

"I'm okay."

"When this lunch is over, why don't we walk back to Tengboche. Just you and me. We'll spend a few days at the monastery, like we've talked about doing. It's a beautiful day for a walk."

For Asia and me, the next day is an easy but long walk from Namche Bazaar downvalley to Lukla, site of a dirt airstrip that looks like the top of an aircraft carrier aground in a sea of steep ridges and valleys. An adjacent village of hotels and restaurants services the twenty thousand trekkers and mountaineers who come through this region each year. One of the hotels is Nima's, and that is where we spend the night. We are scheduled next morning to depart on one of the several Twin Otter flights that arrive daily (weather permitting) from Kathmandu, discharge arriving trekkers and climbers, load those who have completed their adventures, and leave as quickly as possible for the return flight before warming air makes takeoff problematic.

Next morning the plane arrives on schedule, and by nine Asia and I are in Kathmandu, loading our packs into a small taxi for the ride to our downtown hotel. Our driver chooses a shortcut through narrow side streets. We swerve to miss a bicycle rickshaw that in turn has narrowly missed two women in cotton saris who have stepped into the line of traffic to avoid a sacred cow standing motionless in the street. The driver honks at a small child with a distended belly protruding below her stained T-shirt (her only clothing), and Asia gasps as we miss her by inches. We slow as the driver honks again to open a passage through a sea of people pressing from both sides toward the street's center. Asia stares at a *sadhu* with long beard and dreadlocks, naked save for his soiled *dhoti* and painted face, and when he catches her eyeing him, he reaches out with his arm and steps from the pack of people toward our taxi, and we are thankful for an opening in the crowd that allows us to speed away.

We arrive at a small hotel that Asia and I like. It's modest and has an enclosed garden that offers refuge from the clamor of Kathmandu's noxious traffic. I'm relieved to find that Jon Meisler has arrived as planned. He is a thirty-two-year-old adventure-travel outfitter specializing in trips to remote mountain regions in Tibet, and he is coming with us on the next leg of our journey. Fluent in Mandarin Chinese, Jon has a traveler's knowledge of Tibetan, and a keen interest in Tibetan culture and Buddhism.

Jon tells us that the necessary permissions have been approved, and he expects tomorrow to be able to pick up our Chinese visas. He is concerned, however, that the bombing of the Chinese embassy in Yugoslavia may complicate our plans and even compromise our safety. The Chinese have reopened the border crossing between Nepal and Tibet to travelers with American passports, but selectively; some are being turned back at the whim of the officials. Of much graver concern is that the Chinese citizenry is inflamed, and a mob in Chengdu has burned the American Consulate. The U.S. State Department has issued a travel advisory for Americans in all rural areas of China, especially the rural areas of Sichuan that surround Chengdu.

I've made a resolution on this journey to try and emulate the equanimity with which Jonathan seemed always to meet any challenge, and this is a good place to start. On the positive side, I remind myself that the Chang Tang is inhabited mostly by drukpas, the hearty Tibetan nomads, who are unlikely to have any views on the bombing, if they have even heard of it. On the other hand, we are almost certain to encounter well-armed patrols of the People's Liberation Army. Jon explains that the Chinese army is so well disciplined, however, that officers and enlisted men alike, no matter how remote their postings, would never think of harming us for fear of reprisals from their superiors.

Jon is worried, though, about the second half of our journey, in Sichuan, where we will have to drive through dozens of rural villages on our way to Minya Konka, and where local peasants might not show the same restraint as army personnel. Before leaving, I promised Asia's mother I would never expose her daughter to any situation that was potentially dangerous. At the time, I had assumed this to mean prudence when I took her climbing; I never imagined dangers from political tensions. The frustrating thing is that I am old enough to have seen enough of these kinds of international incidents, either firsthand or in the news, to know that five years from now, or even one year from now, it is unlikely many people will remember the bombing of the Chinese embassy in Belgrade. The only thing that could promote it above a minor footnote in the history of political events—for us anyway—would be if this particular minor event resulted in Asia getting injured, or worse.

"What do you think?" I ask Asia.

"I'm going to do whatever you decide. I trust your judgment."

"Let's stay with the plan," I tell Jon, "but at the same time we should fax and E-mail everyone we can think of who might know more about what's going on in Sichuan."

"And if the news is bad?" he asks.

"We cancel and go home."

We have hired to go with us to Tibet as our expedition cook a twenty-two-year-old Sherpa named Dawa Lama. I don't know him, but he was recommended by friends in Nepal for his cooking skills and his perennial good cheer. We meet Dawa in the courtyard of the local outfitter who employs him. He is the same height I am, five foot five, and has what seems to be a permanent smile. He has short hair and bright, intelligent eyes, and he doesn't walk from place to place as much as hop in small, spring-loaded leaps. He says he has been cooking for trekking and climbing groups since he apprenticed as a kitchen boy when he was fifteen.

When we ask Dawa if we can help him complete his chores, he says he has only a few more vegetables to purchase in the local market, and he insists he do this on his own. Likewise, Jon says it's a "one-man job" standing in line at the Chinese embassy to pick up our visas, so I decide to show Asia some of her father's favorite places in Kathmandu.

We load into a motorcycle rickshaw, and as the contraption coughs clouds of two-cycle smoke, we make a dash through congested streets toward the remaining old quarter of the city. Durbar Square, in the center of this section, may still retain some of the character it had when Jonathan first saw it. From what I've seen of Kathmandu so far, though, I am not hopeful. The city appears to have doubled or even tripled in size since the 1970s, and that growth has seen a sprawl of shanties on the city's perimeter, thousands of additional cars and motorcycles and small trucks on the streets, and the conversion of the Tibetan quarter into a hip shopping zone for world travelers. That's not to say these changes weren't already under way in the 1970s: they had actually started in the 1960s when Kathmandu was the final stop on the overland hashish trail that began in Istanbul. You have to go back to the 1950s to find the original Kathmandu.

I was lucky to be able to do that, at least vicariously, when, just before leaving on this journey, I spent a few hours with a venerated old mountaineer named Charlie Houston. Charlie in 1950 became the first Westerner ever to visit the Khumbu when he and his party scouted the approach route the British team would follow three years later on the first successful ascent of Everest. Recently Charlie had discovered in his attic several reels of old Kodak 8mm home-movie footage he shot during his trip, then forgot even existed. He had it transferred to video, and when he saw it again, he was amazed what a small city Kathmandu was in 1950.

"Hardly larger than a village," he said. "And the sky, it was so blue. There were no cars, only Prince Mahendra's Rolls-Royce that had been carried in pieces over the hills from India. Even more astounding was once I had looked carefully at every scene, I realized there were no beggars in the streets. Not a single one."

The rickshaw stops, and even before Asia and I step into the rumpus of Durbar Square, we are approached by a young woman with a pleading expression, a baby on her hip and a skinny three-year-old clinging to her soiled sari. Behind her an old man in a tattered jacket and pants, stained the same swarthy color as his scabbed skin, hobbles toward us on a homemade crutch supporting his clubfoot. I quickly pay the rickshaw driver and indicate to Asia to follow me as we walk in the opposite direction, but I see this is not easy for her.

"I don't know what to do," she says.

"There's nothing you can do, except remember what your father wrote in his journal. 'Never pretend that you don't see them.'"

The square appears as it did twenty-five years ago: the vegetable hawkers and spice sellers and barbers shearing the hair of patrons seated on small wooden stools, the hundreds of supplicants circulating before the surrounding temples and shrines. We stop at the diminutive Ashok Binayak, the smallest shrine in Durbar yet the one that attracts the densest crowd. It houses the much-loved Ganesh, the elephant-headed god who proffers safety to pilgrims and travelers like us about to set out on the long journey north.

We climb the nine steps of the Maju Deval temple of Shiva with its three-tiered pagoda roof, and sit on the top step to gaze down on the hubbub. "I remember one morning in 1976 several of us came down here to film a scene," I tell Asia. "Your father was with us, and we were all wearing T-shirts that said 'American Bicentennial Everest Expedition.' In his journal he wrote about how at first he felt puffed up to walk around town with the expedition logo on his chest, but then caught himself, like he usually did, realizing his ego was taking over.

"Anyway, we were filming when Chris spotted a sign in front of a shop that said 'Hash for Sale.' If my memory's accurate, it was right over there, where those people are selling vegetables. So Chris went in and bought a ball of hash the size of a grapefruit, saying he was stocking up for the climb. Maybe it was the logo on the T-shirt, but somehow the local newspaper found out and the next day there was a front-page article headlined 'Everesters to Smoke Pot on Mountain.' It said we had bought a very large ball of hash in order to do medical experiments at high altitude. The leader of our expedition was a fairly high-placed official in the State Department, and the article caused a flap back in Washington."

"Were there a lot of people on the team who smoked hash?" Asia asks.

"There were a number, myself included. The heaviest users were the two doctors, including Chris. Your father didn't smoke, but he wasn't moralistic about it, either. He just decided after staying in that Buddhist monastery for twenty days that he wanted to experience the world as it was. But Chris was much different, and it was interesting having them as my two main friends on the climb. Chris was always pushing things, and that was one of the traits that drew me to him. Even on Everest. We were climbing the standard route, so to up the ante he dropped acid on the climb from the South Col to the High Camp at 27,500 feet. He didn't mention it to me until some time later, so I knew he wasn't trying to impress anybody. He wasn't like that, anyway. He just wanted to take the experience to the limit."

"Did he tell you what was it like?"

"Yeah, he laughed and said it was about as wild as he expected."

"What did you think of it?"

"My reaction was a mix of envy and caution. The part of it I was drawn to was the idea of pushing yourself. In some ways I think it was just part of being young and in your twenties, that attraction to trying to find your limits. But remember how I told you I had that funny feeling about the empty champagne bottle Ron left on the summit of Huascaran, in Peru? Well, I had the same feeling about Chris taking acid at eight-thousand-plus meters."

I take Asia in the afternoon for a drink in the Yak and Yeti Hotel, a few blocks from the Royal Palace. There are a few good hotels in Kathmandu, and the Yak and Yeti is arguably the best. We enter the lobby and I am pleased to see everything is still arranged as it was when I was last here. I pass the concierge, walking toward the bar, and see that the couch and chair around the small table are still in their same place.

There is an Indian family sitting in them, but they appear to be leaving, so I ask Asia please to wait because I don't want to sit anyplace else.

"Is that where you first saw her?" Asia asks.

"Yes, in that chair."

While we wait I can see her in my imagination as though it were still that April afternoon eighteen years ago. Her brown hair cut in bangs, her white T-shirt, and her jeans. They were good jeans, and she had a good haircut, although it would take some time for her to teach me things like how to distinguish a good haircut from a bad one.

I've already told Asia that in the months that followed the avalanche, I wasn't sure what I was going to do. I didn't know if I would ever climb again. I told her that by then I was making my living writing and working on films, but since most of my projects involved mountaineering, or river rafting, or exploring in remote or potentially dangerous regions, I wasn't sure of my occupation, either. I explained to her that I wasn't feeling sorry for myself—I was too thankful to be alive for that—but I simply had no idea what I was going to do.

Then *National Geographic* called and said they wanted to complete the story on Mount Everest National Park. They planned to send in Jonathan's place one of his boyhood friends, who was also an established photographer with the magazine, and they wanted me to write the article. They asked if we could leave in late March. There was no climbing involved in the assignment, and as the article would run with a number of the photographs Jonathan had already taken, it seemed important to follow through on the assignment, for no other reason than that the article would be a keepsake for Geri, for Jonathan's parents, and, when she was older, for Asia.

The photographer and I checked into the Yak and Yeti, and our first day there I was in the lobby looking for a place to sit to order a drink. That's when I saw Jennifer sitting where the Indian family is now.

When they stand and leave, Asia and I take their places. "I'm not sure why I told her the story," I explain to Asia. "Maybe it was because she looked as forlorn as I felt; maybe it was because I detected in her an intelligence that made me want to confide my own grief. Part of it might have simply been a need to explain the dour way I was acting. Whatever it was, I sat here in this same chair and told her about the avalanche, about your father's death, and about my own near death. I hadn't talked about it since you and your mother came to visit a month after he died. Jennifer listened carefully. When I finished, she paused and cleared her throat. She then told me she too was traveling as an antidote to her own grief."

Our drinks arrive, and I toast Asia. She has brought only her trekking clothes on this trip, but she has carefully selected the colors, and they all match nicely. She has her hair in a cute ponytail, and she does not look out of place. I take a sip of my drink and continue my story.

"She told me that a little over a year before, her husband had been sailing around the world. They had a large yacht, seventy feet long, and several of their friends were on board as crew. She wasn't a sailor herself, but she would fly in on occasion and join her husband and friends on short legs. She was with them transiting the straits north of Australia when, unknown to anyone on the boat, a strong earthquake hit the south coast of New Guinea, sending an enormous tidal wave across the water. Her husband always made her wear a life jacket when she was out of the cockpit because she wasn't a very good swimmer. When the wave hit, she was sitting on the afterdeck, and she remembers that, as the boat pitched up, the boom swept the deck and hit her husband on the head. The boat then broke in pieces, and that's the last thing she remembered. When she gained consciousness, she was inside an Australian Coast Guard helicopter. It was some hours later before they would tell her that out of the thirteen people on board, she and one other were the only two who survived.

"I could see she was a discreet person," I tell Asia, "and it had been difficult for her to tell me her story. I had the sense, in fact, she had told it only occasionally, if at all. I was going out to dinner that night with some friends who also had known your father, and I invited her to come. It was a pleasant evening, and it seemed like a good distraction for us both. Back at the hotel we exchanged addresses, and it was a few months later when I was back in California that she called. She was in Los Angeles for the day, and she wondered if she could come up the coast to visit. Yvon was rooming with me while his house was being rebuilt, and his own family was spending the summer in their cabin in Jackson Hole. The three of us had a nice dinner. Then two weeks later I was in Wyoming climbing with Yvon when he asked if I had heard from Jennifer. I said I hadn't, and he suggested calling her and inviting her to join us. She showed up the next day and stayed for two weeks. We were married a few months later, and within a year Carissa was born."

"You guys always seem like such an incredibly tight couple," Asia says.

"We're very different, though. People always assume Jennifer is a strong outdoor type, and I think they're surprised when she tells them she only goes as far as the last good hotel. When I first met her, sitting right here in that same chair, I asked her if she wanted to come along on my trek to Everest Base Camp, and she laughed and said the farthest she'd ever walked was from a cab to the front entrance of Bergdorf Goodman. She also said later that if she had accepted, it probably would have been a disaster, and we never would have married.

"But obviously the attraction was there, and it started in our stories of the deaths of people we were close to, one in a tidal wave and one in an avalanche. But even more, it was our own near deaths in both those things. After we were married and Jennifer was pregnant, I read her Saint-Exupéry's *The Little Prince*. It seemed a good story to read to someone who was expecting a child. In the story the Little Prince tells Saint-Exupéry that the trouble with grown-ups is that they are always confusing matters of consequence with matters of inconsequence. That became for us a shorthand. We would be at a dinner party and someone would be pontificating about one thing or another, and I would whisper to Jennifer, 'Is that a matter of consequence?' and she would grin and say 'I don't think so.'"

Asia and I finish our drinks. We stand, and I take one more look at the chair and couch.

"There's one last thing for you to know," I tell her. "It's that I wouldn't have met my wife, and I wouldn't have the family I have now, if your father hadn't died. And had he lived, your life most certainly would have had a different trajectory. I'm not sure I know what either of those things mean, and I'm not sure I expect to find out what they mean on this trip. But I'm thinking about it. Every day."

Part 2

Chang Tang
June 1999

4

In a gray dawn under a leaden sky, we drive across the Kathmandu valley and into the great southern rampart of the Himalayas. The back of
our minibus is loaded with fresh vegetables and potatoes by the basket-
ful, eight plastic drums of additional foods, four large duffels with gear
for trekking and climbing, two crush-proof cases containing camera and
video gear, and three pairs of skis, should we find the Crystal Mountains
bordering the Aru Basin good for ski mountaineering. We ascend a road
cut into the near-vertical sides of a deep valley that is heavily forested.
The sky is weighted with dark clouds that mist the air, but high above,
through an occluding window in the clouds, a cliff of dark rock creates a
vertical band of black, and near its top a small ledge supports in silhouette a solitary silver fir.

"It looks like a Chinese watercolor," I say.

"This country is *so* beautiful," Asia replies. Asia seems as excited as I
am relieved that we have committed to this next portion of our journey.
I say "relieved" not because anything has happened to ease the political
tension in China, but because we are leaving behind the city, the traffic,
and the poverty. When we received replies to our faxed requests for

additional information about the situation in rural Sichuan, all we could learn was that it was still volatile. So I decided to commit to the next stage of our adventure: the drive westward to Mount Kailas and the *khora* trek around the sacred peak, the exploration of the Aru Basin, and possible climb into the Crystal Mountains, then the long drive eastward to Lhasa. Once there we can get a new read on the political situation before continuing to Sichuan.

For now we still have to get across the border. Officials apparently are still turning some Americans back, and we have been warned we might have a further problem: Dawa, our Sherpa cook and a Nepalese citizen, is on our group visa and his last name is Lama. Apparently "Lamas" are sometimes denied entry, even though the surname has no more to do with religiosity than "Smith" does with ironmongery.

When we arrive at the border, Jon explains to Asia and me that the passport control is actually three miles farther up the road, but to get there we first have to transfer our gear from the minibus to two vehicles that he arranged for weeks earlier and that he now hopes are awaiting us. We cross a bridge that separates Nepal and Tibet, and we are all relieved to find the Toyota Land Cruiser, the double-wheel Chinese truck, the two drivers, and the government liaison officer who have come down from Lhasa the day before.

I am also relieved they are all Tibetans, including the liaison officer, whom Jon says he knows from a previous trip. "These guys are apolitical," he says. "We won't have any problem with them."

We transfer the food and equipment to the big truck, placing our supplies alongside several aluminum tanks of propane for our camp stove, and twelve large drums of gasoline for the two vehicles, then drive the three miles to the passport control and park behind a logjam of trucks and minibuses. We get out to stand in the back of a long line of mostly young travelers waiting to get their visas stamped. It's good to see the *Wanderjahr* alive and well, and I imagine my own kids hitting the road.

When it is close to our turn at the window, I'm encouraged: so far it doesn't appear that anyone has been turned back. But it does appear that most are being hassled. We step to the window and present our passports and visa. The first officer, a Chinese woman in her twenties, studies the documents impassively, then hands them to her associate, a Chinese man who looks to be in his forties. He alternates between the front page of each passport and a scrutiny of each of our faces. He takes Dawa's passport, compares it to the name on our group visa, then eyes our young Sherpa cook with a palpable disdain. Dawa is smiling, as he has been every minute of the four days I have so far been in his company. How can anyone be anything less than heartwarmed by Dawa? But this bureaucrat has the kind of face that starts dogs barking, and I fear that our expedition is about to end before it even starts. Then, with mocking condescension, the bureaucrat stamps the visa, tosses the passports back to us, and tilts his head indicating we are to move on. We're in.

After a victory lunch of Chinese noodles and Pabst Blue Ribbon beer, brewed under license in China, we continue two hours up the road and spend the night in a truck-stop town. The next morning we leave early. Jon, Asia, the liaison officer (or L.O.), and I ride in the Land Cruiser with one of the drivers while Dawa keeps company with the other driver in the truck. We climb out of the river valley and onto a broadening upland coursed by runlets that diminish as we gain altitude. On the opposite hillside I point out a lone copse of small trees stunted by their bold foothold at this advanced altitude. Jon says they are likely the last trees we will see for a month. The road makes a long switchback up a rounded hill covered only with occasional dwarf shrubs and cushion plants, and a thin steppe land grass. I point excitedly to two kiangs, the wild ass of the Tibetan steppe, grazing not fifty yards from the road. Asia asks about a compact range of glaciated peaks to the south, and I reply they are small mountains, probably with no names.

"They're the kinds of mountains I would like to climb," she says.

"That's good, because where we're going none of the mountains have names."

The clouds begin to break, and with the opening country and the opening sky, I have the feeling of approaching a threshold. Then ahead we see a dozen tall poles strung with prayer flags and a large adobe hearth holding boughs of smoking juniper. This marks the pass that divides the watershed of the highest mountain range in the world from the highest plateau. We stop and get out, and Jon points to the northwest, toward open sere hills that extend to a distant horizon.

"That's where we're going," he says. "And that's what it will look like for the next month."

We reach a fork where the long dirt road that crosses the southern margin of the Tibetan Plateau joins the Kathmandu-Lhasa road, and turn left toward Mount Kailas, still some 450 miles away. Jon warns that in places it will be nothing more than a dirt track—difficult in good weather, impassable in bad. We expect to take three days to get to Kailas, and our drive will be luxurious compared to that of the pilgrims we pass, loaded cheek by jowl into the backs of two lumbering trucks.

To millions of Buddhists and Hindus, the 22,000-foot-high Kailas is the most venerated mountain on earth. The peak lies only a few miles from the headwaters of the Indus and the Bramaputra. These two great rivers, the former coursing west and the latter east, flow for hundreds of miles, then turn around both ends of the Himalayas. There are also two lesser rivers coursing off Kailas, one flowing north and one south. As the heart of these four cardinal rivers, Kailas is the geographical reflection of the Buddhist *mandala* and the Hindi *yantra,* the center of a great four-sided universe. To devotees, the mountain is the *axis mundi,* the pillar connecting Earth to heaven, and to make the coveted *khora* around it is to reduce sins that have accumulated over a lifetime.

For two hours we drive traveling northwest, making good time as we pass Shishapangma, smallest of the world's 8,000-meter peaks, although no peak of 8,000 meters seems small. Then the road crests a rounded hill, and we see ahead in a shallow basin a gathering of trucks halted because one of them is up to its rear axle in soft sand; the others hesitate to go around for fear of even softer sand to the sides of the track. We stop short of this jam, and our two drivers huddle to discuss their strategy. They decide to take a wider route, and we stand aside as the Land Cruiser accelerates before it leaves the track, then slows as it enters the wallow of sand, but has enough momentum to carry it through to firm ground on the far side. I am not optimistic the truck can repeat this, and consequently I am not surprised when it gets stuck.

The Land Cruiser backs up and the two Tibetan drivers connect a rope to the rear of the truck to try to tow it back to the starting position. They leave slack in the line, however, and when the Toyota charges forward the rope breaks. The Tibetans then rummage in the back of the truck and produce a steel cable that is frayed but large enough in diameter for the task. But the Land Cruiser lacks sufficient power to pull the truck free, so I ask for shovels. Jon, Asia, and I are all incredulous when the drivers admit they have forgotten to bring any. The three of us then begin to gather rocks and toss them under the tires, and the Tibetans follow our lead. The Land Cruiser once again pulls while the rest of us push, but the tires continue to spin and Asia, looking down at the front tires of the truck, yells to the driver, "Straighten your wheel!" The driver, not understanding, leans out the window of the cab, and Jon translates.

With the wheels now straightened, we once again push while the Toyota pulls, and this time it works. When the truck is back to its previous starting position, the driver guns the engine and the vehicle lurches forward. We give the driver shouts of encouragement, but then he slows just as the truck approaches the sand. Asia yells, "Don't slow," and then more shrilly, "Don't slow!"

Once more the truck bogs down, and we face the prospect of repeating the same procedure. As we get in position, I tell Asia, "Don't yell at the truck driver this time, okay?"

"Yeah, but he slowed down when he should have speeded up."

"But yelling's just going to make him mad."

"I have a hard time being quiet when people screw up."

"Me, too, but just have Jon tell him he's got to keep as much momentum as possible."

She thinks about this for a few seconds, then nods her head and says, "Okay," then turns to Jon, who has already overheard us. "Okay, I'll tell him," Jon says, then passes Asia's suggestion on to the truck driver. We lower into position on the front of the truck, like linemen on a football team, and once more push with all our strength. This time the truck succeeds in backing up, and then, keeping full momentum, makes it through the wallow as we cheer it on. We climb back in the vehicles and continue, soon passing another truck whose wood-sided cargo hold is filled with pilgrims en route to Kailas, and as we pass they return Asia's wave.

Jonathan was familiar with the Kailas *khora.* In early 1980 he had been tantalized by a bush pilot's description of flying the border in the western part of Nepal and seeing in the north the emblematic white mountain, shaped like a diamond, rising in isolation above the sere steppe. That was the year China began to open its borders to mountaineers and adventure trekkers, and Jonathan dreamed of making the revered pilgrimage. Later that year, after he and I had been invited to join the expedition to Minya Konka in eastern Tibet, he talked to me about the possibility of getting a permit to go to Kailas, but western Tibet was still closed.

By then we had enough projects planned to keep us busy for at least a year. After Minya Konka we had lined up the *National Geographic* story on Mount Everest National Park, and the following year we hoped to make a crossing of Borneo. But we kept the idea of going to Kailas as a possibility for the future.

By then Jonathan had achieved his goal of making a living as a professional photographer focused on adventure travel, and I was on the cusp of achieving the same as a writer and film producer. Four years earlier, after returning from Everest, I had faced the consequence of my earlier decision to go on the expedition at the cost of going back to school. For a while I painted houses, but I was yearning for an occupation to match my passion for adventure and near addiction to periodic sojourns in wild country. At first I wondered if perhaps I was born in the wrong era. It seemed that a century earlier it had been easier to find an adventuresome occupation. If you were on the East Coast, you could pack your family in a Conestoga and head west, or you could sign on a full-rigged whaling ship and head for the South Seas.

Then the railroads replaced the wagon trails, and steamboats displaced sailing ships. One of my heroes from that era, an experienced sailing captain named Joshua Slocum, refused to make the conversion to steam. By 1894, however, he felt like flotsam bobbing uselessly in the wake of a new technology. Then he found the answer to his dilemma marooned in the tidal flats of a cow pasture. It was an abandoned sloop—cast aside like himself—and after resurrecting the old boat, he became the first man to sail alone around the world.

Slocum was one of the first to take an adventurous occupation and convert it to an adventurous sport. One day during the Everest expedition I had an epiphany that caused me to begin to wonder if I could convert adventurous sport into an occupation. I was helping the television crew film a scene climbing ice on the Lhotse Face when I realized that they were doing the same thing I was doing: having fun climbing an ice slope in a stunning location. But they were getting paid for it. Back home I called the director of the film, Mike Hoover—who was then one of the leading adventure filmmakers in the world—and asked how I could get into the business. He told me that it all started with good ideas.

I had in fact a four-drawer file cabinet labeled, from bottom to top, "Bad Ideas," "Good Ideas," "Great Ideas," and "Fantastic Ideas." I had made the labels as a joke, but, in fact, I did keep files of ideas, and one of them contained notes from reading Baron von Humboldt's 1802 account of his *Travel to the Americas*. The book described a botanical expedition in which Humboldt crossed from the Amazon to the Orinoco and reported seeing in the distance, rising out of the jungle, mysterious mountains with vertical sides and flat tops. I thought it would be interesting to explore and climb one of these remote formations. After getting the tip from Mike about how to get started in the documentary business, I began to research this area known as the Guiana Shield. I found a report of one peak shaped like a great tree stump that was said to have a cave just below the summit that went through the mountain side to side, like the eye of a needle. It was, in fact, known as the Eye of the Gods, and was also rumored by the surrounding Maquitiare Indians to be the lair of a dinosaur creature that occasionally descended the mountain and raided villages.

"Sounds like perfect TV," Mike said. I helped him write a proposal; he sent it to ABC, and three weeks later they sent a check for $55,000.

"That was easy," I told Mike.

Mike was in charge of organizing the film and the crew, and I was in charge of the climb and the climbers. When we landed at a small airstrip on the upper Orinoco, we hired a large dugout with a thatched canopy. I found a discarded board, painted on it in large letters "Amazon Queen," and nailed it to the front of the awning. We hired several Maquitiares to go with us as porters. We motored up narrowing rivers for three days, hiked through the jungle for another three days, then took six more days to scale the vertical walls of the spire to reach the cave. We found no dinosaur, but looking out from the huge window of the cave's opening, I watched pairs of blue and gold macaws veering in syncopated flight over the jungle canopy two thousand feet below. In the floor of the cave, at the opening of the enormous window, a gurgling spring supported enough shrub growth to give us firewood to cook our meals.

We camped in the cave for three days. The ceiling of the main chamber was nearly a hundred feet high and rounded like the dome of a cathedral. There was a labyrinth of side tunnels, and we were exploring one when we heard our feet crunch on the rock floor. Looking down we discovered hundreds of tiny skeletons. At first we thought they were bats, but picking up one we saw that it had a beak. They were skeletons of some unidentified species of bird, and we wondered if perhaps this was their burial ground. If it was, did that mean they were all guided by an inherited sense of navigation to come here on their final flight? Or maybe this was the feeding aerie of some jungle raptor. But there were too many skeletons here for one bird, so did that mean one generation showed the next this secret location?

It was an easy climb from the cave to the summit where Mike filmed us giving each other bear hugs. The TV show was a success, and more jobs with Mike followed. He taught me how to shoot a scene so the editor had all the pieces with all the angles needed to tell a story on film. More important, he taught me how to pick projects that by their nature were dramatic: stories with interesting people going to interesting places with goals that had built-in obstacles to overcome.

During this time I was hoping I could get together on one of these jobs with Jonathan, but he was busy with assignments for *National Geographic* in Baja, Baghdad, Hong Kong, and the high Arctic. Then in 1979 he was hired by ABC to be cameraman filming the ascent of Ama Dablam. One of the expedition leaders called to ask if I was available to join the team, but by then I had already signed on with Mike to go on a skiing and climbing adventure to Antarctica, and there was insufficient time to go from one trip to the other.

Once we were both home from our journeys, however, Jonathan called to say he had won approval for the Everest Park project, and he wondered if I was interested in being the writer. I jumped at the chance, and we scheduled the trip for fall 1980. Then we both received invitations to join the Minya Konka expedition. Jonathan was invited as a cameraman, and I was asked to be both a member of the climbing team and a coproducer of the film, a new role for me. Since the expedition was also scheduled for the fall of 1980, we made the plan to travel to Lhasa once the climb was concluded, then to Kathmandu, then to Everest. Since Lhasa was just opening to outsiders, *National Geographic* was also interested in a story on that part of our adventure.

I was then thirty years old, and Jonathan was twenty-eight. We had both realized our dream: we were doing what we loved, and we felt as if we were on top of the world.

Asia and I gaze out the window of the Land Cruiser as we pass an expansive alkaline lake. We are on the edge of the Chang Tang, and we see for the first time the colors emblematic of the high steppe: turquoise water, sienna hills, cerulean sky. We parallel a drainage entering the lake, and in marsh sedge I look for waterfowl, hopeful to see the black-necked crane that summers on the Tibetan plateau, then crosses back over the Himalayas to winter in its remaining sanctuaries. The cranes are few in number and, since they spread widely across Tibet, it is uncommon to see them; but I have faith we will be lucky.

In midafternoon the road drops into the valley of the Yarlung Tsangpo, the great river that drains all of southern Tibet. Downriver, to the east, the Tsangpo eventually makes a sharp turn into India and becomes the famed Bramaputra: upriver, to the west, it has its origins in the feeder streams east of Kailas. Like all rivers that flow in deserts, its existence in this dry, treeless steppe seems a miracle. Our Land Cruiser stops at the road crossing, and all of us get out to wait for the attendants who operate a small ferry moored on the opposite bank. Our driver honks his horn, and in a few minutes a young woman and an older man appear from a hut across the river. The young woman hops aboard a small twin-pontoon barge that is tethered to a cable spanning the three-hundred-yard width of the river. The older man drives a tractor away from the water, pulling a towrope looped through a sheave so that it ferries the barge to our side. We drive aboard, the young woman switches the towrope and signals the old man, who now drives the tractor back toward the river, and we start across.

Most travel accounts by visitors to Tibet up to the time of the Chinese occupation described crossing the Yarlung Tsangpo on tender coracles of inflated yak stomachs, and this present-day contraption seems an equally resourceful use of whatever materials you have to get the job done. The young woman on board the barge is dressed smartly in the jacket, pants, and cap of the Chinese maritime. It is a photo op, and Asia and I both take out our cameras.

Although Asia has a new electronic Canon, at home she prefers her father's old manual Olympus cameras. She left them behind because she was concerned about damage or theft, and we also realized if she had the same camera body as mine we could share lenses, which in turn would pare down a little the amount of gear we would have to carry. For the past year she has been enrolled in a fine-arts curriculum at the University of Colorado, with an emphasis on photography. She knows following in her father's footsteps will be a challenge: She is aware of how hard he worked to earn the coveted rank of *National Geographic* photographer. She has also told me she is undecided whether to make the same commitment. She is dissatisfied with the photography program at the university but uncertain if she has the resources to switch schools. I've been watching her take pictures for two weeks, and I'm also questioning if photography is the best match for her talents. She is good in some situations, including taking pictures of kids, but hesitant in others. As we cross the Yarlung Tsangpo, for example, she seems only to be taking overview shots, instead of climbing to the top of the truck or getting close up to the young woman in the maritime suit.

I step to the end of the pontoon that is athwart the barge and confirm it a good position for a wide-angle shot. I motion Asia to come out, and I give her a hand as she steps into position, gets the shot, and gives me a smile. She knows I'm here for her if she wants my advice. But I tell myself that this is like my approach to teaching her to climb, that I am happy to do it, but first she has to decide if it's something she wants to pursue.

That evening we drive off the road, set up our first camp, and the next day pass through the Chinese outpost of Zhongba, about one-third of the way to Kailas. The town is a depressing collection of mud-wall huts and abandoned trucks half stripped of their parts, like carcasses half eaten by vultures; of broken bottles, strewn garbage, and dried excrement. Half the place has been reclaimed by drifting sand, and it would be none too soon if the dunes were to cover the remaining half.

Five miles later, however, the only sign of our species' imprint is the primitive dirt track we follow, and it parallels a wetland with a large assembly of ruddy shelducks and common mergansers. As we bump along, I'm reviewing the flocks, looking for a pair of shelducks in a good position to photograph, when I see on the far side of the bog two birds that look distinct.

"Stop!"

Our driver brakes hard and I hop out with binoculars in hand and focus on whatever it is on the far side of the grass and sedge.

"Cranes. Black-necked cranes. Two of them."

They are about five feet tall, with black necks, as the name describes, pale white bodies, and drooping black tails. They are too far away to make out the red patch on their crowns, and too far away to photograph, but that doesn't bother me, knowing their image is recorded in my memory. We take turns looking at them through the binoculars, and I am relieved that both Jon and Asia seem to share my enthusiasm—it can be difficult explaining bird-watching behavior to noninitiates.

It feels as if we are at last in the remote heartland of Tibet. To the south we see a wide breach in the rampart of the snowy Himalayas, and this can only be the pass that leads to the Kingdom of Mustang, and farther south, to the great valley of the Kali Gandaki, bordered on one side by Annapurna and on the other by Dhaulagiri. To the right of the breach are the glacier-covered peaks of the Kanjiroba, above the Land of Dolpo, where in 1973 George Schaller conducted his survey of blue sheep, described by Peter Matthiessen in *The Snow Leopard.* Now we pass two horsemen dressed in lambskin *chubas* with embroidered mucklucks to their knees; they urge their white and gray mounts to a canter so that the horses and horsemen pace our two vehicles, and as we travel in parallel we watch them cross the steppe land against a backdrop series of sharp peaks whose summits are capstoned with the sediment of the ancient Tethys Sea.

We stop to refuel the vehicles from the drums in the back of the truck, and while the two drivers finish this chore I walk away from the dirt track until I am absorbed into the vastness. There is wind today, but this is a land that is used to wind, so the wind picks up no dust. The visibility is over a hundred miles, and the tips of mountains that appear above the distant horizon could be as much as 150 miles away. If I were a Buddhist, this would be the place I would meditate, and, in fact, there is a practice within the "old school" (*Nyingma-pa*) that requires lengthy meditation of vast expanses. There is an attraction to this: the thought of sitting alone on this hardscrabble steppe, enough food and water at close hand only for minimal sustenance, contemplating this openness until, as Jonathan's teacher Goenka taught him, "the unruly mind is sufficiently calmed."

We stop in late afternoon to set up camp next to a stream of clear water meandering in full turns through a broad alluvium. Asia and I sit on the bank as sunset clouds spill over the crest of the Himalayas, and we watch two Mongolian plovers forage insects from the riverine rocks. That evening in our tent, sitting in my sleeping bag propped against my folding backrest, I go back to my photocopy of Jonathan's journal of his first trip to the Himalayas. I have chosen this one to read this evening because it describes Jonathan's twenty-day retreat under Goenka's tutelage. I want to examine it again, and also to read part of it to Asia, in anticipation of our *khora* around Mount Kailas.

S. N. Goenka was a Burmese Buddhist who practiced a technique of meditation said to have originated with Gautama Buddha himself and to have survived for the past thousand years only in Burma, where a chain of devoted practitioners passed it down from one generation to the next. Goenka wanted to reintroduce the practice to India, and the result of his effort was the monastery Jonathan entered in 1973.

For the length of his retreat, Jonathan remained silent, talking only when he had a question to address directly to his teacher. He did not read or write. Each day for ten hours he was expected to sit in meditation and try to follow a "path to mental purification through self-observation." This was a technique called *vipassana*, a Pali word from the first Buddhist texts that means "to see things as they are."

"After he left the monastery he caught a flight to Kathmandu," I tell Asia, "and started writing again in his journal. Here's the entry as he's flying to Nepal: 'I have been introduced to a path that will take a lifetime to follow. Now that I know the technique, it is up to me to work so that I can progress along the path. Already I feel a big change, more peaceful, more aware, a better understanding of myself and how to cope with everyday life.'"

Then he filled these two pages with phrases he learned in talks Goenka gave after each day's meditation practice. "Listen to a few," I say, holding up the photocopy to show her the pages.

"We look at animals in cages. But each of us is caged within an animal. Do we look at ourselves?

"Your name or your person, which is dearer? Your person or your goods, which is worth more? Gain or loss, which is the greater bane?

"The first fact of existence is the law of change or impermanence.

"*Annica* equals change."

Asia says, "So that's what that means."

She is referring to the frequent references to *annica* that Jonathan made in nearly all his journal entries over the years following his retreat with Goenka. "He wrote it again at the end of this section, in huge letters," I say, holding up the journal and showing her. "I've kept notes on some of the places where he's used it."

I set down the journal and pick up a ringed binder in which I've listed many quotes from Jonathan's journals, filing them under headings such as "Living in the Moment," "Knowing Yourself First," "Containing Your

Desires." Now I read her three of the ones I have categorized under the label "Change":

> "*11 March 1975, Dharan, Nepal.* The old man who used to sell me tea and bread in the shop where I have always stopped has passed away. He was kind and wise, and I shall bring a photograph of him for his sons. All is *annica*.
>
> "*8 April 1979, Camp 2 (Ama Dablam).* For 12 hours I have tossed and turned with a splitting altitude headache, and I am very disappointed in my inability to experience the *annica* of this situation, and handle it with the appropriate equanimity.
>
> "*October 6, 1980, Ruins of Konka Gompa Monastery (near Minya Konka base camp).* My heart cries out in anger at the Chinese for this destruction. But tears will not change the reality or the *annica* of all that exists. From a man to a mountain, from a thought to a nation, it is all in the same cycle of birth and growth, death and decay.

"That last entry" I tell Asia, "was also the last thing he wrote before he died."

I wake early, and while Asia is still asleep I dress quietly, slowly open the tent door to keep the zipper noise to a minimum, and crawl out. I stand and stretch, my arms straight above my head. The sky is clear. The stream next to camp reflects the orange and yellow alpenglow on the snow summits to the south. The basalt volcanoes to the north, even in warm light, remain black. Grazing stock have cropped the feather grass on the foreground hills to a soft bristle that is pale yellow.

In a few minutes everyone is up, and it is still early when we leave. At midmorning we pass a narrow but long lake the same turquoise as the necklace gemstones that measure the wealth of Tibetan women. The lake is held between mineral hills of yellow and red hues, and the sky is the color and richness of a sapphire. At noon we reach Maryum La, an 18,000-foot pass marked by two rock cairns on each side of the road, and we stop to rest. After three days of travel in the vehicle, I feel a need to use my legs, so I tell Jon I am walking the road, and when they leave, they should pick me up at whatever point I manage to reach.

The air is cold and dry, and there is wind out of the west. Along the road, caught on the lava stones leached to the surface of the desert pavement, are dozens of tissue squares printed with various mantras and icons of Buddhas and bodhisattvas. The wind picks up one of these papers and skips it over the bare hill like a flitting bird, taking with it as it goes its admission that life is suffering, its recognition that the cause of this suffering is desire, and its wisdom that to be delivered from this desire is to follow the right path.

My knowledge of Buddhism is limited to a traveler's exposure that began in 1976 when Jonathan and I visited the old lama living alone in the cave near Mount Everest, and continued after the climb when we stayed for a few days at Tengboche. During that stay Jonathan had been circumspect talking about his twenty-day retreat under Goenka, and I assumed it was because he was sensitive about even me taking him for another flower child of the *dharma*. But he did reveal enough of the experience that I had a sense of how much it had transformed his life. While he wouldn't talk about it in detail, he did offer to take me to Goenka's retreat, saying the only way to understand this practice was to experience it. I meant to take him up on the offer but never did.

If Jonathan detected in me a reluctance to embrace Buddhism in any organized manner, he was right. It wasn't that I had anything less than complete respect for his beliefs, but rather that I had been exposed, living in Hawaii and later California, to two or three gurus who I was convinced were wheedling as much money and as many sexual favors as they could from their gullible followers. It was also the beginning of Hollywood's celebrity fascination with Tibet, and my skepticism that this rapture with Buddhism had less to do with commitment to self-restraint than guilt over self-indulgence was only confirmed by an incident shortly after I returned from Everest.

I was sharing a house in Malibu with several surfers, and we lived near an actor named Michael Parks who was then starring as a motor-cycle-riding outcast in a popular television series called *Then Came Bronson.* Parks was being touted as the next James Dean, but he was friendly and unpretentious, and he asked to see my slides of Everest. After he saw them he said he had a friend who lived in L.A., another actor named James Coburn, who was also interested in Nepal and Tibet.

As a kid I had watched Coburn in perhaps a dozen movies, and think-ing it might be fun to meet him, I accepted Parks's offer to arrange a visit. I navigated my Volkswagen bus up a long drive lined with tall palms to a large house with a pillared entry. As I walked to the door, I could hear inside the house the unmistakable chanting, drum beating and horn blow-ing of a Buddhist *puja.* It sounded like the ceremony that had been per-formed for our expedition at Tengboche, and my first thought was that Coburn had one hell of a sound system. I rang the bell, and when the maid answered, I could tell the sound of the *puja* was coming from a room out of my view but just beyond the entry. I introduced myself, and she asked me to wait. In a moment a well-coiffed man in a dark suit who looked like a Mafia consigliere came to the door. As so many of us did in those days, I wore my hair long and I had a mustache. I was wearing an aloha shirt and had my slide trays in one hand and projector in the other. He looked at me, then over my shoulder at my VW bus, and I saw one eyebrow raise. I told him who I was, and he nodded perfunctorily and said, "Follow me."

Past the entry we turned a corner and suddenly I was in a large living room with a vaulted ceiling. The furniture had been rearranged to allow room for a dozen or more Tibetan monks dressed in burgundy robes who sat facing each other in two lines on either side of the lama leading a *puja.* It was the real thing, just like I had seen in Nepal. The consigliere told me to wait, and in a few minutes Coburn came down the wide stairs. It was midmorning, but he was dressed in a silk robe and smoking a cigar. I sat my projector down to shake his hand.

"Thank you so much for coming. Parks said your slides are fantastic."

"They're not just mine. I have dupes from other climbers on the expedition."

"I can't wait. Everest! Imagine that. But it's noisy down here, so let's go to my bedroom."

"Who are these guys?" I asked, pointing to the Buddhists.

"Tibetan monks staying with us while they're in town. I'll introduce you when they finish their chanting. The leader is a high lama by the name of Karmapa."

I knew enough about Tibetan Buddhism to know that Karmapa, measured by the number of his followers, ranked only behind the Dalai Lama. I followed Coburn up the stairs, along a balcony that allowed me to look down on the *puja,* and then into his bedroom. I had my next surprise seeing a beautiful woman sitting in front of a large vanity with a robe draped loosely over her shoulders, leaving her substantial breasts in view. Coburn introduced us, and when I shook her hand I did my Buddhist best to keep my eyes focused on her face. There were two large stuffed chairs in the room, and Coburn sat in one while I arranged my projector on a small table. Then I sat in the other chair and told Coburn I was ready.

"Can I get you anything before we start?"

"No, thank you, I'm fine."

"Are you sure? Coffee or something?"

I paused for a moment, listening to the sound of the Karmapa and the monks chanting, and stealing a glance at the woman who by then had resumed combing her hair but had not closed her robe.

"Actually, maybe I'll have one of those cigars. And some cognac, if you don't mind. I know it's early, but what the hell."

We descend from the Maryum La, and in less than half an hour we round a bend, and there it is, Mount Kailas. We pull off and stop alongside another Land Cruiser whose owner, a Tibetan woman in her fifties, is some yards in front of her vehicle, on her knees bowed to the mountain. Kailas, perhaps twenty miles away, is familiar to me from the photographs I have seen in books on Asian exploration: singular, with no other mountains to diminish it, rising from the steppe like a great white egg.

We get out of the car and stand looking at the mountain. The older Tibetan woman is still prostrate, and her driver waits next to the vehicle. We are quiet, conscious of not intruding on her privacy. Slowly she rises off one knee, then the other, stands, and clasps her hands and bows again toward the mountain. She is wealthy. She owns a new car that in China costs nearly a hundred thousand U.S. dollars. She wears a traditional but very well-made Tibetan dress, and has a necklace of large pieces of turquoise and *tzee*, the coveted zebra-striped agate that can sell for twenty thousand U.S. dollars or more. On her knees before Kailas, however, her wealth means nothing. Here she is a pilgrim among pilgrims, and when she walks past us, she turns and smiles. I can see that she has been crying, and although I must guess, I have the intuition her tears are not for atonement, but rather that she has been dreaming all her life of seeing this mountain.

She climbs in her vehicle and leaves, and in a few minutes we do the same. Three hours later we arrive in Darchen, the town at the base of the mountain from which all pilgrims begin the *khora* of Kailas. Once through the town's mud-wall gate, I remember my friend Gretel Erlich—the writer, traveler, cowgirl, and Buddhist—telling me before I left that if I were to take from this journey all that it had to offer, it was essential I "see things as they are." (Reading Jonathan's journals, I have now realized this was the same thing Goenka had told him, and the same thing Gautama Buddha had told his pupils twenty-five hundred years earlier.) I have Gretel's admonition in mind because I had expectations for this town. After all, it is the starting point for arguably the world's holiest trek, gateway to one of the planet's most sacred places. It's a small town full of mostly Tibetan pilgrims. Nearly everyone is here for spiritual enlightenment, spiritual redemption, or some combination of the two. I wanted it to be a great place. But if I truly "see things as they are," what I see in Darchen is a fucking mess.

Jon, Asia, Dawa, and I are sharing a dormitory room in a guest house that we are told is not quite two years old, but already the paint has peeled and large hunks of plaster and adobe have fallen out of the walls. The pit in the outhouse has filled, so everyone has taken to using the surrounding dirt courtyard. There is a stream of erstwhile springwater flowing through town, into which everyone throws their garbage and also takes their drinking and cooking water. You can see at the edges of the stream that some of the shit also gets deposited there. I have been passing through places like Darchen since I started my adventure travels at age eighteen, and thirty-two years later I am feeling a strain on my commitment to what an anthropology professor convinced me back then was an admirable ethic called cultural relativity.

Outside the guest house I squat on my hunkers, working with Dawa to assemble and test our backpacking stoves to make sure they've survived transport in the back of the truck. I begin to consider the possibility that I am becoming a curmudgeon, so I ask Dawa, unflappable and perennially cheerful Dawa, what he thinks of Darchen.

"Darchen? Very dirty, very ugly. I think it's a good idea we try to leave tomorrow."

"Thank you, Dawa. I appreciate that."

In fact our plan is to leave tomorrow, if we can contract yaks to carry our camp gear. I am reluctant to ask Asia to carry a heavy pack until I see how she does at high altitude with her asthma; and in addition, one of our drivers and our L.O. want to come, and they do not backpack. We finish organizing food and camping gear, and I'm relieved when Jon returns to say he has succeeded in contracting a yak driver with three animals who will arrive first thing in the morning.

That evening, before we go to sleep, Asia tells me quietly that she has to pee but she's afraid of the dogs. She's referring to the town's population of feral dogs that during the night gather in a ferocious pack and make stepping outside a serious consideration. Her fear brings to mind a story she told just before we left. She said that two months earlier she had been at her maternal grandparents' house, going through her baby pictures, when she found a letter from her father written in 1980, at the beginning of our journey to Minya Konka. In the letter he said he hoped Asia was recovering from her dog bite.

"What dog bite?" Asia asked her grandmother.

"A dog once bit you right here," her grandmother said, pointing to Asia's hip.

"How old was I?"

"Only a little over a year. You were too young to remember."

But Asia wasn't so sure. In fact, she had a vivid memory of a dog biting her. Could it be the same incident? Was it possible she could remember anything that far back? The more she thought about it, the more she was convinced it was the same incident, which meant she had a memory of something that happened at a time when her father was still alive. So if she could remember the dog, she told herself, maybe she could remember him. For several weeks she struggled to conjure an image of her father. Any image, any memory. But nothing came forth, and slowly she had to accept the fact that no memory was there. The initial excitement, followed by the growing disappointment, put her into a mild depression that began to lift only as the date of our departure began to approach.

I tell Asia to wait just a second while I get my headlamp, and then we head out. In the courtyard we stop to listen, and after a moment we can hear the howl of the dogs. They seem to be on the far side of town, so we venture outside the walled enclosure. I turn off my headlamp and look south. Under the gray and black light of a waxing moon I can see, across the sloping alluvium of the Barga Plain, the edge of Lake Manasarovar. Asia steps a few feet away and, as discreetly as possible, takes care of business. On the horizon there is a distant electrical storm whose brightest discharges illuminate the glacial flanks of Gurla Mandhata, a 25,000-foot massif that is thirty-five miles away. When she is finished, Asia joins me and we watch the lightning.

"Thanks for taking care of me like this," she says.

"I'd do the same for my own daughters."

"You better watch out, or I'll move into that guest room of yours."

We both laugh, then wait for more lightning. The foreground plain and background mountain are no more than ghostly shapes under the half moon, until a sudden flash of lightning reveals ridges and valleys and the lake and the glaciers that leave their imprint on our eyes until the images again fade into vague shapes. Asia and I stand motionless next to each other. We are quiet, waiting for more lightning, but instead we hear the howl of the dog pack, and now it sounds as if it is approaching. Still we wait until another flash again illuminates the steppe.

"Maybe we should go back in," Asia suggests after the light has faded.

"Maybe we should," I reply, my hand on her shoulder.

Our three yaks and yak driver show up on time, and after loading the duffels on the backs of the animals we depart Darchen walking west, leaving Kailas to our right, in the Buddhist manner of circling all sacred objects clockwise. The trail is marked every fifty feet or so with small cairns made mostly of white stones that have been brought from elsewhere for this purpose. The path bends to the north, parallels a long wall of *mani* stones, then passes through a gateway arch that frames a view of the Lha Chu Valley. The floor of the valley is flat and wide, but the walls are steep and composed of dark conglomerate that at higher elevations is capped with snow that drips like icing down the chocolate-colored rock. The great west face of Kailas now emerges, and below it a smooth dome of dark rock called Guru Jator that is believed to represent a ritual offering of *tsampa*—the barley-paste staple of Tibetans—made by Padma Sambhava, the tantric master who introduced Buddhism to Tibet in the eighth century. In the same way nearly every physical feature of the mountain and its surrounding ridges, valleys, streams, and cliffs is imbued with legend and animated with spiritual power.

A slight breeze is cool against my skin. There are no clouds, and the whiteness of Kailas is brilliant against the deep blue of the sky. The yaks and the driver set a comfortable pace. Because these animals have circled Kailas so many times, it is believed that when they die they will surely be reborn to a higher life. Likewise, it is believed that any pilgrim who makes the sacred number of 108 circumambulations will achieve instant enlightenment. Many pilgrims, in fact, make the thirty-three-mile circle around the peak three times, and some do the route in one day, an admirable achievement considering the trail ascends and descends the Drolma La, an 18,600-foot pass a little more than halfway around the *khora*.

We plan to take the standard three days (although the last day will be very short), and even then we may be slow if Asia has trouble over the Drolma La. So far, however, she is doing fine, although walking up the gradually ascended floor of this valley is easy. We are making this trek only one week before *Saga Dawa*, the first full moon of the fourth month of the Tibetan calendar, the period of the Buddha's birth, death, and enlightenment, and the time of year considered most propitious for completing the *khora*. The trail is therefore busy with pilgrims, many slower than us, some faster. We pass four nuns making a full-prostration *khora*. With each step they fall to their knees, extend onto their stomachs, touch their foreheads to the ground, stand again, clasp their hands over their heads and advance another step, all the while chanting a mantra. It will take these women several weeks to complete their *khora*, and at the end they will be bruised and bloodied. As we pass, I clasp my hands and make a short bow of respect. They all have dirt smudges on their foreheads, and one already has a cut over her eye. They stop and smile at us, then drop again to their knees.

These prostrations are actually a form of yoga. As every bone and joint touches the ground, you are suppose to think of a different visualization. The goal is perfect harmony of body, speech, and mind: body is the prostration, speech is the mantra, and mind is the visualization.

Tibetans believe that if you do one such prostration perfectly, you will gain instant enlightenment. My own goal on the *khora* is to hike in harmony with the landscape by avoiding extraneous thoughts. But already this morning I have caught myself thinking about the deficiencies of our truck driver, about the political heat between China and the United States and whether it will cool sufficiently to allow us safe passage from Chengdu to Minya Konka, about the monsoon and whether this year it will arrive early.

Now I take a deep breath and absorb the view from the top of a small rise that reveals a stream braiding through the broadening valley. I clear my mind, concentrate on listening to my shoes crunch the gravel. I slow so that Asia can catch up to me, and as we walk side by side I take her arm in mine, and more strongly than at any previous time on our journey, I feel the presence of her father who, like Asia, is also walking next to me, walking even as *part* of me.

I wonder whether Asia understands how I feel. I wonder whether to say something to her to try to explain it. But I hesitate. It's the same reluctance I sometimes feel with my own daughters, a reluctance to express my emotions that I suspect I share with most men (a trait my daughters laughingly call "a guy thing"). I realize I should tell Asia how at this moment I am feeling not only like a father, but like her father, like her *real* father. Then I decide maybe she can sense that just by the way I am holding her arm.

I take another deep breath and hear up the trail the crow call of an orange-billed chough, and say to myself, Here and now, here and now.

By midafternoon we begin a gradual ascent up a northerly fork of the Lha Chu Valley, and the north face of Kailas is slowly revealed so that at first its broad but near-vertical expanse is but a compressed ribbon of snow and rock. A stiffening south wind whisks tendrils of spindrift off the summit ridge. Asia is slowing, and I cut back my own pace so I don't pull too far ahead. The altitude is over 16,000 feet, and I am watchful should her asthma begin to impede her breathing. I stop and wait, and when she reaches me she says, "I'm so tired."

"That's normal at this altitude."

"But I'm *so* tired."

She seems to be breathing okay, and I am about to tell her she has to try to ignore her discomfort and her lethargy—to make her mind tell her body what to do—when I hesitate, realizing this is a lesson that she has to discover on her own. I think Jonathan would agree with this strategy, too. When his wife became pregnant with Asia, he wrote in his journal that "I hope my child grows up with understanding and with wisdom, living life with equanimity, but I know this will happen only if I allow the child to experience the truth of life on his or her own, without imposing my will."

We continue for another ten minutes, then Asia stops again, sits on a rock, and lowers her head to her lap. Now I am concerned less with life lessons than with whether or not Asia can get over the Drolma La tomorrow, or even as far as camp today. I stand next to her, not saying anything. A full minute passes, and she still has her head in her lap, her hands over her eyes. Then she looks up and forces a smile.

"Okay," she says. "Let's keep going."

In less than a half hour we arrive at our campsite directly under the north face of Kailas. There is still a stiff wind. Asia and I set up our tent, and she crawls inside. I help Dawa get the cook tent up and then start our two small backpacking stoves. When the water is hot, I take a cup of tea to Asia. She takes a sip but draws it quickly away from her lips, then sets the cup down to cool.

"It seems like I spend half my life," she says, still trying to smile, "getting my body, or the things I put in my body, or the things I put on my body, at just the right temperature."

"You won't have any trouble getting your tea to cool here," I reply, returning her smile.

Striated clouds have now occluded the sky, but in a half hour a narrow break in the cover allows the slanting sun to shine on our camp, and I talk Asia out of the tent for a photograph.

"Feeling better?"

"A little. But I'm worried about tomorrow."

"Don't. Just set your mind to the task. You'll be surprised what you can do."

The morning sky is clear, and the air is calm. Dawa has prepared a fine rice pudding, and I am pleased that Asia eats a portion larger than what she usually takes for breakfast. Again she tells me she is apprehensive, and once more I tell her she can make it if she wills her mind to put one foot in front of the other.

Direct sun is on our camp by the time we are packed and ready to leave. There are dozens if not hundreds of pilgrims in front of and behind us on the trail. We have only seen one small group of Americans, one group of Italians, and a lone Frenchman; more come from India, but the multitudes are from Tibet, who have come from all quarters. One tall pilgrim is from Amdo, over a thousand miles to the north and east, and belongs to a group called the Goloks whose men never cut their hair. He has his hair inside the cowboy-style hat so commonly favored by Tibetans, and when at a rest stop I ask if I can take his photograph without his hat, he smiles and obliges, and his hair falls broadly across his shoulders. As I am using a flash to fill the shadows on his face, I have Jon ask the Tibetan if he would mind taking off his mirrored sunglasses, and this time he hesitates, but then removes them, and I am shamed by my own brashness because he has cataracts. This ailment is common in Tibet, especially on the high steppe where there is an average thirty-four hundred hours of sunlight a year. I quickly take his picture, and just as quickly he replaces his glasses.

We pass the curious *Siwatshal Durtro,* known to Hindu pilgrims as the Cool Grove Charnel Ground, said to be a replica of a graveyard in India. It is a boulder field perhaps an acre or more in extent where pilgrims have left thousands of shirts, pants, sweaters, belts, shoes, hats, combs, socks, and other personal objects. All the rocks that are even approximate in shape and size to a human torso are pressed into service as manikins and dressed with shirts and hats. We watch a pilgrim stop to remove a shirt from her pack and position it on a rock. In doing so she enacts a ritualized death, thus preparing herself for the ascent to the Drolma La where she will experience a ritualized birth, and at that point enter a new life.

Between death and birth, however, is a Buddhist purgatory, a state of consciousness called *bardo* that has a physical representation in a field of granite boulders we now hike through. (We have passed a geological contact zone from sedimentary to igneous.) Between two of these glacial erratics is a narrow tunnel where pilgrims now stop and line up to squeeze through. It is believed that if you fail to make it through the tunnel it is because you have accumulated too many sins and your soul will be trapped in this netherworld. The tunnel has a diameter a little less than that of a basketball hoop, but we all worm through without mishap.

We hop rock to rock over a small creek, and the trail steepens as it ascends toward the Drolma La. The altitude is over 17,000 feet, and we all slow. I say nothing to Asia because there is no need to: she is keeping a slow but steady pace and she passes Tibetans who have passed her but who now must stop to rest. We follow a morainal ridge winding between granite rocks, stepping up stairs of stones placed in the steepest sections. The altitude is now 18,000 feet or more. I am a short distance above Asia, and when she stops and glances toward me, I give her a questioning thumbs-up. She nods affirmatively and keeps coming. When she arrives, I say, "You're going to make it."

"I'm slow."

"You're steady."

"I guess I'll make it."

"You'll make it, and remember from the Drolma La it's downhill all the way to Darchen. You've got it in the bag."

She is having to dig deep to do this, and I'm proud of her. I turn and continue, and in less than a half hour I can see the Drolma La fifty yards ahead. There are two tall poles supporting dozens of long lines that in turn hold hundreds of prayers flags that themselves are in the foundation colors of the Buddhist cosmology: blue, green, yellow, red, and white. Each flag is printed with a mantra that is carried by the wind horses aloft to the snows of Kailas. I reach the pass and walk among the hundred or more pilgrims, many smiling, many crying, all joyful in laughter or in tears. Now comes a man in his twenties, young and strong, circling the summit flags in full prostration, chanting his mantras as he throws himself bloodied on the boulders and sharp stones, dedicated to the pilgrim's pact that the more you suffer, the more you gain. There are dozens more on their knees, bowing and chanting their prayers toward Kailas, recognizing their suffering as the fact of their existence but joyful in their acknowledgment that they are but one being among millions of beings, and here, on this high pass, one pilgrim among a hundred pilgrims.

Asia, in her fleece pullover colored a daffodil yellow, her pants a complementary sage green, and her hair in a smart ponytail through the back of her billed cap, is only a few yards away, and she looks up and gives me a confident nod, and I smile and give her a thumbs-up. I watch her approach with the same stride her father had. She arrives at the prayer flags and takes out from her pack the *kata* scarf given to her by the lama of Tengboche. I stand up to give her a hug, but stop short when I see that instead of tying the *kata* to the prayer flags, as the lama had suggested she do in memory of her father, she stands holding the silk scarf and is crying.

We have been on this journey for nearly one month, and in that time she has never revealed any of her emotions in any way that could be called dramatic. Now her shoulders rise and fall, and her sobs come from far inside her. I step to her and put my hands lightly on her shoulders. She is still looking down at the silk scarf in her hands, and between her sobs she says, "All my life, I've wanted to know him."

She clears her tears and ties the scarf between two prayer flags and holds it in her hands, reluctant to let it go. Finally she lets it slip through her fingers, turns, and steps to me, and I hold her while she cries once more.

5

An hour's drive past Kailas we can see in the distance to the southwest the rock and ice crown of Nanda Devi, the highest mountain in India. At middistance on the open steppe is a mixed company of kiang—the Tibetan ass—and also Tibetan gazelle. This is the first time on our journey we have seen gazelles. They are small and stocky animals whose range extends across the Chang Tang and the adjacent highlands to the east. George Schaller had told me that as we approach the Aru we should also begin to see the antelope-like chiru. Out of the six species of wild ungulates found in the Chang Tang, he considers the chiru the most distinctive: it is the only representative of its genus, and is found only on the Tibetan steppe. "Chiru look as if they have somehow strayed from the African plains," Schaller has written. "Their lanky legs seem designed for striding toward the horizon, and their large, bright eyes are ideal for sweeping the steppe for danger." Jon, in his previous trips to the southern margins of the Chang Tang, has only once seen a solitary male chiru, and we are all excited at the prospect of visiting a region still remote enough to safekeep at least a few of these striking animals.

In the Aru we also hope to see wild yak. If Schaller regards chiru as the most distinctive ungulate, he considers wild yak the most emblematic, the animal that with its woolly appearance and irascible temper embodies the wildness of the Chang Tang. All of the Chang Tang once harbored enormous herds of wild yak and chiru and gazelle, but now they have been extirpated or reduced to remnant groupings in all but the most remote enclaves like the Aru Basin, bordered as it is on one side by the Crystal Mountains, rising to 20,000 feet, and on the other side by a range of mountains that, although rising to over nineteen thousand feet, has no name. That is why I want to experience the Aru, and why I want to take Asia there: not only to see the wild animals, but to feel the wildness.

The Aru, however, is still several days away, and for now we follow this dirt road that arcs northward around the western margin of the plateau of Tibet, toward the great ranges of Central Asia: the Karakoram, the Kun Lun, the Pamir. By afternoon the country is noticeably drier, and there are only patches of grass on the hardscrabble hills. I try to follow our progress on a U.S. government "Operational Navigation Chart." These ONCs, as they are referred to by military and civilian aircraft pilots, cover the globe, and are accurate in physical features, but in some remote places, including Western Tibet, they have unreliable positions and names for roads and towns. I'm not sure where we are, so Asia unpacks a GPS unit we have brought, sticks the antenna out the window, and begins roaming for a three-satellite fix. It is a prototype model, loaned to us by the manufacturer, that is supposed to have short E-mail transmission and reception capability, but so far, even with her knack for such things, Asia has been unable to get that part of it to work. In a minute, however, she gives me our coordinates, and I plot them on the chart.

We know where we are, and we know it with precision, but I have mixed feelings that we have this knowledge only because we have plugged into a global electronic web, and in truth I'm relieved the E-mail doesn't work. Most Himalayan expeditions these days have satellite uplinks and Internet sites. Maybe I'm a Luddite, but having these connections to the outside world for me takes away some of the mystery of traveling to remote places like the Chang Tang. Even more than reducing mystery, Internet sites and satellite phones on expeditions also alter the interrelation with wildness because the expedition members are no longer committed to relying only on their own resources for their survival. If they make a mistake, they call for help. To me, this is significant because it reduces self-reliance, and self-reliance is the single most important contribution to character that comes from contact with wildness.

"Contact!" Thoreau wrote. "Think of your life in nature—daily to be shown matter, to come in contact with it, rocks, trees, wind in your cheeks!"

We drive over seasonal flood beds on concrete bridges constructed in the last two years by the Chinese government. We follow a flat-bottom valley with a winding stream that irrigates the banks, and set up camp on a small bench covered with grass cropped by sheep to the height of a golf green. After dark, Jon, Asia, Dawa, and I are in our cook tent when we hear a vehicle slow and stop. We are about to investigate when suddenly three Chinese soldiers from the People's Liberation Army open the door flap and, without asking or saying anything, step inside. We motion them to sit on the ground cloth that serves as our floor, and they are no sooner seated than they demand, in Chinese, to know where we are from. Jon is hesitant to answer, and risking the chance they could speak some English, I tell him we can't mislead them about our national identity because they may ask for passports.

"We're Americans," Jon tells them in Chinese.

"How come you bombarded our embassy in Yugoslavia?" they demand.

"What embassy? What bombing?" Jon replies, following a strategy I had developed several days earlier in case we had an encounter such as this one.

"You haven't heard?"

"No, we've been traveling for several weeks, and we don't have a radio."

They then explain the bombing, and Jon tells them we are sorry but as individuals we didn't have anything to do with it. This seems to mollify them, and one even goes back to their vehicle and returns with apples to share with us. We respond by offering them some of our chili-cured yak jerky, which they seem to enjoy. Soon they are back on the topic of the bombing, however, and we are relieved when they finally depart.

"Let's hope that's our last encounter with the army," Jon says.

We arrive midafternoon in Shiquanhe, the principal city of Western Tibet, a sprawl of shoddy concrete buildings, most of which appear to have been built only within the last five years. We would prefer to drive through without stopping—we are only two days away from the point George Schaller has penciled on our map as the place to leave the road and venture cross-country into the Aru—but we must spend the night to give our Tibetan staff time to purchase supplies. There is only one hotel here, a gray concrete box that must have at least fifty rooms, but none has a toilet. Behind the building the solitary outhouse is so foul none of us, Tibetans included, can use it; instead we relieve ourselves around the outside of the hotel, ignoring as much as we can the street traffic and pedestrians. From the stench surrounding the building, it is obvious other guests do the same. Putting up with this is one thing if you're well traveled, but it is another for a novice like Asia who also has tidy personal habits. But, bless her heart, she is not complaining.

Using enameled metal basins filled with hot water from thermoses brought to our room, she can at least wash her face and hair. At lunchtime we walk toward the city center looking for a restaurant, and as we pass a medical clinic I comment that if rural Chinese hotels are any measure, I wouldn't want to be injured here.

"The hospitals are actually quite good," Jon says. "They have a higher priority than the hotels."

"Wasn't Kim in a hospital after the avalanche?" Asia asks. "Once you guys got back to Chengdu?"

"Only for X rays," I reply. "It turned out he had two broken vertebrae in his back. But by then the hard part was over. On the way out after the avalanche we had carried him for a day on a jury-rigged litter, but that was so painful he decided to walk. We wrapped a foam sleeping pad around his chest, put Ace bandages on his knees because they were blown out, and gave him quite a lot of morphine. It took four days to get to the road head."

"Was Yvon hurt?"

"His ribs were broken and he had a concussion, but otherwise he was okay. I tore my bicep nearly in half, so my arm was in a sling."

"Was my dad cut up very badly?"

"Only a little. That's where the blood came from on that baseball cap you have that your mom gave you. His injuries were mostly internal."

"Did he say anything to you? I mean, before he died?"

"He couldn't talk. I asked him if he was okay, and he tried to speak and shook his head no. Then I told him we were all still alive, and we were going to get out of this okay, and he nodded again. He understood what I said."

Asia doesn't ask any more questions, and in silence we continue to walk down the street. I'm not sure what is going through her head, but I know in mine I once again, as I have many times in the past twenty years, see the image of Jonathan's face as I held him in my arms, his eyes looking into mine.

We leave Shiquanhe in the predawn darkness, and one hour later we discover a leak in the truck's radiator. We have no choice but to drive back to town in the Land Cruiser to buy a new one. At the parts store I suggest to the drivers they also purchase antifreeze, but they reply they don't think it will be that cold where we are going. I tell them it will be that cold, and I insist we buy the antifreeze, so they do. We drive back to the truck, install the new radiator, and continue. These drivers are both from Lhasa, and this will be their first time venturing onto the alpine steppe of the northwestern Chang Tang. They are both middle-aged, and the older of the two—the driver of the truck—has told us he is a monk who only recently left the monastery to take up driving. It is clear they have no idea about the kind of place we are going to.

We quickly transit the town of Rutog, passing a full convoy of military trucks transporting soldiers. We reach Purong Co, a large lake the far shore of which defines the border with India. On the near shore there are ducks, geese, and grebes, and across the lake a backbone of glaciated peaks that descend abruptly into the water.

"Those mountains over there are the southern terminus of the Karakoram," I say.

"Isn't that where K2 is?" Asia asks.

"Yes, about two hundred miles north of here." I show her on the ONC chart the unnamed point marked "28,250 feet."

"Have you been back there since your expedition?"

"This is the closest."

I've already told Asia the broad story of the 1978 K2 expedition, but I intend to fill in more details because I came home from that climb realizing what I could do if I set my mind to a task and didn't give up. It was a lesson that has stayed with me all my life.

Ours was only the third expedition to climb to the top of what is regarded by mountaineers as the most difficult high-altitude peak in the world. Chris Chandler had been invited to join the K2 team as doctor and climber, and as happened on Everest, he introduced me to the team and recommended I also be invited. Chris and I looked forward to making up for our involuntary split up on Everest. Moreover, K2 would be a more exciting peak to summit together. I told Chris that my only worry was a return of the lung problem I suffered approaching the South Col. I knew that getting down quickly on K2 might not be as easy as on Everest.

"It was probably just bronchitis or pleurisy exacerbated by the altitude," Chris replied. "Anyway, there's only one way to find out. Go back to eight thousand meters!"

Before we even started the approach march, however, other fears arose. A British team led by the expedition veteran Chris Bonington also had been given permission to climb K2 that season, but because there weren't enough porters in the area to support simultaneous expeditions, ours was scheduled a month later than theirs. When we arrived in Pakistan, we heard that they had gained the base of the mountain without mishap and were already beginning their ascent. Then a day before we were to begin our own trek one of our group came into the room and said, "Bonington is here." We all froze in place. No one said anything until the news bearer broke the silence.

"It was Escourt," he said. "A slab avalanche. They never found the body."

Nick Escourt, a close friend of Bonington's, was one of their lead climbers. We saw Bonington later that day, after he had filed his report with the district commissioner. His blank eyes and sunken cheeks told even more than his story of how a slab eight feet thick broke away and swept Nick to his death. Seeing the grief on Bonington's face brought back that morning on Everest when I climbed to the South Col wondering each step of the way whether or not my partner Chris had bivouacked, and if he had, whether or not he was still alive, and if he was alive, whether or not he was at that moment watching the sun rise above Lhotse, knowing only with a detached consciousness that its warmth was too late to save him.

The approach march to the base of K2, like that to Everest, was long, 110 miles from the roadhead, where our caravan of jeeps and trailer-pulling tractors was met by hundreds of Balti men from the surrounding hills. We needed 280 porters to shoulder our loads to the base of the mountain, but because much of the way was through uninhabited country, we would need 70 more porters to carry food for the 280. Then we realized we would need 15 more to carry food for the 70.

On the fourth day of the approach march we shared a campsite with Bonington's homebound expedition. He had organized the most elite high-altitude mountaineering team in the world: They had made the first ascents of new routes on many of the major Himalayan peaks, including the south face of Annapurna and the southwest face of Everest, and first ascents of giant rock and ice tusks like Changabang and the Ogre. But K2 had turned them back, and it had taken one of their strongest compatriots.

"We were all a bit surprised," Peter Boardman, one of their team, told me. "Too much hard climbing too high, as you'll soon find out." I remember very clearly how he paused and shook his head, and then concluded, "It's a big hill, that. A bloody big hill."

After a week we arrived at the foot of the Baltoro, the longest temperate-zone glacier in the world. For the next week we hiked over this giant ice stream, following a faint track over the rock rubble that covered most of the glacier. On the third day we crested a rise that revealed an enormous pyramidal mountain so steep that much of it was bare rock. I stood transfixed. I was still staring at it some minutes later when Chris caught up and joined me.

"How are we ever going to climb that?" I asked.

"We're not," he said. "That's not even K2."

I was looking at a smaller but similar-shaped peak called Gasherbrum 4. Two days later we reached the head of the Baltoro, where two lesser glaciers branched in opposite directions. At the end of one of these spurs, standing singular and four-sided like the Great Pyramid, and rising two vertical miles into the air—so high it appeared more as a painting from a book of fables than something made of real rock and ice—was the second-highest mountain in the world.

That afternoon I walked away from camp to sit alone looking at K2. There was a thin haze in the air, blown in from a dust storm off the Taklimakan Desert, that softened the light and made the great mountain appear even more mythical. Once again I wondered if a month from then, when I was high on that mountain, I would wake at night with the congested windpipe and lungs I had suffered on Everest. And if that happened, would I be able to get down fast enough to stay alive? Even if I remained healthy, would I own the strength, and the resolve, to get down if we were trapped high on the peak by a storm? And if we made the summit late in the day, as we most likely would, was I willing to sacrifice fingers and toes to the bivouac that would most likely follow?

Against these fears, I remembered the strength of the disappointment I had carried home from Everest when I had failed to reach the top, a disappointment I continued to harbor. But to climb K2—especially with Chris—would more than make up for that past shortfall. Looking at the mountain, however, considering it bottom to top, the magnitude of the endeavor seemed impossible. Then I remembered what Bev Johnson, a climbing friend, always told herself when looking at a seemingly impossible task. "You go about it the same way you would go about eating an elephant," she told me. "You take it one bite at a time."

We enter Domar, the last town we must pass before turning off the dirt road, and we are relieved there are no roadblocks, and no officials in front of the police station. We drive through town as fast as we dare, and on the other side I begin carefully to track our position as we approach the turnoff Schaller has penciled on the ONC chart. I do this by combining the advance of our odometer with an estimate of our compass direction, and plotting this dead-reckoning position on the chart's contours.

"I think we're close. It's got to be right about here."

We pull off the road at the opening of a latitudinal valley that as far as we can see provides a promising route east. It's a seasonal drainage bordered by sand dunes and possible bogs that don't appear on the chart, however, and I am uncertain whether Schaller's pencil mark is on the south or north side. We don't want to start on the wrong side with the risk of becoming trapped in loose sand and mud. I'm trying to match the large-scale contours on the chart to the reality of the terrain around us when Asia takes out her GPS, and in two or three minutes connects to her satellites and reads me our coordinates. I plot them on the chart.

"This is it all right. We leave the road right here."

"See," Asia says. "Aren't you glad we brought this thing?"

I'll give in only a little, so I reply, "I guess so," but I say it with an acknowledging grin.

We leave the road, thankful to be out of view of further army patrols, and head into the vast open steppes of northwest Tibet. There is a feeling similar to journeys on jungle rivers when you start on a tropical coast and travel up a large river until it branches, then branches again, then again, each time narrowing, each time the jungle growing nearer, until finally you reach that single moment when the canopy on each bank touches overhead, and you are enclosed. Only here, as we progress further into the heart of wildness, the country is opening and the sky widening until now it has become a great dome so vast it seems to be pushing down the circling horizon.

We follow the dry valley, keeping an eye for signs of water as we have no reserves for this evening's camp. We see three nomads crossing the open steppe, bent to loads on their backs supported by forehead tumplines. There is nothing to be seen in any direction on the open steppe that might be their destination. Their presence here in this vastness leaves me strangely unsettled, as though they own no past or future, as though they have no story.

When we reach them we stop, and they tell us they are carrying ice from the frozen riverbed to their tent. They nod to the low hills to the south—their camp is apparently hidden in a cross-drainage adjacent to a spring. In a few minutes we see their black yak-hair tent, and we stop a half mile away to set up our own camp. Asia and I hop out of the vehicle on opposite sides, and as I walk out on the broad gravel bed, she runs around the car and over to me, then gives me a hug.

"We're here," she yells. "Off that road. No more army, no more filthy towns!"

Jon and one of the drivers take the Land Cruiser to the nomad camp to fill our water containers. Meanwhile we set up our tents and Dawa, singing one of his Sherpa songs, prepares a fine meal. After dinner I watch the sun set as the moon rises, and later walk alone across the hard-scrabble expanse. This is the evening of the full moon of *Saga Dawa* when, during the day, Buddhists replace prayer flags at passes along roads and trails across Tibet, at hilltop chortens, and at monasteries now rebuilt since their destruction during the Cultural Revolution. I cross the firm gravel floor and climb a small rise behind camp. In brilliant silver light I see in the near distance the round bare hills emblematic of the Chang Tang, and closer, in the dried flood bed of the wide drainage, a mosaic of cracked mudcake.

I have an urge to keep walking, to cross this steppe land through the night and into the dawn, toward a mountaintop in the distance the snowy summit of which is illuminated by moonlight. I consider how some day I might be able to make a long foot-journey across this land. Yet there are so many things to do, I tell myself, and we have only this one lifetime in which to do them. Or perhaps, as every Tibetan believes, there is no "one lifetime," but a continuum of birth and death, birth and death. With this thought I return, accompanied by the moon shadow of my own form, toward camp, the only sound the crunch of my boots and the inhale-exhale of my breath into the cool thin air.

We wake to snow flurries, but, between squalls, visibility opens to twenty miles or more. The truck fails to start, and when the battery runs down we begin taking turns hand-cranking the engine, each of us working until we are out of breath. I take off the distributor cap and reset the points, and after nearly an hour of additional cranking, the engine finally catches and we leave. As morning light falls in shafts between squall clouds, we follow a faint track parallel to a series of dry lake beds and sand dunes. It is spectacular, yet I find myself worrying about the bad weather and a truck clearly prone to breaking down. Then Asia points excitedly to a sand dune a hundred yards away.

"Look, a wolf!"

A loping wolf crests one of the dunes, then continues running a sand ridge parallel to our track. My mind clears as I fix on this heraldic animal, leading us up this broadening valley as though it were gatekeeper of the eastern wildness. A quarter mile later the sand dunes give way to a rising alluvium, and the wolf, now on the open, crosses our course a hundred yards ahead, and the driver accelerates. When I realize what is happening, I say, "Don't chase him; he'll collapse from exhaustion."

Jon immediately tells the driver to slow, but he only grins and drives the Land Cruiser even faster.

"Stop," Asia says, and when this doesn't work she leans forward to within inches of his ear and screams, "Stop!" This needs no translation, and we slow to a stop as the wolf continues to run until it finally disappears behind another dune. It feels as though Asia's scream continues to fill the silence that follows it, and as we bump along, no one saying anything, my initial wince gives way to the realization that she has saved the wolf's life.

"I think we've just witnessed one way these animals are hunted down," I finally say. Then I turn round to Asia and add, "Good job."

"Thanks," she replies.

A few miles farther I see at the base of a bordering hill a series of tawny animals angling away at a gallop, too distant to identify with an unaided eye. When I ask, this time the driver stops quickly, and I focus my binoculars.

"Kiang. Eight of them."

We continue when suddenly, as though appearing from nowhere, four male chiru broach our flank at full gallop and cross our vehicle's path no more than thirty yards ahead. Their rapier horns seem as long as their bodies, and they run with the speed of phantoms. I scramble for my camera, but by the time I have it raised to the window they have come and gone. I turn to see Asia holding her camera; she nods and says, "I got 'em."

"There's more," Jon calls, and turning we see four more males. They are small animals, only two and a half or three feet tall at the shoulder, with long horns curved slightly outward at the tips that add another two feet to their height. On the ONC I note their number and location for George Schaller.

"We're here!" Jon exclaims. "Wild Tibet."

"Eight more on the right," Asia says.

By midmorning we have covered twenty-five miles and counted fifty-three chiru—nearly all males, as the females are in migration to their calving grounds this time of year. We have seen numerous kiang, and the one wolf. Then we pass a nomad's tent, and in a few miles another. Both are made of black yak hair fabric guyed out with numerous lines of black rope—they look like a desert species of sea urchin. The nomad's herd of goats and sheep graze on the hillsides, and as the domestic stocks have reappeared, the wild animals have disappeared save for a few kiang.

We drive through the day, following the sometimes faint track of other vehicles, likely trucks that the wealthiest nomads now own. Soon we see a tent with a truck parked in front, and as we pass it two mastiffs run after us, snapping at our vehicle. Only ten years ago or less the nomads all migrated to their summer pasturage with tents and house-wares on the backs of their yaks. Trucks are expensive, and we can only assume that the money to buy them comes not from selling milk and wool, but from the much higher earnings to be had from the trade of *shahtoosh,* the fine undercoat wool of the chiru.

"*Shahtoosh*" is Persian for "king of wool," and chiru fur is finer than cashmere, finer even than the vicuña fur of South America. Measured by the micron diameter of each hair, it is the finest wool in the world. For hundreds of years there has been a trade in *shahtoosh* out of the Chang Tang and over the Himalayas to Kashmir, where Indian master weavers produce the world's softest scarves and shawls. In the past two decades these shawls have become chic in urban fashion centers from London to Los Angeles, where a full-length *shahtoosh* shawl sells for close to twenty thousand dollars. The same shawl also requires the wool of about three adult chiru, killed by Tibetan nomads mostly during the winter months, when the undercoat is thickest.

Schaller's studies have revealed that poaching has increased significantly since the late 1980s. Less than a hundred years ago, Captain C. G. Rawlins, one of the so-called gate-crashers trying to gain entrance to the forbidden city of Lhasa by crossing the Chang Tang and coming in through the back door, wrote that "almost from my feet away to the north and east, as far as the eye could reach, were thousands upon thousands of doe antelope (chiru) with their young . . . we could see in the extreme distance a continuous stream of fresh herds steadily approaching; there could not have been less than 15,000 or 20,000 visible at one time." One can only guess what the total population was in those years, but it seems certain to have been in the hundreds of thousands. When Schaller first visited the Aru in 1988, and again in 1990 and 1992, he still saw herds of up to 2,000 and estimated the entire population in Tibet to be about 75,000 animals. On his last visit, in 1994, he followed vehicle tracks into the basin that had not been there two years before, and in places where previously there had been herds of chiru, there were now flocks of sheep. Schaller was therefore curious to get our report to see what had happened in the five years since.

We camp a half mile from another nomad who comes to greet us. He wears a lambskin *chuba,* the traditional knee-length robe, folded down on one shoulder because of the heat, which is a little below freezing, but on the Chang Tang that is considered hot. His hand rests at chest level in the garment's fold, Napoleon-style. His felt-soled mucklucks are constructed in a harlequin patchwork of red, green, blue, and black fabric. He stands at the edge of our camp, quiet and polite, and when we finish putting up the tents we invite him in for tea. He takes the mug in both hands, inhales the steam and drinks the brew, thanking us before he returns to his own tent.

Next morning new-fallen snow covers the faint tracks we have been following. We strike camp, and, concerned about finding our route in these conditions, drive to the nomad's tent to see if we can negotiate a fee to have him come with us. As we park in front of the tent, he steps out and waves to us. His tent, made from woven strips of yak hair sewn together into matching halves connected along a ridgepole, is covered in a layer of snow. He motions us to step in. His wife, smiling widely, is pumping a goatskin bellows to fan a small fire of burning sheep dung, and the air is filled with its aromatic smoke. Two young girls, perhaps three and five, peer at us from behind the heavy homespun of their mother's ankle-length skirt.

The nomad motions us to sit, and his wife pours us each a cup of yak butter tea, the gesture of hospitality universal among Tibetans. Asia makes eye contact with the little girls, and points to the corner of the tent where three young sheep lie in the corner on a bundled blanket. (Sheep birth in late winter, and in this harsh country they must be reared inside their shepherds' tents.) The young girls glance at the sheep, then back to Asia, who motions them to come to her. After a minute or so the older one overcomes her caution, steps from behind her mother, and sits next to Asia, who smiles and puts her arm around the little girl who then relaxes and sets her hand on Asia's knee.

We agree on a fee, finish our tea, thank our hostess, and leave. The nomad sits in the front seat of the Land Cruiser. All the land is blanketed in snow, and through an occasional thinning in the cloud cover, diffused sunlight reflects off the whiteness until all features are lost to overexposure. Both driver and guide have borrowed Asia's and my ski goggles. As neither of them has bathed in weeks or perhaps months, the goggles make them look like military veterans of a desert legion at the end of a long and difficult campaign.

We take turns glancing behind to check on the truck, and soon we see it is stuck in a mud wallow. We turn around and spend a half hour digging a trench in front of the rear wheels with shovels purchased in

Shiquanhe, then position in the troughs two fifteen-foot logs we have carried in the bed of the truck to give traction to the tires. Under way once again, we travel through country free of nomads and their stocks, and again the wild animals return. We pass a solitary Tibetan gazelle that pronks away in spring-loaded leaps; there are frequent groupings of male chiru mixed with an occasional female and yearling.

We have traveled about fifteen miles when we leave our guide at the tent of another nomad who agrees to accompany us from here. He tells us we have missed the female chiru migration, which passed through here two weeks before. He estimates the count this year to be between two and three thousand animals. This migration is a mystery that has fascinated George Schaller for years, because no one has pinpointed where the animals go from here.

If our guide is accurate, this year's migration is significantly less than the 7,500 females Schaller counted passing through the Aru in 1992. Then, as though in timely confirmation of Schaller's suspicion that nomads are moving permanently into the area, we approach a new settlement of a dozen adobe dwellings. We stop so Asia can get a fix with the GPS. I note the location, take a few pictures for Schaller, and enter in my log what our guide had to say about this year's migration. I know, of course, all this data will only confirm Schaller's fears.

We leave our guide in the settlement, and continue, navigating now by the route Schaller has penciled on our ONC chart and the fixes Asia secures with her GPS. We expect to cross a high pass into the Aru Basin by day's end. Schaller has warned me that this pass could have snowdrifts even in June, and although it has stopped snowing for now, the sky is clouding. At a nomad's tent we stop to ask directions to the pass. He has a truck parked in front, and Asia points to the chains dangling from hooks below the rear gate.

"Maybe we should try and buy them," Asia suggests.

Since they didn't even bring shovels, it is certainly no surprise to learn our drivers also are without chains. I know Asia's suggestion has merit, but I also know buying the chains would require a lengthy barter, and with the weather building, I don't want to delay.

"I doubt they'd sell them," I say, "because they can't replace them out here."

"Whatever you think," Asia says.

Jon, who is in charge of logistics, doesn't say anything, so we drive away, but in the back of my mind I am already second-guessing myself. Asia may have the better tactic—to prepare for the weather rather than to try to outrun it.

We enter a narrowing valley that leads toward the pass, and it begins to snow. The faint track of the nomads' trucks soon disappears under accumulating snow. There is only one way up the valley, however. I look back to see that the truck is once more stuck in mud. We turn around, go back and dig it out, and continue. In another hundred yards we look back and see the truck stopped again, and once more we turn around. This time there is something wrong with the throw-out bearing, and it takes an hour to repair.

The angle of the road eases, and it feels as though we are approaching the pass. Visibility is only a few hundred yards, but the surrounding slopes disappear steeply into the clouds—an indication that we are being enclosed by higher mountains. The drifts are more frequent, however, and we have to make multiple charges in the Land Cruiser to push a track through the deeper ones now nearly two feet thick. Ahead I see what appears to be the pass, perhaps only three hundred yards ahead. We hit one drift close to three feet deep, and it stops us. We get out to shovel a trench through it, back up, rush at it again, and this time push through. I look behind for the truck, and we are all encouraged when it makes it. In another minute we reach the top of the pass.

"We'll be in Aru in an hour or two," I predict optimistically, although I feel as though we are stepping through a door that is rapidly closing.

For a few minutes we make good progress down the gradual grade. Then the route starts to climb again, gently at first, then more steeply.

"I guess that wasn't the pass," Jon says.

We hit more deep drifts, slow, and stop. I look back for the truck.

"They're stuck again."

"They'll never get through this."

We turn around and work our way back to the truck. We find the truck driver and Dawa digging a trench in front of the rear tires to create a channel for the logs. The two drivers now huddle with the liaison officer and Jon, who then comes to give me the report.

"They say they can't go on."

"I'll admit it's getting tough."

"They want to go back to that first pass, so if it keeps snowing we won't get stuck in this basin."

I am loath to backtrack, however, to admit defeat too early and set a tone of giving up before we really try. I want these guys to know it's going to take a lot more than this to turn us back.

"I think we should camp here," I tell Jon, "and wait for the weather to improve, then push on."

"I'll try and convince them."

"It's important to our larger goals that we get to the Aru."

There is a small area next to the parked vehicles that has been blown free of snow, and the Tibetans erect their tent there. I find it's too rocky, so I suggest to Asia we position our tent on the flat snow. She's fine with this, and we are just finishing staking the guy lines when the Tibetans come over to tell us we can't camp on the snow.

"Why not?"

"You'll freeze to death."

"We have inflatable pads to put under us. We'll be fine."

"No, you must not camp on the snow."

"Listen guys," Asia says, "Rick has camped on snow for *years*. Like he's been on Everest *twice*, and he's climbed *K2*. He's been on five expeditions to *Antarctica*. He's more comfortable sleeping on snow than he is on *dirt*."

I find Asia's promotion of my mountaineering prowess embarrassing, but I also have to admit it's endearing. I think to myself, Wait until we go rock climbing together, then she'll find out. (The truth is, I am an average rock climber at best, mostly because my legs are just too big to haul up steep rock.) Then I think this would be the same evolution I'm going through with my own daughters, who as young kids regarded me as larger than life and now, as they are getting a little older, realize that I have foibles and weaknesses just like everybody else.

Jon tells the Tibetans that we know what we're doing, and they don't need to worry. They shake their heads and go back to their tent, but as they depart they say, "You'll get *sick* sleeping on snow."

When the tents are up and we are moved in, I have the idea to walk to the pass and investigate conditions on the far side. I calculate that I have a full hour and a half to complete my excursion, but I take my headlamp just in case. I leave camp heading toward the pass, and the walking is reasonably easy as long as I take care to scout a route around the drifts. I note that it will still take some digging to get the truck through.

This pass we are trying to negotiate is an east-west crossing over the southern foothills of the Crystal Mountains, and in clear weather I imagine the view from here to the north probably includes at least one if not more of the major summits of the range. A few miles ahead I can see, rising into the clouds, the flank of what must be one of those peaks. The slope I am ascending now begins to ease as I approach the top, and I can begin to see into the opposite drainage. When I reach the crest, I note I am higher than the actual pass, which is off to my right a few hundred yards. The route from here down the other side is steeper than I anticipated, and it disappears from my view as it enters the narrow canyon. I convince myself that even if the snow doesn't melt in the bottom of the canyon, we should have enough momentum going downhill to push through.

But enough of these logistics. I take a deep breath, exhale slowly, and clear my mind. I stand still, close my eyes, and listen. There is no wind. There is no sound. I remain as motionless as possible, and then I hear it, a faint hum. It requires concentration to pick it up. I have heard it before, but only in places completely without noise: the Haleakala Crater, the Western Cwm, the Antarctic ice cap.

Then there is a light zephyr just strong enough to take away the hum. It's not enough, however, to carry away the joy I feel being alone in this wildness. I open my eyes and look in the direction of the Crystal Mountains. I decide enough daylight remains that I can descend a little ways down this other side and into the canyon. Before I began the descent, however, I glance across the ridgeline to my left, and suddenly I freeze. I feel my pulse quicken, feel a tightening in my chest.

Stay calm, I say to myself, calm and still.

I slowly turn my head to catch the zephyr on my cheek, to gauge its direction. The air, thank God, is moving off the ridge, drifting down the slope. Up the slope, perhaps 150 yards from me, are a large brown bear sow and her cub. The sow is digging furiously in the snow, pulling in unison with both foreclaws as she rips tough cushion plants from the ground. Then she noses into the hole she has created, and the cub moves forward. The sow comes up with what could be either a marmot or a pika in her claws, although I'm not sure she has either. I chide myself for forgetting my binoculars. Both she and the cub are distracted, so I judge this to be a good chance to retreat. I turn around and walk toward camp, and when I think I am far enough away I start running, not to escape danger, but to get my camera to photograph the bears before they leave. This is a rare sighting.

In camp I call to everyone and point to the hillside where the two bears are easily visible. We mount our spotting scope on the tripod and focus. The sow is still digging, and the power with which she uproots the cushion plants is awesome. While we take turns looking through the

scope, I photograph the animals with our telescopic lens, pausing to consider how lucky I was to have been in a downwind position when I first
noticed them. Had I surprised them, the sow probably would have
charged and perhaps mauled me. Tibetan brown bears are closely
related to grizzlies and, if anything, are even more temperamental.
Schaller wrote that on his second trip into the Aru in 1990, his wife,
Kate, and a Chinese driver encountered a bear and two cubs that
"rushed at them from a dip in the plain, her head threateningly low, hair
bristled, and with utter fury chased the car, then chased twice more
when they paused at a distance." Kate added that "I have never, ever,
seen such an angry animal." After that Schaller remained alert whenever
he was on foot. When I met with George, I asked him about bears, and
he said they were rare, adding that it would be unlikely we would see
any. But if we did, and we were on foot, we would realize very quickly, he
said with an amused chuckle, "that the tallest tree in the Chang Tang is a
stunted dwarf about one foot high."

That evening in the tent, as Asia and I write in our journals, I recall
what Dave Foreman, the advocate of preserving wilderness sufficiently
large for big predators, calls "the reality check of walking in a neighbor-
hood where the locals have big teeth." This will be a good experience for
Asia, to see a place that is still intact, that still has all the pieces in place,
all the predators and all the prey. Not only to see it, but to feel it.

6

In the morning I wake to the sound of windblown snow graveling against the nylon fly of our tent. I look out the door and see the spindrift scudding at ground level over sculpted snowdrifts. I can hear Dawa singing as he does most mornings. When he sees me, he smiles and brings over two insulated mugs of tea, one for Asia and one for me, which we drink sitting up in our sleeping bags. Then I dress and walk to the cook tent, stopping to scan the hillsides, but see no sign of yesterday's bears.

After breakfast I ask our Tibetan driver if he can take me in the Land Cruiser to the col so I can have a safe refuge from which to scout the route down the far side. But the Tibetans first want to use the Toyota to tow-start the truck, whose battery has again drained. I watch as the Land Cruiser pulls the truck through the snow, but it doesn't start, and soon both vehicles are stuck. Frustrated, I decide to walk to the col on my own, realizing I must maintain a constant scrutiny of the hillsides and remain mindful of wind direction.

At the col I first scan the slopes, then descend into the opposite canyon. I approach a small promontory that obscures the slope below it.

The wind is at my back, which leaves me upwind if there is a bear ahead, but there is nothing I can do about it. I move cautiously to the top of the promontory and look over: no bears. I continue downward, and now the drifts are thigh deep, and I realize that unless some of the snow melts, it will be difficult if not impossible for the lumbering truck to get through. I return uphill, my eyes sweeping the open snow slopes. At the col I see that the clouds have broken sufficiently to reveal a snow peak with sharp ridges that must be one of the higher summits of the Aru range. It is brilliant white against a patch of blue, and as I stand admiring it I have an idea: While we wait for the snow over the col to melt, Asia, Jon, and I should climb this peak.

My only concern is the bears. Despite my enthusiasm for exposing Asia to direct "contact" with wildness, I know I can't heedlessly place her in harm's way. But if we approach the mountain along a ridgeline to my right, and the wind continues to blow from the west, we'll have an uninterrupted panorama of the entire basin yet stay downwind of our advance. That should eliminate the risk of either surprising a bear or telegraphing our smell. We can then traverse the basin, following a high contour that will continue to give us an open view. Above that the terrain should be too steep for a bear to venture into. To be completely safe, we can camp at the base of the ridge that leads to the summit, higher than any bear would normally wander.

I return to camp and tell my plan to Jon and Asia, who are both excited, but then Asia looks concerned. Finally she says, "I'm sort of afraid of bears."

"We can control the risk," I tell her.

"I know you wouldn't do anything to get us in trouble," she says, admonishing me. Before leaving on the journey Asia's mother said the same thing in more or less the same tone.

While Jon would like to go, he is more immediately focused on the challenge of getting our vehicles over the pass. He and the Tibetans have decided they should return in the Land Cruiser to the last nomad settlement, to see if they can purchase both a better battery and the set of chains Asia saw the previous day. I agree that chains are probably essential to getting through.

"If we're not back in the morning, you and Asia should climb the peak by yourselves."

"Okay," I answer, then turn to Asia and tell her that we should have listened to her in the first place. I am learning to pay better attention to her ideas, and apparently so is Jon: he asks her if she can think of anything else we should do.

"Fill three plastic gunny sacks with gravel," she answers, "and put them in the back of the Land Cruiser. The weight will give you better traction coming back up, then we can use the gravel to line mud pockets if the truck gets stuck. Also tell the driver to keep it in four-wheel compound low. He's staying in high way too much. If he doesn't like it, tell him too bad, just do it."

"Okay," Jon says, turning and putting his pack and sleeping bag into the Toyota, in case he has to spend the night out. After they depart I turn to Asia.

"Where did you learn about that stuff?"

"From an old boyfriend who was into off-roading."

Asia and I go back to our tent to wait. The clouds have again closed in, and once more it is snowing. She crawls into her sleeping bag and reads a book while I lie on my back listening to the snow build and then slide down the nylon walls.

"I figured out once that I've spent about three years of my life living in tents," I tell her, "and the majority of that time was waiting out storms."

"What was the longest one?"

"I've never been in a really long one. Ten or eleven days on K2, I guess. Yvon was once stuck in an ice cave in Patagonia for over a month. It helps to remember those past storms because when you're in the middle of one you sometimes think it's never going to end. But it always does, and there's usually enough time afterward to keep going. On K2, though, we had six storms all together, and by the end of the last one we were out of everything, food, fuel, strength, patience, time. Everything."

"How long did the whole thing take?"

"Sixty-eight days above Base Camp, and five of those were above eight thousand meters, the so-called death zone."

If those of us on the 1978 K2 expedition had been told it would take more than two months to get up the mountain and down, we would not have believed it. At the onset we thought we could do the climb in a little over one month. As soon as we arrived at Base Camp we set to work organizing our equipment. Next morning Chris and I left early to scout a route to our Advanced Base Camp. It felt good to be leading with Chris again, as good as it had felt in the icefall on Everest. But I noticed he was slower than usual, and the next day he needed to take a day off. Nevertheless, we continued to make good progress, reaching Advanced Base Camp, and then Camp 1, at the base of the ridge we proposed to climb. I was thrilled when Chris and I were selected as part of a lead team to set up Camp 2. The weather held, and for two hours we climbed quickly. Then Chris took the lead up a steep section of mixed rock and snow. He started to slow, and several times he knocked rocks down on us.

"He's taking forever," one of the other climbers said.

Another barrage of rocks came down and hit the guy standing next to me. He rolled back his sleeve, and a large bruise was already forming on his forearm.

"I don't think it's broken, but it hurts like hell," he said.

Chris yelled down that he was sorry, and we yelled back to be careful. He continued, and in a few moments another barrage of rocks came down.

"Get off the rock and back on the ice!" I screamed. "You trying to kill us?"

"Look, the ice doesn't go much higher than this anyway!" Chris yelled back. "I am being careful."

By next day we had ropes secured to the site of Camp 2. While another team began to scout the route to Camp 3, the rest of us ferried food, climbing gear, fixed rope, oxygen bottles, tents, stoves, and fuel up to the growing gear stockpile at Camp 2. Once the route to Camp 3 was fixed, we waited anxiously for the expedition leader, Jim Whittaker, to announce who would lead to Camp 4. The northeast ridge we were attempting had a knife-edge traverse at its midpoint. We knew this section would be the most technically difficult part of the ascent, and whoever got to scout it would have the most demanding—and satisfying—lead-climbing on the expedition.

Jim made his choice: the three climbers on the first team would be led by John Roskelley, the strongest and most skilled climber on the expedition. They would push the route for two days. Then Chris and I would take over for the next two. We all felt that, weather permitting, we had a good chance of completing the task in four days. All of us chosen huddled to discuss the equipment we would need: ice screws, pickets, fixed rope, aluminum deadmen, locking carabiners. I was encouraged to see Chris's enthusiasm for the challenge: maybe he was past whatever it was that seemed to be holding him back.

My hope, however, was short-lived. When we began ferrying supplies to Camp 3, Chris still moved slowly, and he didn't carry as much as most of the others. He was underperforming, and I wasn't sure why. I knew that in the previous year he had been too busy to get much climbing in, and he wasn't in great shape. Maybe he was just worn out from working hard.

As his climbing partner for the previous five years, I should have talked to him. As Emerson said, the only way to have a friend is to be one, but instead I found myself privately angry at him for not trying harder. I began to wonder if there was some way I could team with John Roskelley. He and I had been getting along well, joking and telling stories. At times I felt guilty for wanting to change partners. But I also knew that when Jim Whittaker chose the summit team, he would go for the strongest one or two pairs, and I wanted to be included in that group.

The day before John and his crew were to cross the knife-edge, the first storm hit. Most of us, including John, were in Camp 2, and for the first two days we felt it made sense to stay there: if the storm were short-lived, we would then be in a better position to resume our various tasks. On the third day, however, we realized we were eating food and using fuel we had worked hard to get into position, and it made more sense for most of us to go down to Camp 1. We decided to leave two people at Camp 2 to shovel snow off the tents, and once the storm cleared, to break a trail downhill through the new snow to make it easier for everyone else to come back up. Cherie, one of the three women on the team, said she wanted to stay, and so did Chris. The rest of us descended.

After the storm went on for four days, then five days, we all felt it made more sense for Chris and Cherie to join us in Camp 1. On the sixth day, using a walkie-talkie, Jim asked them to descend. But to everyone's surprise they refused, insisting they preferred to stay at Camp 2 to acclimatize. Rumors began to circulate whether their pairing involved more than friendship. If it did, it had the potential to be disruptive: Cherie's husband was also a member of the team.

The storm continued through the seventh day, then the eighth. Each day the rumors about Chris and Cherie notched up. Then Jim decided that when it cleared Chris and Cherie should return to Camp 1. We knew that he was also going to reshuffle the lead teams for Camp 4. Then he said it: John and I would lead the first, and most difficult, section of the long traverse.

On the ninth day the storm cleared, and after waiting one more day for the snow to consolidate, John and I climbed to Camp 3 to begin the traverse. We passed Chris on his way down. He had already seen some of the other climbers ahead of us, carrying loads to the upper camps, and they had told him about the rumors.

"Whittaker's not mad at you," I told Chris. "I think you should just apologize to him for not coming down when he asked. Then start working hard and you'll have as good a chance at being included in the summit teams as anybody."

"Okay," Chris said, but I could tell he was upset. He turned and continued descending, and I continued climbing, knowing against hope that things with Chris were not settled. Why wasn't he more enthusiastic? He shouldn't have refused Jim's request to come down. Didn't he know he was setting himself up to be excluded from the summit team? Wasn't that why we were both here, to do everything we could to be included?

The sky was cloudless when John and I left Camp 3 early the next morning. In a half hour we were on the knife-edge, a ridge that had been scoured over the eons by glaciers grinding on both sides until they left a thin, serrated blade a half mile in length. Rising several thousand feet on each side above the bordering glaciers, it formed the border between Pakistan and China, and in one wide step over its crest we crossed from one country to the next.

"I'm not sure I have my visa," John said.

John belayed the rope while I crabbed sideways across the flank of the ridge. The two crampon front points on the toes of my boots and the tips of my two ice axes were my only connection to the steep ice. Every fifty feet or so I would turn an aluminum screw into the ice slope, or, in places where it was hard snow, hammer in a picket, then clip my rope into the anchor and continue. When I was two hundred feet out, I placed two screws and tied off the rope. John jumared across while I flaked out a new length of rope, then I belayed while he led the next section. The altitude was about 23,000 feet. We both felt strong, and we were in sync, pausing only now and then to exchange a grin or a nod to confirm that the climbing was fantastic.

By noon we had fixed seven hundred feet of rope. By midafternoon, one thousand feet. I was belaying John, hanging from two ice screws. Under me, the slope fell away steeply, into glaciers that eventually melted into the brown expanse of the great plateau of northwest Tibet that I could see over my shoulder. I paid out the red rope, watching it gently saw up and down on the snow slope as it reacted to John's movements, creating rainbow refractions in the snow crystals. Then I watched a butterfly land next to the rope. It was piebald orange and black, similar to the painted lady butterfly at home. I used to catch butterflies like that when I was a kid, in my cheesecloth net.

A butterfly, at 23,000 feet? I yelled to John, and he called back that there were more where he was. I looked around and saw two, three, four more. Soon there were dozens all around, hundreds of them across the slope, a cloud of butterflies migrating upward on an air current, carried higher and higher above the great snow peaks of the Karakoram.

It was my lead, and I strung out another two hundred feet. Then it was time to return to the lower camp. We pulled ourselves back on our own fixed lines, and as we regained the top of the knife-edge, we balanced on the crest. The sun was dropping toward the far horizon.

"John, look. On the glacier."

A vertical mile below we saw the twin shadows of our two figures cast by the lowering sun across the glacier. There was a nimbus, glowing in opalescent hues, encircling the heads of our shadow figures. We each waved our arms, and the arms of our giant puppets waved in reply, sweeping their hands over hundreds of yards of glacial ice.

Next day we managed to fix another twelve hundred feet of rope, then two others took over and soon we reached a place to position Camp 4. Before we could get the tents up, however, a second storm hit, and once more we had to abandon the mountain. This one lasted a week. While we waited in Camp 1, Jim called a meeting to announce that he had chosen the summit teams. We glanced at each other, awaiting his decision.

"I think the first summit team should include Jim Wickwire and Lou Reichardt on one rope," he said, "and John Roskelley and Rick Ridgeway on another."

I had made it. I was ready to take the final bite, to eat the elephant. Then John announced he wanted to climb the mountain without using oxygen. While no one had ever climbed K2 without oxygen, the year before Reinhold Messner and his partner, Peter Habeler, had ascended Everest without it. We had heard, however, they had suffered some impairment, possibly permanent, of their short-term memory. I was also worried that climbing without oxygen would trigger a recurrence of the lung problem I had suffered on Everest.

Lou said we should all climb in the same style, and if John was climbing without oxygen, he would, too. Wick then said he would also climb without oxygen. Everyone looked at me, and I realized I had no choice.

"Sure," I said. "I'll go without oxygen."

When good weather returned, we all began carrying to the high camps. A few of us planned to reach Camp 4 ahead of the others, to dig tent platforms. Chris and his rope partner would follow, continuing on to the next goal, a rounded hill at the base of the summit pyramid christened the Snow Dome, where we planned to position Camp 5. At Camp 4 John and I worked to create the first platform by chopping off the top of the ridge crest with our ice axes and snow shovel. This would have been a strenuous task at sea level, and since we didn't want to expend any more energy than necessary, we made the platform big enough to accommodate only the footprint of the tent and a narrow catwalk on one side. Once the tent was up I went inside to start a stove to make tea. Outside, through the fabric wall, I could hear John laughing.

"What's so funny?" I called out.

"It's great out here," he yelled back. "I'm taking a shit into China and a pee into Pakistan without even moving."

On the next day Chris and his partner had made it only halfway to the Snow Dome when the third storm hit. This one lasted another week. We had now been working at 18,000 feet or above for forty days. We had supplies for about two more weeks, three if we stretched them. When the storm cleared, it took two days of hard work to dig the ropes from under new snow, excavate and repair damaged tents, and haul more supplies to the higher camps. When we were done, Jim instructed John, Lou, Chris, and me to push on to Camp 5. We got an early start, and by late morning we were halfway there. Lou took the lead while Chris belayed and John and I rested.

"You know, Chris," John said, "I don't imagine we'll ever be good friends, but we can clear this up enough to at least get along for the rest of the trip."

I looked at John and gave him an encouraging nod, thinking at last we'll get this in the open and behind us.

"Maybe we can," Chris said positively.

"So there's just one thing to clear," John said, "and that's the fact I don't like you and Cherie blaming me and Rick for what's going on between you two, because it's clear to anyone that has two eyes in their head."

The two of them started yelling at each other. Lou was fifty feet above, concentrating on getting over a difficult crevasse. Suddenly he disappeared and the rope dug into the snow and went tight around Chris's waist. Chris held Lou's fall by instinct, and he didn't miss a beat cursing John.

"My personal life has nothing to do with whether we get up this mountain!" he screamed, holding the rope, not even bothering to look up to see what had happened to Lou.

"Bullshit!"

I climbed as quickly as I could at nearly 25,000 feet to the hole into which Lou had disappeared. By the time I reached it, Lou's head popped up as he jumared his way out. He was covered with snow, and his glasses were askew. He dusted himself off and said, "What's going on down there?"

"A little argument."

Lou continued on, and when the last of the rope fed out, Chris was forced to start climbing. When he was thirty feet up he turned and yelled down to John, "I'm just sick of your redneck values."

"At least I have values," John yelled back.

We reached Camp 5 late in the day, and snow began to fall again. By morning, we knew we were in another storm. Everyone rappelled back to Camp 1 except John and me, who stayed at Camp 4 to maintain the tents. It was the worst storm yet, and we feared we might be blown off the top of the narrow ridge. Outside we reset the guy lines, and inside we held our feet to the tent walls to stay the strongest gusts. By radio we were told there had been more arguments about Jim's choice of summit teams. Now it was decided that there should be two summit pushes. The four of us on the original team would try to climb directly up the summit headwall, and Chris, Cherie, and perhaps one or two others would try to traverse from Camp 5 at the eight-thousand-meter contour to the Abruzzi ridge, the route by which the two previous successful ascents of K2 had been achieved.

This fourth storm lasted eight days. When it broke, John and I worked our way down, clearing ropes and resetting the route for those coming up. It was the twentieth time that I had crossed the traverse—counting the original lead, the retreats before all the storms, the loads carried to the higher camps. Lou, Jim, and some others decided they would climb from Camp 1 to Camp 4 in one day. They arrived, but not until after dark, and next day, despite good weather, they were too exhausted to continue. Camp 4 was now too crowded to receive the next group of climbers who, by radio, voiced their fury. Chris, weary from the arguments, sat cross-legged in his tent, working to change a gas cartridge in a stove, unwilling to get involved. Suddenly there was a loud *whhumpf.* The others thought it was an avalanche; instead Chris's stove had exploded, burning off part of his hair and beard. Without saying a word, he stuffed his sleeping bag, gathered his personal belongings into his pack, and quit the expedition.

Afterward, I lay in my sleeping bag, asking myself what I could have done to prevent it from coming to this. I told myself I should have tried harder to talk to Chris. He had been a good friend, teaching me so much about mountaineering, arranging the invitation for me to join the Everest expedition and then the K2 climb. I knew that, in addition to the problems he was having on the mountain, he had recently been through a messy divorce. But I also knew it was too late.

Asia and I are in the cook tent finishing lunch. Jon and the Tibetans are still gone, and outside it's snowing. Dawa hands each of us a cup of tea, and while Asia waits for hers to cool she studies the sagging walls.

"If the guy lines on this tent were angled differently," she says, "there would be a lot more room in here."

She goes outside and starts resetting the lines. I set my tea down and go to help, following her instructions by placing ski poles as spreader struts under the guy lines so they pull out rather than pull down the sides of the tent. I have noticed Asia owns a natural aptitude for figuring out how things work, as well as how to fix things that don't work.

"That's better," she says when the last line is guyed properly.

"Much better," I agree.

An hour later we're still in the cook tent, and it's still snowing when Jon and the Tibetans return. Jon reports success in purchasing the chains and a used battery, but the Tibetans have been charged the equivalent of six hundred U.S. dollars. On other trips to China I have been impressed by how astutely the Chinese—and now apparently the Tibetans as well—understand the principles of supply and demand. I am also relieved that Jon was astute enough when arranging for the lease of the truck and Land Cruiser to negotiate a flat rate, with any extra costs picked up by the company that the L.O. and drivers work for.

Even though we have the chains, we all agree not to try the pass until the weather improves.

"We can't climb the mountain, either," I say. "Not until there's absolutely no chance of avalanche."

"The Tibetans still want to move back to the first pass," Jon tells me, nodding to the L.O. "They're afraid of getting trapped."

"And I'm still reluctant to do that," I reply.

Jon translates this, and our L.O. squeezes his face like he's tasted a lemon, then speaks to Jon in an angry tone.

"He says he can't understand," Jon translates, "why you and Asia didn't go to Everest Base Camp, instead of coming here. He's saying the roads there are good, and there are lots of other climbers and trekkers to talk to."

"There's no way to explain that one in one sitting," I tell Jon.

"I know, but these guys are getting upset. They're genuinely worried."

"Okay, we'll move back to the first pass. But make sure he understands that we don't go any farther. We stay there until it clears, and then we come back here, and then we go down to the Aru."

Jon translates and the L.O. smiles broadly, stands, and shakes my hand. It takes an hour to break camp. Even with chains the truck gets stuck twice, and it requires nearly three hours to drive the approximately two miles to the lower col. Once we arrive Asia and I again go about setting our tent on snow, and again the Tibetans shake their heads in disbelief. Then the driver of the truck begins talking excitedly, and points toward the ridge between us and our previous camp, the same ridge I am proposing to ascend to gain the mountain I hope to climb. I look and don't see anything. The driver holds his circled fingers to his eyes, indicating he wants me to get my binoculars. Once I've retrieved them, I look in the direction he is pointing and bring into focus the two brown bears. I study them for a moment before I realize they are both fully grown, and not the mother and cub I saw before. So much for George's fear that bears have been nearly extirpated from this range. Instead, the place is crawling with them.

The bears are directly in the path we will take to approach our climb. Asia once more reminds me that she is afraid of bears, and although I don't tell her, I am getting apprehensive myself. But I decide to go through with our plan to try to climb the mountain. That evening, as we go to bed, the sky is clear. When I wake early the next morning I open the tent door to large patches of open sky among the clouds.

"It's partially clear," I say. "Good enough to move. How do you feel?"

"I'm pretty good."

"Let's have some breakfast, then get out of here."

I sit up and begin to sort through the items I will take with me: headlamp, toothbrush, fleece cap, journal. Asia brushes her hair and then puts it in a ponytail.

"I'm a mess."

"You look fine."

"I've had the same long underwear on for a week."

"After a while you reach an equilibrium where you don't smell any worse. We may not be there yet."

"I'm not sure that's anyplace I want to get," she says, grimacing.

"On K2 I went the last month without changing my long underwear. I remember when I finally got down to Base Camp, I peeled it off my legs like an old bandage. Roskelley was sitting next to me, and there was a feather that must have been held in the same place by the underwear because the quill had worked into my skin. I guess it was from my down sleeping bag, but it looked like it was growing out of my leg. I said, 'Hey, John, look at this,' and he glanced over and said, 'Oh, man, we gotta get out of here. We're starting to adapt.'"

We both pull on our shell climbing pants, push our feet into our double boots, and then fasten our gaiter leggings. From the cook tent I can hear Dawa preparing breakfast, and in a moment he is outside our tent with two mugs of steaming milk-tea. We thank him, and when we finish dressing we carry our packs to the cook tent to finish organizing our gear. Jon joins us, and after we have breakfast I go outside only to see that storm clouds have started to encroach on the remaining patches of open sky. In a few minutes it begins to snow. It's only a light flurry, but the clouds are gathering, and I know it will only get worse.

"I hate to say it, but we've got to wait."

"I don't mind," Asia says. "My dad said in one of his journals that it's good to learn to be patient."

I know she is right. This is only the third day of the storm, and I remind myself that compared to other trips, especially the K2 climb, three days is nothing.

After Chris quit the K2 expedition, the four of us on the summit team climbed back to Camp 5, carrying supplies we would need the next day to go to Camp 6 and, we hoped, to the summit. My companions still planned on trying to reach the top without oxygen, and to complicate things even more, Jim and Lou argued that we had a better shot if we all traversed to the Abruzzi ridge rather than climbed the headwall. John was adamant, however, that the headwall would be a more elegant, if more difficult, conclusion to our route. After a four-hour discussion we compromised by splitting into two teams: Wick and Lou would make the traverse, and John and I would go straight up.

My doubts only increased. Could I do it without oxygen? Could I climb the band of steep rock and snow that cut across the summit headwall on the direct finish at nearly 28,000 feet? I wasn't sure, but I had got this far, and once again, I swallowed my doubts.

In the middle of the night I went out to pee. I looked up and saw the stars had disappeared, and I was just acknowledging what that meant when I felt them landing gently on my cheeks: big, wet snowflakes. By dawn wind-driven snow was buffeting our tent. It was hard to accept we were facing yet another storm. We had now been above Base Camp for fifty-five days. We knew that in most years winter arrives in the Karakoram in early September. It was now the end of August. Once again, we retreated, but this time only to Camp 4, hoping against hope the storm would be short-lived.

While we waited we talked again about climbing without bottled oxygen, and this time I voiced my concerns. Wick and Lou admitted that they too were less than certain they could do it, and finally we decided we would use oxygen, though John was reluctant. He still insisted on attempting the direct finish, however, so we still needed to divide into two groups of two. At least I didn't have to factor the possibility of permanent brain damage into the list of obstacles that yet separated us from the summit.

Three days later the storm broke, and once more we trudged through deep snow back up to Camp 5. The next morning we left shortly after daybreak, and on the backside of the Snow Dome we stopped and embraced, each group wishing the other the best of luck. If things went as planned, John and I would meet Wick and Lou the next day on the summit.

John and I continued in a direct line upward. There was deep snow from the last storm. I had to lean into the slope, packing the loose powder with my body, then my knee and then my foot until I could get a foothold. Then I would step up and my boot would sink into the snow despite my efforts to pack it, and I would gain maybe six inches. One hour passed, then two. I heard a voice, like someone yelling far away. I looked down and there was Wick.

"Soft snow," he yelled. "Turned back. Follow you tomorrow."

Late in the day John and I reached Camp 6 at 26,000 feet. We pitched our tent and, at last light, crawled in. John's feet were numb, and he removed his triple-layer leather boots and put his feet and stub toes—the ends missing from his summit day on Dhaulagiri—on the bare skin of my stomach. I lit the stove. In those days the butane stoves we used were inefficient and slow to melt the snow into water, but we knew we had to drink as much as possible. By the time we each consumed a liter of water, melted another two liters for the morning, and had dinner, it was twelve-thirty A.M. We went to bed, and an hour later sat back up to start melting more snow. Hours passed as we slowly fed snow into the billy. It was after six before we were ready to leave. We were already late, and we left the tent knowing but not admitting that, even as we started, we were defeated.

I belayed John as he left our campsite and rounded a corner behind our tent. I knew there was a big slope above him, leading to the rock band. In a few minutes he came back.

"Extreme avalanche conditions," he said. "It's not worth the risk." We had a radio, and we called the others in the lower camps.

"Well, I guess that's it," Jim radioed back. "We gave it a hell of a try."

John and I lay in our tent, too exhausted and too demoralized to pack up and go down to Camp 5, pick up Lou and Wick, and begin the long descent off the mountain.

"Maybe we should give it one more try tomorrow," I said. "In the chance that this sun consolidates the snow."

John was certain there would be too much potential for avalanche, but he agreed. We woke once again at one-thirty in the morning to start melting snow, and once again it was after six before we were ready to start. I belayed John, and he disappeared for a few minutes around the same corner. When he came back, I was sure I knew what he was going to say, but I was wrong.

"I just got a call from Camp 1. They can see Lou and Wick through the telescope. They're going for the summit."

We realized Lou and Wick must have returned for another try, and presumably found favorable snow conditions. We decided to follow them, traversing to their Camp 6, and then tomorrow going for the summit via the Abruzzi ridge. We broke down camp, and with everything in our packs, including oxygen, we each had about sixty pounds. As we struggled through soft snow at eight thousand meters, we were approaching our limit. To conserve strength for the summit, John said we should ditch our climbing hardware, and I pointed out that with no hardware we didn't need a rope. We abandoned that, too.

It was late afternoon by the time we reached Lou and Wick's campsite. We slowly dug a platform for our tent, then once more started the time-consuming business of melting snow. We received a garbled radio call from Base Camp: those below could see Lou and Wick on the summit. By eight P.M. they hadn't returned, and we were getting worried. We had a policeman's whistle, and leaning out the tent door we blew it at the same time we clocked our headlamp like a searchlight, sending the beam into the black, cold night. Nothing. Another hour passed.

"Did you hear something?"

"Blow the whistle again."

We listened. Then we heard it: Lou's voice. In a few minutes he was outside the tent. We were just unzipping the door when he stuck his head in the back vestibule. John and I both turned.

"Good God," John said.

Lou's face was sheathed in ice. Not just snow, but large pieces of clear blue ice in his beard, a large icicle coming out his nose, his lips puffed and split and bleeding. But even through his exhaustion, his eyes glowed. We pulled him in by his shoulders. He was shaking, too cold to speak. I poured a cup of hot lemonade but then couldn't get it past the large pieces of ice in his beard. I grabbed one of them and pulled it out, along with a clump of hair, then got the cup to his lips, and he drank. He leaned against John and looked as if he were about to fall asleep.

"We made the summit," he said, his voice shaky.

"We know."

"I made it without oxygen."

John and I nodded at each other, knowing the effort implied in that simple statement.

"Where's Wick?"

"I don't know."

"Where did you last see him?"

"On the summit. He stayed to take a picture. I think he's bivouacking."

The wind had started to blow in strong gusts. It was very cold. Lou went to his tent, and John and I continued to melt snow in our ongoing effort to hydrate. Finally about twelve-thirty we turned the stove off, slept for an hour, then started it again at one-thirty. It was our third night at eight thousand meters, our third with one to two hours of sleep. While the snow melted, we packed our gear. The wind was still blowing.

"What do you think Wick's chances are?" John asked.

"I think we're on a body detail instead of a summit bid."

John didn't answer.

We left the tent at three-thirty A.M.

"Good luck," Lou called. "I have a feeling Wick will be okay."

John and I did not share his optimism. The wind was abating, however, and in the clear sky the half light of the stars illuminated the slope. With no rope between us we climbed each in our own world. Within an hour we were several hundred feet above our tent. I switchbacked up the slope, thankful when I changed direction for the chance also to change the hold on my ice axe, as the cold of the metal was conducting through my mittens, and my fingers were numb. I knew I would likely suffer frostbite, but there was nothing I could do about it.

At dawn we stopped at the site of the high camp of the Japanese expedition the year before. We looked across the valley to Broad Peak, another of the world's eight-thousand-meter mountains, and we were even with its summit.

"Wick might be moving by now."

"I hope so."

"If he's bad, we're going to have trouble getting him down without a rope."

"If he's bad, we can't get him down."

In another hour we entered a narrow couloir. John was just above me, and craning my neck I saw the ten points of his crampons above my head, and I thought, Don't fall, John. I moved into the narrows, finding handholds on the side, seeing between my legs the slope fall away steeply to the Abruzzi shoulder, and ten thousand feet below that, the Godwin-Austen glacier. I moved up to the next handhold, testing it with my palm, then gripping tightly even though my fingers were wood. Two more steps, and I was out of the couloir.

I looked up and the wind was blowing small snow-devils that danced over the surface, catching the morning sun, bright against background shadows. John, in his blue nylon jumpsuit, was fifty feet above me, and above him another figure, legs slightly spread, arms down, stiff and unmoving, like a scarecrow. It was Wick. Was he frozen? I watched as John approached. Wick remained motionless. John made another step. Then I saw Wick raise his arm. A greeting. At least he was alive.

As I neared, I could hear their conversation.

"I was on a small flat spot, a little below the summit."

"Frostbite?"

"I think so."

"Can you make it down?"

"Yeah, the hard part's behind. That traverse up there."

Wick indicated with his ice axe another steep section of rock plastered with a veneer of snow. We joked about the bivouac, then Wick said, "Good luck. See you back at camp."

"Be careful, Wick," John said, patting him on his cap.

We wouldn't realize until later that John's small pat was the first human contact Wick had had in fourteen hours. We wouldn't know until Wick told us in the days ahead—as we struggled down in yet more bad weather, as we then left Base Camp and had to carry him on a litter until finally a helicopter whisked him as fast as possible into emergency surgery where they had to cut away the tissue from his lungs damaged during his bivouac, and remove the ends of several of his toes—that for fourteen hours he had counted each minute. That during the coldest hours after midnight he had to keep saying to himself, Wiggle your toes, move your fingers, it will end, stop shaking, control yourself, you must survive. That after the dawn finally came he had sat there, not wanting to move, enjoying the magnificent sunrise, thinking he would just take a nap and go down later, until he saw the image of his wife, and then his kids, and he forced himself to stand, saying to himself, over and over, I'm going to make it, I'm coming home, I love you, I'm going to make it. It was later, when Wick told us these things, he would also add that John's small pat on the head brought him to tears.

I told John it was time to go on oxygen. We were a little above 27,000 feet, and with a steep section of mixed rock and ice in front of us, and no rope, I wanted to be as clear-headed as possible. We unshouldered our packs, and I was attaching my regulator to my bottle when I saw John reshoulder his pack and start up, leaving his oxygen bottle in the snow.

"What are you doing?"

"There's no way I'm hauling that thing to the top. I know I can get up without it."

He was right. *He* could get up without it. John waited while I turned the valve on my bottle and checked the gauge: 3,900 psi, full pressure. I fitted the mask around my face and put my pack back on. But something was wrong with the mask. I couldn't get it to seal around my face. I took it off, readjusted the straps, but it still hung loose.

"I'm going," John said. "See you up there."

I continued to adjust the straps. John finished the traverse and disappeared around a corner. I rerouted the straps, taking longer than I cared to because my fingers were frozen. I put the cap and mask back on. It was worse than before. How long had I been fiddling with this? Five minutes? Ten? Fifteen? How far up was John? Could I catch him? What else could I do? Keep trying to fix this mask? Or climb K2 without oxygen?

I thought back to Everest. What if I got pulmonary edema? But so far my lungs seemed fine. I was doing okay. What about brain damage? Was it worth the risk? I looked around. Above me was a steep rock and ice traverse. Below me was the steep gully. Far below that, the glacier. I was by myself. There was no rope.

I smiled and thought, What brain damage? You're already crazy.

I took off my pack, set the bottle and regulator in the snow, put the near-empty pack back on, and started climbing. I made the traverse, rounded the corner, and saw John above. He wasn't that far away. When he saw me, he slowed until I caught up. We stopped and rested. It was only about ten o'clock, and we were well above 27,000 feet. The wind had died, and the sky was cloudless. A perfect day. The slope above us was moderate. The snow was a little soft but not too bad. All the hard climbing was past us. We stood and continued, lifting one foot slowly, kicking a step, breathing a few times, kicking another step, every once in a while switching the lead.

It took four hours to climb to 28,000 feet. But then something happened. I would lift my foot and place it, and breathe and breathe and breathe, and then go to lift my other foot, but I couldn't, and I had to say to myself, do it, do it, do it, and finally I would lift the foot, then say, I have to rest, have to rest, no you can't rest, can't rest, can't rest. Finally I would lift the next foot, and then start the same argument until I made the next step. Then I leaned over my axe and heard my mind say, I can't make it. And then I heard it say, You have to make it. I can't. Have to. Can't. Only two hundred more feet, you have to. And I lifted my foot.

Then I started to get dizzy. I had to breathe five times, ten times, between steps to regain my balance. I would stop and breathe and breathe until I could make the next step. But the dizziness was almost constant. John took the lead. He was stronger than me and moved ahead. Lift another foot, I told myself. Then another. John was above me, stopped. I made another step, another, until I was close to him.

"It's a gentle slope . . . from here."

"The summit . . . ?"

"Fifty feet . . . fifty feet to the summit."

We locked arms and started stepping, more quickly now. There it was. Fifteen more feet. Ten feet, then John stopped.

"It might be corniced," he said.

"Good thinking."

Neither of us seemed to remember that Lou and Wick had been there the day before and reported no cornice, the sometimes dangerously thin lip of snow caused by prevailing wind that is often found on tops of mountains. But we were operating on instinct. John held my ankles while I belly-crawled to the top and looked over. No cornice. John crawled up behind me, and we grabbed and held each other, too tired to speak, too exhausted to stand. We sat on the summit, holding each other. The sky was cloudless. There was no wind. As I breathed, my dizziness began to clear, but it was still as though everything were echoing, as though I were in a dream. I looked north to the peaks of Chinese Turkistan, east across the Chang Tang, south to the great Nanga Parbat. I looked at my partner, sitting next to me, staring as blankly as I was at the view, neither of us smiling, only breathing, breathing, breathing.

7

At midday in the cook tent Jon proposes an idea so obvious I shake my head. Since the snow is too deep to move the vehicles, and the upper slopes are too unstable to climb, he suggests we use our cross-country *randonnée* equipment to ski down to the Aru Basin.

"It might not take too long to get down there," he says.

"We could be there before dark," I answer.

"You mean leave today?"

"Why not?"

Asia likes the idea, but our L.O. and two drivers frown when Jon explains the plan, admitting they are nervous about remaining alone for a few days in this desolate place. They confide they are afraid of the *tremo,* a half-man, half-bear creature they believe inhabits these high mountain slopes, and they are especially fearful now because they believe the *tremos,* with all the recent snow, will be especially hungry.

"If you shoot one," our truck driver says emphatically, "the *tremo* stuffs rocks into its wounds and keeps coming for you."

Jon does his best to reassure them, and an hour later, when we are ready to go, they give us an enthusiastic farewell, although the truck driver tells Jon several times we should come back as soon as possible. The snow is perfect, and we glide away. We use skins to ascend to the col, then remove them to go down the other side. The angle is steep enough in places to skim over the new snow in a lazy slow motion that allows me time to scan the slopes for bears. A half mile down we cross a single set of bear tracks that comes down one slope, crosses the drainage, then disappears up the opposite side; we are relieved to see nothing of the animal other than its marks in the snow. In another hundred yards we cross a set of tracks that belong to what we think might be chiru, and just past that a set of tracks belonging to a large wolf.

We drop into a steep drainage with tight, blind turns, proceeding cautiously to minimize the possibility of surprising a bear. We wind through the narrow corridor for a mile, then two, rounding one turn to discover a small herd of five blue sheep. When we cross the path of their snow prints, we realize that the tracks we saw earlier belong not to chiru but to these sheep. Since blue sheep are one of the principal food sources for snow leopard, it seems probable that the most elusive of all Himalayan creatures still inhabits this remote fastness.

We round another tight bend, and with a startling suddenness the canyon opens onto a broad basin with a large turquoise lake set like a jewel in the bottom. It is now late afternoon, and we pitch the single tent we have brought. We all three crawl in and start the stove, thankful when the tea water is hot for the warmth of the cups on our fingers.

Next morning the sky is clouded, but it is no longer snowing. We build a cairn, in order to find the narrow entrance to the valley if, on return, visibility is poor. Then we snap on our skis and continue toward the lake. The snow is only a few inches thick, but skiing conditions are excellent.

We approach a nomad's yak-hair tent, and because his mastiff is barking fiercely, and no one appears, we keep going. In another few hundred yards we see in the distance a herd of chiru: eight males, one female, and two yearlings. By noon, sun breaks between parting clouds, and the snow melts. We remove our skis and strap them to our packs, which makes our loads even heavier. We angle toward the lakeshore and by midafternoon set up camp. Asia returns from the lake with a small aluminum billy in each hand, and as I watch I fasten the long lens to my camera to take her picture. She is framed by the background lake, and the quartering light reveals the high cheekbones and almond eyes she has inherited from her mother. It's a photograph that could make the front cover of *Elle* (if they were to do an issue devoted to the outdoors), and as I push the button for a second exposure, I tell myself that it is also a photograph that Asia will hate.

As a young girl she was asked frequently by Colorado photographers to work as a model. Most of these shoots were for the Patagonia catalog, or magazines like *Outside,* and she enjoyed them because she wasn't modeling but doing what she normally did such as snowboard or hike. Then later she accepted a job acting in a video for a United Airlines commercial, playing the role of an Aspen teenager, giggling at boys as they walked by. "It was such a stereotype," she said when she told me the story. "When I saw it I hated it because it had nothing to do with who I was." She was offered a job modeling at a runway show, but turned it down. "To me it's not a compliment when somebody tells me I'm beautiful. I guess that's one of the reasons I got into the baggy clothes thing, and I still am, a little."

Even though she is self-conscious about modeling, she is still interested in fashion, not in the glamour but in clothing design. The previous summer, while staying with us in California, she had designed a set of kids' snowboarding clothes for Patagonia. I regarded that as a considerable accomplishment for someone so young, and since we've been on the trip I've considered that perhaps design is a sister talent to her instinct for knowing how things work.

Now she sets down the pots of water, assembles our backpacking stove, then pumps, primes, and lights it. I have had to show her how to do this only once. She places one of the pots on the stove, wraps a skirt of aluminum foil around it both to steady the pot and to trap the heat, then, using a phrase learned from me, smiles, and says, "I think it's time for a brew."

Next day Asia and I leave Jon in camp, and with only day packs we walk the shoreline, heading north. To the west, the Crystal Mountains border the basin. There is no wind. The only sound is a faint lapping of water, and the call of bar-headed geese far out on the mirror lake. With binoculars I spot, above the opposite shore, two yaks on a hillside. They are black and large and very possibly wild. Near our feet a ground jay hops away, its rounded back suggesting a hunched-shouldered old man. Ahead of us, melting snow reveals patches of green-gold feather grass. Between cotton-white clouds the sky is cobalt blue. Every once in a while we flush from the shoreline pairs of gooselike ruddy shelducks that paddle away, escorting to safety their small lineups of downy ducklings. In the middle distance, toward the mountains, we see chiru galloping over the snow-patched alluvium.

With the mountains, the lake, the chiru, the ducks, comes a joy that brings memory of a passage from Jonathan's journal I read two days before, while waiting at the col for the storm to clear. "In the early morning the air is cold and the surrounding hills bright in a fresh cover of snow. A few low clouds, and then above, through an opening, the banner plume off the high summit of Dhaulagiri. It is awesome."

It is a simple passage, describing the first time Jonathan saw at close hand the crest of the high Himalayas, and reading it left me with a longing, perhaps more than at any time since he died, to be with him, to share again the great joy he took witnessing the wild beauty of this Earth. Now, as I continue on this walk with his daughter, I spot at water's edge a Saker falcon feeding on a kill. We approach slowly, and the raptor eyes us but continues to reach down and pull flesh from its prey. We are less than fifty feet away when it abandons its meal and takes wing, then sets down at a distance to eye us. We walk to the site and see in a scattering of feathers the white and red bones of what only this morning was a snow finch taking seeds from the spring grass. I stoop down and study the remains.

"What is it?" Asia asks.

"This small piece of red flesh, it's its heart. Normally the first thing a falcon would eat."

I stand and look around. The falcon has departed.

"Only its heart," I repeat.

Asia remains silent, and we walk away, maintaining our northward track. In an hour we stop on a small hilltop free of snow, overlooking the lake, and have lunch. Viewing the length of the Crystal Mountains, we see five or six summits above twenty thousand feet, and the one we want to climb, if we get that opportunity, is one of the higher peaks. Even if we don't have the opportunity, however, sitting at this place looking at these mountains—surely among the most remote peaks on Earth—is satisfaction enough.

"Listen," I say.

"To what?"

"To a hum. A kind of distant hum. You'll barely be able to hear it."

We are quiet. There is the distant chirp of a snow finch that lasts only a moment before it is absorbed into a silence that permeates the land and the sky so thoroughly it feels as though it has weight.

"Hear it?"

"Yeah, I do. What is it?"

"It's the background sound of silence."

Two days later we are skiing back up the narrow canyon toward the col and our waiting vehicles, and our no doubt anxiously awaiting Tibetan colleagues. The morning is cloudless, and snow conditions are perfect.

"Asthma okay?" I ask Asia.

"I'm feeling good. This is *so* pretty."

The direct sun reflects off the surrounding snow-covered slopes, and the white is brilliant against a clearing sky with openings between clouds as blue as a luminous sapphire. The storm appears to be breaking, and I have the thought that we can rest this afternoon and tomorrow start our climb. If we camp at the base of the summit ridge and ascend the mountain the following day, we could be back to the vehicles by that nightfall. By then the snow should be melted from the col, and we can drive down to the Aru.

We reach the first col by noon, and I offer my plan, but Asia complains that her feet have started to hurt. She takes off her boots and I don't see anything unusual, but she says she thinks she has blisters under her calluses. She puts her boots back on, and I tell her we have less than a mile to go and that we'll be there in no time. She gets up and starts sliding one ski forward and then the next, but I can see a slight pause between the glides, and as much as I wish it were otherwise, I suspect my plan to climb the mountain may be in jeopardy.

It is only midafternoon when we arrive back at camp. The Tibetans are relieved to see us. Dawa, wearing a grin larger than usual, tells us he has a late lunch prepared, and taking Asia by the arm, leads us into the cook tent. Asia takes off her boots and examines her feet. She shows me where it hurts, and when I touch the spot she flinches. Despite the clearing skies and stable weather, I realize we are not climbing anything tomorrow, and the disappointment must show on my face.

"I'm sorry, I'm not the kind of person who can just suck it up."

"Well, I can't make you into something you're not," I reply, and I regret my words as soon as they are out. "I'm sorry, I shouldn't have said that."

"It's okay," she replies. I take a deep breath, and then she says, "You could climb it without me?"

"But that's not why we're here."

"If it's worth anything, I really had a good time down there skiing with you."

I try to smile, then say, "Yeah, I would say that's worth something."

I go outside, confirm that the weather is still stable, then tell Jon that if conditions remain like this in the morning, we can move the vehicles over the col and into the Aru Basin. Then I go to the tent Asia and I share, crawl inside, sit against my folding backrest, and tell myself I should be ashamed for what I have told Asia. I'm acting as though this were my trip alone and not hers. I admit to myself that I arrived at the beginning of this journey with a preformed ideal of who she was. As the daughter of my dead friend, I expected her to be a young woman who would climb with me to the top of an unnamed peak in an unexplored range where together we could look over unknown lands. In that way she would understand what pulled her father to the high mountains, and I would have achieved what Jonathan dreamed of doing when she was yet inside her mother's womb, to bring her to these lands and "teach her the truths of life, the truths I have learned."

But I have never assigned these kinds of expectations to my own daughters, and what right do I have to expect them of Asia? "I'm sorry I'm not the kind of person who can just suck it up." Why should she have to be? I tell myself that she's certainly done a much better job of accepting me for who I am, with all my foibles—my bullheadedness among others—than I have done in accepting her.

Next day the weather is still stable, and in only an hour we break camp, load the truck, and are on our way. But I have underestimated the combination of the softening snow and the tubercular condition of the truck's engine. Even with chains, the lumbering vehicle gets stuck in one wallow of snow after another, and each one requires shoveling trenches in front of the rear wheels to place the logs. We regain the position of our previous campsite, but it is still five hundred yards to the col, and now we must shovel the entire distance free of its two-foot snow cover, and it takes eight hours. Since I am the one who has pushed to make this move, I feel obligated to work harder than the others. Still, as I pause to catch my breath and massage the blisters on my hands, I can't help but divide the total cost of this Chang Tang portion of our adventure by the number of days I expect it to take, and use this daily rate as the measure of my privilege of shoveling to near exhaustion a half-mile trench.

[177]

By late afternoon we reach the col. I tell everyone we will be in Aru within an hour, and we all give a cheer. Then we start downhill, and in five minutes we are stopped again by a short but steep hill buried in a thigh-deep drift. It is nearly dark, but I know how important it is to shovel a path before the snow freezes. We take turns at our shovels, but the others, one by one, give in. Then I am alone, shoveling toward the hilltop, now only forty feet away. We have pitched the tents next to the vehicles, and there is no sound from camp. The only noise is the scrape of my shovel into hardening snow.

At eleven P.M. I pause to consider my effort to convince Asia that when you want to influence people, or convince them to do what you want them to do, it's a more effective tactic to work hard yourself and that way set an example. At the moment, I must admit this strategy isn't working too well. I wonder what she thinks of me out here in the middle of the night, in this wild and distant corner of Tibet, shoveling a trench to nowhere. Maybe she thinks I'm some kind of crazed Himalayan Fitzcarraldo. She's probably too young to have seen the movie, but if she did she might find in the main character something that seemed familiar.

The snow isn't getting any softer, so I take the shovel and resume my work, finishing the task just before midnight. I walk back to camp, sit in our tent's vestibule, and take off my boots.

"How did it go?" Asia asks.

"I made it to the top of the hill, so I'm pretty sure we can get the truck up in the morning."

"So am I," she says encouragingly.

I am quick to fall asleep, but despite my weariness I still wake at first light. I pull on my boots and walk to the cook tent, and when I open the flap Dawa jumps out of his sleeping bag, apologizes for sleeping in, and starts the stove to heat tea water. Asia joins me in a few minutes, and as soon as we finish breakfast the Tibetans borrow Dawa's propane stove, place it directly under the grease-caked oil-pan of the truck's engine, and turn the flame to full volume. Following a habit ingrained through years of being exposed to potential danger in remote places, I go through what I call my "what-if" analysis. In this case, I say to myself, What if the engine, and then the truck, catch fire. There are twelve fifty-five-gallon drums in the back, eight still full of gasoline, and nine large cylinders of pressurized propane, five still full. I decide the best strategy would be first to order Asia to run, then to grab our tent—pitched about thirty feet from the truck—rip it out by its stakes and drag it with its contents as far away as possible. At least we would then have the equipment we would need to walk down to the Aru and camp with the nomad who owns the tent we skied by earlier, and live off him until we could figure out how to get out of here.

The truck doesn't catch fire, however, and the engine, preheated nicely, coughs a few times as it turns over and then starts. Backing up to get as much speed as possible, the truck gets a charging start and chugs successfully up the hill I have spent half the night clearing. My vindication, though, proves to be short-lived when, after another hundred yards, the Land Cruiser bogs down in a snow-covered creek. The Tibetans are hesitant to enter the ice-choked water, so I take a shovel and wade in. Still the Tibetans hesitate, so Asia takes the other shovel to help me. At first she straddles the water by keeping one foot on the vehicle's bumper and the other on a curb of snow. This position keeps her feet dry, but also prevents her from getting any leverage on the shovel.

"It's okay, Asia," I say, "I can get it. It's hard to get leverage standing like that."

To my surprise she wades in, the ice water rising to her knees and filling her boots, just as it has filled mine. She doesn't complain, and I'm thinking that perhaps my stories of Everest and K2 are having some influence. I'm also regaining confidence in my Tom Sawyer strategy. The Tibetans, after several minutes of watching Asia and me, offer to relieve us. They take the shovels and wade into the ice water as Asia and I wade out. She then follows my lead, stomping her feet to get blood into her toes.

"So we got the Tibetans to help out," I say to Asia, as I continue to stomp in place.

"Don't worry," she says. "I'm learning."

"I know you are. And I'm not worried."

It takes another half hour of shoveling to open a lead through the ice water sufficient to free the Land Cruiser. Once it has crossed, we stand back while the truck gets a running start and enters the creek, sending a thirty-foot curtain of water mixed with ice spraying out from each side. Halfway through it begins to slow.

"Go, go, go!" Asia yells.

The driver coaxes all the power he can from the anemic engine. Dragged by the water to a near stop, he has just enough momentum to make it to the other side, and we all cheer. We continue slowly down the valley, stopping every hundred feet or so to shovel snowdrifts. By early afternoon we are past what we hope is the last drift, but then the driver signals another halt and crawls under the truck. It's some minutes before he crawls out and huddles with Jon, who then walks over to Asia and me.

"Apparently the clutch is broken."

"If an adventure is an outing where things go wrong," I say, "then this is one helluva good one."

"They said there is a gold mine within a three-day drive of here," Jon replies. "They want to take the Land Cruiser and see if they have a clutch we can buy."

"Doesn't sound like there's an option."

"I should go with them, but there's no more room, so you guys would have to stay here."

"That's okay," I reply. "Especially since there's no choice."

While Dawa prepares a box of food for Jon and the others to take, Asia and I pitch our tent. Since we've done this nearly every day for the last two weeks, we go about the task with a quiet efficiency. As I tension the guy lines to stakes, I am also noting that the weather is good, and we'll be at this camp for at least two days, maybe three. I remind myself that only yesterday I vowed not to push Asia against her will, but I can't keep myself from raising the question.

"How are your blisters?"

Asia Wright and Rick Ridgeway, Chang Tang Plateau, Tibet, June 1999 *Jon Meisler*

Jonathan Wright, Minya Konka Base Camp, October 1980 *Edgar Boyles*

Rick bidding farewell to Jonathan, October 14, 1980: "The breeze blew across the grave, carrying aloft, as the Tibetans believe, our prayers." *Edgar Boyles*

Asia Wright at the Bodhnath Stupa, Kathmandu, May 1999: "Someday I will bring this child [to this country]," Jonathan wrote in his journal, "to experience the truths in life, the truths that I am learning." *Rick Ridgeway*

View from the hill above Namche Bazaar, May 1999: "At the head of the valley the transverse wall of the Lhotse-Nuptse ridge looks like the rampart of Valhalla, and above it, as though rising from the inner sanctum, we can see the tip of Everest."
Rick Ridgeway

Asia and the Lama of Tengboche, May 1999: "He looks much the same as when I first saw him in 1976, when he performed a *puja* ceremony to bless our Everest expedition against 'bad luck on the mountain.'"
Rick Ridgeway

Into Tibet, May 1999: "Jon points to the northwest, toward open sere hills that extend to a distant horizon. 'That's where we're going,' he says. 'And that's what it will look like for the next month.' " *Rick Ridgeway*

Loading the yaks at our first camp on the Kailas *khora*, June 1999: "To devotees Kailas is the *axis mundi*, the pillar connecting Earth to heaven, and to make the coveted *khora* around the sacred mountain is to reduce sins that have accumulated over a lifetime." *Rick Ridgeway*

The northeast ridge of K2, 1978: "We were on the knife edge . . . scoured over the eons by glaciers grinding on both sides until they left a thin, serrated blade a half mile in length."
John Roskelley

Resting a few feet below the summit of K2, 1978: "The sky was cloudless. There was no wind. As I breathed, my dizziness began to clear, but it was still as though everything were echoing, as though I were in a dream."
John Roskelley

Dick Bass (left) and Frank Wells during their attempt to be the first to climb the Seven Summits, the highest peak on each continent, 1983: "When they invited me to join them, after an initial hesitation I began to get interested. Not that I gave them much of a chance of pulling it off, but that they were committed so whole-heartedly to it." *Rick Ridgeway*

Yvon Chouinard (left) and Doug Tompkins on the summit of an unnamed and unmapped peak in Bhutan, 1985: "It added to the sense of adventure that [we were] looking into territory so remote it was unclear which country owned it." *Rick Ridgeway*

Yvon (left) and Doug "enjoying" a freeze-dried dinner during our climb and sea kayak expedition north of the Straits of Magellan, 1988: "Back in the camp, we watched the rain sheet off our kitchen tarp. Three days passed, then four, then five. . . . Six days, seven, eight. . . ." *Rick Ridgeway*

Queen Maud Land, the first big wall climb in Antarctica, 1998: "When I think back to the climb, two images come to mind. One is a vertical band on one side that is gray—the granite wall—and a horizontal line on the other that is blue above and white below—the sky and the ice. . . . It is a Rothko of the Antarctic." *Gordon Wiltsie*

Snowed in below the pass over the Crystal Mountains and into Aru Basin, June 1999: "I am loath to backtrack, to admit defeat too early and set a tone of giving up before we really try. I want [the Tibetan drivers] to know it's going to take a lot more than this to turn us back." *Rick Ridgeway*

Asia hiking in the Aru Basin, the Crystal Mountains in the background, June 1999: "We walk the shoreline, heading north. There is no wind. The only sound is a faint lapping of water, and the call of bar-headed geese far out on the mirror lake."
Rick Ridgeway

Asia on the summit of an unclimbed and unnamed peak in the Crystal Mountains, June 1999: "She steps onto the summit and is blown down as the wind sends her skidding across the ice. She struggles back to her feet and waves her ice axe over her head, then gets knocked down again. When she's back on her feet, I can see her eyes are still beaming." *Rick Ridgeway*

The last day of our trek to find the grave of Asia's father, July 1999: "Soon the moraine squeezes against the river, and we are forced to walk on the edge of the roaring water, hopping boulder to slippery boulder. The river channel is steep, and I find the roar of the cascading water both distracting and disorienting." *Rick Ridgeway*

Minya Konka, October 1980: We had proposed to climb the ridge on the left skyline, but we were stopped by the avalanche that swept us down a buttress just beyond the left edge of the photograph. *Rick Ridgeway*

Asia at her father's grave, Minya Konka, July 1999: "For the second time in my life . . . I pry loose the stones and carry them to the bier and set them gently on top of my old friend. Now I am with his daughter, and we do this together, she and I, and it is good work." *Rick Ridgeway*

Jonathan's photograph taken from the western cwm of Everest, 1976: "We sat . . . watching the wind plumes blow in long banners off the snowy summits. . . . Backlight illuminated these tailing clouds so that they were in stark contrast to the shadow shapes of the peaks. In the cold, calm air I heard the camera click. Jonathan said, 'I think that is the best mountain photograph I have ever taken.' " *Jonathan Wright*

"Still kind of sore, but definitely better."

"That's good."

While Asia finishes tightening the guy lines I take the shovel and dig a trench to divert meltwater away from the front of our tent.

"It's great to finally have some good weather," I say.

Asia tightens a guy line, looks at me, smiles, and says, "Maybe we should try and climb the mountain."

"Only if your feet are okay."

"I could give it a try."

"You sure?"

"Yeah, I'm sure."

Now it's my turn to smile. "Okay, let's give it a go, just you and me. You okay to leave in the morning?"

"Yep."

Jon and the Tibetan drivers leave in the Land Cruiser, and Dawa, Asia, and I have a lazy afternoon organizing food and gear for our climb. The sun disappears early behind the high ridge that borders the narrow canyon, and we both put on our down jackets. Dawa cooks a pasta marinara for dinner, and stars shine in a cloudless sky as we crawl into the tent to go to bed. We're both in our sleeping bags when Asia says, "Rick, I'm starting to figure some of this out."

"Some of what out?"

"That this trip is like kind of a test for me. Well, maybe not a test, but a challenge to see things differently. Like you were telling me earlier, how you have to see where you want to go and work hard to get there. I'm trying to do that with school, to see where I want to go. But I'm beginning to see two ways of doing it, not just in school, but I guess in everything. One is where you don't take the chances because you want to at least be able to estimate the outcome. The other is where you take the risk, endure the obstacles and the discomfort, but keep open the possibility of something truly remarkable happening."

"There's two roads, Asia. The Tibetans can't understand why we didn't take the easy one that goes to Everest Base Camp because this one has trucks that always break down and deep snow and bad weather. But it also has wolves running up sand dunes, and brown bears digging up marmots, and silence you can hear."

Before I go to sleep I record my conversation with Asia in my journal, and that leads to thoughts of my own kids, and then of my wife who, as I am about to go to sleep, is on the other side of the world about to get up. I wonder what her day will be like, but I think I know the answer: driving the kids to soccer practice, doing her volunteer work at their school, helping with homework.

When I married, two years after Jonathan died, I was still undecided whether or not to return to mountaineering and adventuring. My wife knew before we married what I had taken from the mountains and from the world's wild places. She knew how Ron's death had shaped my awareness at an early age of my limits; she also knew how those sixty-eight days above 18,000 feet on K2 had expanded my awareness of just where the boundary of those limits lay. I had told her about the snow butterflies at 23,000 feet on K2, and about the graveyard of bird bones in the cave high on the mountain overlooking the Amazon. She saw in my office the photograph Jonathan had given me of the satellite peak of Everest with the snow plume blowing to leeward, the one he took that morning in the Western Cwm when we stopped to rest, the one he thought was the best mountain shot he had ever taken.

Soon afterward my wife gave me a greeting card with a photo of two baby's feet on the front and a message inside that said, "Guess who's coming?" Later that week I received a call from somebody named Frank Wells, who said he knew I had been to Antarctica and Everest, and wanted to ask me some questions. He told me he worked in the movie business, and that he had recently met another man his age—about fifty years old—named Dick Bass, who was an oil and gas man from Dallas. He said a mutual acquaintance had discovered that both of them shared the same fantasy, to climb the highest mountain on each continent, something no one had ever achieved. Once introduced, they were so delighted by the coincidence that they shook hands and agreed "to take a shot at it."

I asked Frank how much experience he had, and he answered that he had climbed Kilimanjaro and the Matterhorn. Since Kilimanjaro is only a strenuous hike, and the Matterhorn a guided milk run, my first reaction was that I was talking to a dilettante who was having a midlife crisis. Nevertheless, he was courteous, and he asked intelligent questions. I shared with him what I could about Antarctica and Everest, and I invited him to call back if he had more questions. Before we hung up I asked him what he did in the movie business, and he said he worked at Warner Brothers, and it was only when I pressed further that he told me he was the president.

A few days after his call, I drove to Los Angeles to meet him. His secretary showed me into his office where he was meeting with about ten others, reviewing storyboards for the *Superman* sequel. As soon as I was introduced, Frank said, "Okay boys, the meeting is over. I've got some important business." I liked him immediately, and a few weeks later, when I met his partner Dick, I liked him just as much.

I was beginning to get interested. Not that I gave them much of a chance of pulling it off, but that they were committing so wholeheartedly to it. I tried to put myself in Frank's place. He had started at Warner Brothers twenty-seven years before as a junior lawyer in the business affairs department, and he had worked his way up, one rung at a time, to the highest position. Now he was proposing to leave it all behind to attempt something about which he knew very little, and at which he would in all likelihood fail.

He and Dick proposed to climb all seven mountains in 1983, starting on Vinson Massif in Antarctica, then Aconcagua in South America, Everest, Denali in North America, Kilimanjaro in Africa, Elbrus in Europe, and finally Kosciusko, the highest peak in Australia.

Frank talked to other climbers who had ascended the other peaks on the list, and they all told him the same thing: to do as many practice climbs as he could, and to take along the most experienced climbers he could find. A little while later he invited me to go on any of the seven expeditions I might care to join. I thanked him, and then asked for a few days to think about it.

I told my wife I was compelled by the possibility of going to Vinson, 17,000 feet high and only seven hundred miles from the South Pole. Even though I had been on the trip to the Antarctic Peninsula, I knew you had to get to the interior to see the true Antarctica, a place that had been described as otherworldly, like a distant, frozen planet. I also knew it was an ice desert, with only a few inches of precipitation a year, and that meant there would be minimal hazard from avalanches.

Jennifer was then only a few months away from delivering our first child. I explained the yearning I was feeling to return to the mountains, and the curiosity tugging me toward the world's most remote corners. I admitted that indulging my yearning and curiosity was selfish, in light of the obligations I would soon assume as a father. But I also felt that without that indulgence I would wilt. If that were to happen, I told her, I would lose the passion that had motivated my adventures, a passion I hoped to pass to our children because I felt it would stand them in good stead to whatever end they might apply it. My wife replied that she knew I was a mountaineer before we married, and she always expected I would be one after. The decision was mine; she asked only that I weigh the risks I took against my new responsibilities.

I called Frank and told him I would like to accept the invitation to go with them to Vinson. Since that was the most coveted spot on all the Seven Summits expeditions, he said I could come if I also joined the Aconcagua climb, to help as an organizer and guide. I knew that Aconcagua, despite its 23,000-foot altitude, had very little snow and therefore would be a safe climb, so I agreed to go on that ascent as well.

I was back in the game, but on climbs I knew had very few objective hazards. There was room for another lead climber on the Aconcagua trip, and I called Yvon to gauge his interest. Hiking out after the avalanche on Minya Konka, we had stopped at a pass to look back at our last view of the mountain. We could see the scar left by the avalanche, and the place where we had buried Jonathan. Yvon said from then on he was going to stick to human-size mountains in places like Yosemite and his beloved Tetons. No more Himalayan peaks.

I told him Aconcagua would be safe, adding that it would be fun to get to know Frank and Dick, and he agreed to come. It would also be easy to organize, which wasn't true of the Vinson climb. Of all the Seven Summits climbs, including Everest, Vinson was logistically the most difficult. The biggest challenge was finding an aircraft capable of getting us there. Frank managed to locate a one-of-a-kind DC-3 known as the "Tri-Turbo" because it had been fitted with turboprop engines, including a third one in the nose. It also had been fitted with skis and, in theory at least, had the ability to fly to the Antarctic interior *if* it could be refueled halfway there. As the January start date for the Seven Summits year approached, however, Frank still lacked a solution to that rather sizable "if." He and Dick decided to reschedule Vinson to the end of the year—with a departure in November—to have more time to figure out how to establish a fuel cache about three-quarters of the way down the Antarctic Peninsula.

Frank was also hopeful to find sponsorship to offset the rising costs. ABC television agreed to underwrite part of the cost of the Everest expedition in exchange for a position on the first summit team for a cameraman equipped with a handheld microwave transmitter, to get the first live coverage from the summit. The executive at ABC overseeing the project was the one I had worked with on other projects: the ascent of the mysterious rock tower in the Amazon, the skiing and climbing adventure in Antarctica, the attempt on Minya Konka. Soon I received a call from him offering me the position of coproducer and on-air commentator.

I did not want to return to Everest. Even though I knew the risk was small, I was uncomfortable with the thought of once again going through the icefall. But I was even more uncomfortable with the prospect of returning to the death zone above eight thousand meters. Still, the offer and the work were appealing. I told myself that if I went through the icefall only once, that would reduce the risk. And if I could find a cameraman capable of going above the South Col, I wouldn't have to go any higher than the Lhotse Face to file my on-camera reports. I recalled Jonathan saying that on the Ama Dablam climb in 1979 he had helped a young and talented climber named David Breashears learn how to use a movie camera. I called David, and he took about one second to say yes.

It would be a busy year, but at least I would have several months at home between returning from Everest and leaving for Vinson. Then I received a call from a sponsor who had heard about the idea Jonathan and I had hatched four years earlier to make a coast-to-coast traverse of Borneo, a direct distance of about eight hundred miles, but over fifteen hundred miles following the bends of the rivers. They wanted to back the expedition and produce a film for cable television. The reconnaissance would take one month, and the crossing two. The most favorable window of weather was June through August. In theory I could squeeze it between Everest and Vinson. Once more my wife told me to do what I thought best. I explained that the next year I might not have any opportunities. I decided to accept the offer, but it meant that the first full year of my marriage I would be gone nine months.

I started the year with the first expedition to Aconcagua. The climb was easy, and we forced ourselves to go slowly so we could acclimatize. One evening at the 19,000-foot camp there was a beautiful sunset, and I saw Yvon stand by himself away from the tent, holding his mug of tea in both hands and staring at the distant valleys and peaks. I knew him well enough to be pretty sure what he was thinking. We very seldom talked about the avalanche, but he had told me that he too was still in the habit of pausing at least once during the day to remember how he had been sentenced to death, and then given a reprieve.

We all made the summit, and I was home only three weeks before leaving again for Everest. In Base Camp I studied through the telescope the route up the icefall, and after I had acclimatized, I left early in the predawn and I was through the jumble of ice blocks in only two hours. I filed my reports up and down the mountain, and David succeeded in getting to the summit and transmitting by microwave a live signal that arrived in New York at three A.M., but was aired a few hours later on *Good Morning America* while the team was still descending. Frank made it to the South Col, and Dick made it to 28,000 feet but had to turn back when his summit partners refused to continue, even though the hour was early and the weather stable.

Without Everest, Frank and Dick would miss their Seven Summit record, but they went through with their plan, and in the next five months climbed Denali, Kilimanjaro, and Elbrus. Meanwhile I had departed on my Borneo crossing, beginning on the west coast. We chartered a thirty-foot riverboat, and swung our hammocks between the uprights of the open-sided cabin. Recalling the Amazon expedition seven years earlier, I found another plank of wood and this time painted on it, in large red letters, "Borneo Queen," and nailed it to the front of the cabin.

After two weeks the river had narrowed to the point where we had to transfer to dugouts navigated by boatmen from the interior Dayak tribes. After another week the tributaries dwindled, and we transferred our gear to backpacks and marched for three weeks through the remote jungles in the island's heartland. On the second to the last day of our overland march, I woke feeling nauseous and flulike. By midday I had a substantial fever. My companions divided the weight in my pack. Our Dayak guide told us we would reach a village in two hours. It took me four, as I had to stop frequently to quiet my growing nausea. We could see through a wide opening in the forest the top of the village's longhouse, but then we discovered the gap was actually a large slash that had just been burned. The only way to the other side was across a series of fallen trees that were intertwined above a field of still-hot coals. I rested for a few minutes, my head on my knees, trying to quell not only nausea but a growing dizziness. Then I started across. The heat coming off the ground was intense. My torso was drenched in sweat, and my head was swimming. I focused on each step. If I slipped, I would fall only five or ten feet, but it would be into a bed of coals, and there was a chance I would be burned alive, feet and legs first.

My fever had increased to the point that I was only vaguely appreciative of reaching the other side, and my companions told me later they were more relieved to see me make it across than I appeared to be. I was escorted to the chief's room in the longhouse, where two of his wives attended me, mopping my brow. Another of my companions told me later that when I looked directly at him, and mistook him for another member of our team, he knew I was in trouble.

I have only one clear memory from the fever. When my hallucinations must have been at their peak, I could control them by opening or closing my eyes. I decided to close them, and keep them closed, to see what would happen. Suddenly I was in Vienna, in the eighteenth century, attending a waltz. I was in a line of men facing an opposite line of women, dressed elegantly in corseted gowns with puffed shoulders and low necklines. In unison the line of men and women stepped forward, each taking a partner. I held my dance companion by her waist, and we twirled around the ballroom floor. Then I realized I had the ability to telescope my vision. I focused my sight on the woman's shoulder, and I zoomed in until I could see the individual threads in the fabric of her dress, and then the small hairs texturing the surface of each thread. I zoomed back out, to the woman's shoulder, to her bosom, to her face. But now her head had turned into a gargoyle with flaring nostrils and red eyes and matted hair. That was as far as I could go. I opened my eyes, and the vision disappeared.

There was an airstrip at the village, built by missionaries. The chief told my companions that the missionaries visited every fortnight, but they weren't expected for more than a week. The next day, however, we heard the drone of a single-engine plane, and in a few minutes a Cessna landed. The missionary pilot said he had been heading for another village, but a rain squall had forced him to land at this strip, to wait an hour until the weather improved. My companions carried me to the plane. My shirt was soiled, and before I crawled into the back the missionary gave me a replacement he had in his bag. Across the front, in large letters, the shirt said "God Is My Co-Pilot."

I lay on the aluminum-plate floor of the plane, so dehydrated my toes and fingers had curled and I couldn't straighten them. I realized there was a chance I might die. I kept an image of my wife and baby daughter in my mind, and concentrated on breathing steadily to quell my nausea. Two hours later I was carried from the plane to a German doctor who took me to his house and put me in his guest room. With IV fluids I started a slow recovery from what was later diagnosed as a virulent form of typhoid. Most of my hair fell out, and for weeks my legs burned when I tried to walk as my body struggled to purge the wastes concentrated in my muscle tissue by the fever.

Back home, I called Frank and told him the Borneo trip had gone okay, but I had gotten a little sick partway across. He was still working long hours to organize the Vinson expedition. He had made a deal with the Chilean Air Force to have a large C-130 transport make a nonstop flight over Antarctica, and at a carefully chosen site near the bottom of the Antarctic Peninsula, parachute forty-two fuel drums onto the ice. Then he had to insure the DC-3 Tri-Turbo before its owners would agree to charter it. The only firm interested was Lloyds, but they insisted Frank find two pilots unquestionably capable of the task. After dozens of calls Frank finally secured Clay Lacey, a famous test pilot, and Giles Kershaw, who flew for the British Antarctic Survey and had logged nearly five thousand hours in Antarctica, more than anyone in the world.

These problems were no sooner solved than the Chileans called to say that because the price of copper had plummeted, the national economy was in recession and they were canceling their Antarctic program, and with it, Frank's fuel drop. Frank offered to pay them in advance, and that kept the C-130 refueling flight on schedule. Then Clay Lacey dropped out because of health problems, jeopardizing the insurance. Frank promoted Giles Kershaw to chief pilot, found another copilot, and convinced the Lloyds syndicate to stay with the expedition. Then one of the turbo engines blew, but a spare was found and the repair completed in time to stay on schedule. Then the Falklands War broke out, and Peru denied the Tri-Turbo air space because Giles was British. Kershaw told Frank that he would fly offshore of the Peruvian coast, skimming the waves to stay below radar.

More than anyone I had ever met, Frank followed Shackleton's approach of viewing obstacles only as things to overcome. While I tried to take heart from Frank's example, I couldn't help but wonder if in my own case Shackleton's motto might have limitations. I had lost over twenty pounds, and I could walk only short distances before the burning in my legs forced me to stop. I didn't tell Frank that, however, but assured him six weeks was plenty of time for me to get back in shape.

I told myself that if I missed this opportunity to get to the interior of Antarctica, there might not be another one. I also told myself it would be unfair to Frank and Dick to be the weakling on the trip, taking one of the limited seats on a plane they could fill in a quick phone call to any of the dozens of talented climbers clamoring to go. My wife told me only that I had to live up to my commitment to Frank and Dick. I started jogging, pushing myself until the burning in my legs forced me to a walk, then running again, then walking, wondering if maybe I should call Frank and tell him I was dropping out. I had been gone so many months, and I had such a strong yearning to be at home with our daughter, now a year old. When I returned from this last trip, she hadn't recognized me, and I remembered how Jonathan had told me he had had the same experience with his daughter, Asia. Then I would see in my mind's eye the Antarctic ice cap, and on the far horizon, like islands in a frozen sea, the Ellsworth Mountains. And again I would start running.

8

"How are your feet?" I ask Asia.

"Sore, but they'll be okay."

"That's the stuff."

I shoulder my pack that weighs about thirty-five pounds, and Asia reaches down to pick up hers, but Dawa grabs it and holds it while Asia hooks her arms through the shoulder straps.

"Thanks, Dawa," she says.

"Are you sure you have enough food?" he asks.

"More than enough," I answer. "We're only gone two days."

We wave good-bye, and Dawa wishes us good luck and tells us to be careful. I estimate it will be about a six-hour walk to the base of the summit ridge where I plan to set up camp. When we reach the crest above our truck camp, we stay on the ridgeline so we can keep an eye on the surrounding slopes. A cold wind blows from the west, and I stop and study the terrain with my binoculars. As the wind increases, we are forced to stay in the lee of the ridge crest, but we climb to the top every few minutes to survey the area. We are not that far from where we had both sightings of the bears.

"Feet still okay?" I ask.

"Yep."

"Asthma?"

"Throat's a little tight, but not bad."

"Want to take a rest?"

"Sure, for a few minutes."

We sit down between two round cushion plants that look like an alpine transplant of sea coral. There is little graze or browse, and only occasional signs of blue sheep.

"It's unlikely any nomads have ventured this high, when there's so little food for their animals," I say. "Especially since they haven't been in this area that long. When the first explorers came through here around the turn of the century, this place was pretty much uninhabited. East of here Schaller has found sites that have chipped stone tools from early neolithic occupations, but out here, nothing. So it very well may be that we are the first humans ever to pass this way."

"I just feel lucky to be here," she says, which is a good counter to my professorial musing. But she also has other thoughts on her mind, and in a moment says, "I wish my dad were here, too."

I'm not sure what to say, and for a moment we are quiet.

"Maybe he is here," I offer.

She doesn't respond, and I know my answer does nothing to fill the void she must be feeling. I put my hand on her shoulder, and after a moment we push on. In another hour I find a place to pitch our tent in the lee of a rock. It's lower than where I hoped to place camp, but it's the only place protected from the wind. There has been no sign of bears, however, and I hope that they have enough fear of people to overcome their attraction to our food bag.

We start up our small stove, melt snow, and prepare a packet of freeze-dried macaroni and cheese. After eating we make tea, and lying in our sleeping bags side by side in the tiny tent we prop on our elbows and gaze out the door. Our view takes in the southern extension of the range, and we can see a corner of the lake down in the Aru Basin. A Himalayan griffon, four or five feet across, tacks toward our camp, then kites into the wind and for a few moments is suspended above our tent, adjusting its wing feathers to maintain its hover. To the west the slanting sun casts heraldic rays through the tops of clouds, and to the south the snow on the peaks is pink. The wind has eased, and from a valley far below, sounding across the Crystal Mountains, comes the howl of a lone wolf.

I know that I will carry this view across these high steppe lands of Western Tibet with me for the rest of my life, and I am confident this prospect will have a similar claim on Asia's memory. Vast open spaces tend to do that. I can still remember vividly the first views of the interior of Antarctica as I flew south with Frank and Dick aboard the old DC-3. Chris Bonington was also with us (whom I hadn't seen since we crossed paths on K2), and all of us took turns crowding into the cockpit to look over Giles Kershaw's shoulder.

We passed the mountains that the American explorer Lincoln Ellsworth named Faith, Hope, and Charity. We were following close to the route he took in 1935 when he made the first trans-Antarctic flight. Back then, however, he was the first person to see the land now visible out the window of the Tri-Turbo. That our plane was built only seven years after Ellsworth's adventure made his flight seem tangibly connected to our own. Still, there was one major difference between his flight and ours. For us the weather remained flawless, but for Ellsworth, when the weather turned, he had to land and wait for it to improve. The day before, when we had flown from Punta Arenas to a tiny station where the Chilean air force had dropped our fuel cache, we passed through a cloudy section, but we knew by radio that at our destination it was clear enough to land. Giles had only to consult the ONC chart to know how high to fly to stay above the highest peaks. In 1935, however, Ellsworth had no ONC chart. If he had taken his plane to 30,000 feet, he still had no way of knowing whether or not ahead of him lay a mountain higher than Everest.

I have thought often about this simple fact, and the not-so-simple consequences of what Ellsworth's flight meant not only to our knowledge of the geography of our Earth but to the way we think of it, and through that, to the way we relate to it. I find it remarkable to consider that many people who are still alive today were young adults at the true close of the Age of Exploration, an age that started, as we all learn in school, with the Portuguese navigators of the fifteenth century, but ended, as few of us realize, with Lincoln Ellsworth's flight in the middle of the twentieth. Just as the Portuguese ventured into unknown seas, wondering each day what mysterious land or fabled island might rise from the edge of the ocean, Ellsworth flew toward the far horizon—toward that long line that was white below and blue above—not knowing if at any moment the tip of a far and distant mountain might emerge, a mountain that *could* rise and rise, a mountain that *could* continue to grow as he approached, until it became a true Olympus, a mountain higher than the highest clouds.

"There they are," Kershaw said, pointing ahead. We could make out the jagged interruption on the horizon. It was the same view Ellsworth had had, in 1935, of this range that would prove to be the highest mountains on the continent, the range that would someday be named after him.

As we approached we could make out the broad shape of Vinson Massif. Kershaw angled the plane so we could get a close view as we flew over.

"I think the route goes up that plateau," Bonington said.

"Looks like a piece of cake," I added, forgetting for the moment that it was nearly 17,000 feet high, and only seven hundred miles from the South Pole.

We landed on the rough sastrugi at a distance that appeared to be only a mile or two from the base of the mountain. We were fooled, however, by the clarity of the air: after Kenshaw triangulated our position, we realized we were more than five miles from Vinson. We tied the plane's wings to deadman anchors that we froze into the ice, pitched our tents, slept for six hours, made breakfast, packed our two sleds each with 250 pounds of food, fuel, and gear, and with three of us pulling each one, departed for the foot of the mountain. Although the slope was gradual, it was hard work to pull the sleds across the sastrugi, the one- to two-foot-high crescent formations sculpted into the hard snow by the prevailing wind.

Frank and Dick both did their share of the hauling, and after we had set up our first camp we crawled into our bags and slept for six hours, then woke and made breakfast. The twenty-four-hour daylight created a mild disorientation, like jet lag, but at the same time it was a novel treat to be able to get up and move whenever we liked. We ascended a snow gully leading to a plateau between Vinson and its neighboring peak. There we located the next camp at the base of a short icefall. Bonington insisted we dig a "bolt-hole," a shelter we could escape to in case of a windstorm too strong for our tents. With that finished, and the food securely cached, we returned to our lower camp. At the top of the gully we were high enough to see the ice cap stretching to the horizon. A small singular pyramid peak in the distance rose out of the ice. This was Welcome Nunatak, and although it looked close, we knew from the map it was forty miles away. How far, then, was the horizon: one hundred fifty miles? Two hundred miles?

The next day we carried more supplies up the gully and occupied our next camp. When we awoke the faultless sky had been replaced by a portentous veneer of thin cirrus. We waited to see if a storm was coming, and when nothing changed we decided to take the risk of moving to the next camp, comforted with the knowledge that we had the bolt-hole to retreat to.

We left at six in the evening, taking in one carry everything needed for the next camp where we planned to sleep for a few hours, then continue to the summit. With any luck we would be there in another twenty or thirty hours. We climbed into the shadow of a parallel ridgeline, and the temperature suddenly dropped to about thirty below zero. As I stopped to put my down parka over my jumpsuit, I considered that it was cold enough to be dangerous: If I fell into a crevasse, I might freeze before I could complete a self-rescue. In half an hour we climbed back into sunlight, and things cheered up. Soon we arrived at an inviting flat bench just below the edge where the slope dropped away down the steep west side of Vinson.

"Good-looking campsite," I said.

"Bloody exposed campsite if a storm brews up," Chris replied.

"I think everything's gonna be just fine," Dick said. "It seems to be clearing."

The worrisome high clouds did indeed seem to be dissipating. By the time we had pitched camp and finished dinner it was two A.M., and we were all confident we were only hours from reaching the top. We awoke at six, and by nine we were off, carrying only extra clothing and a few candy bars. We followed the ridgeline, and had a grand view of the ice cap eight thousand feet below. Behind us we could see the other peaks of the Ellsworth range running in a line like an island archipelago frozen in an otherworldly icescape.

"This has to be the most fantastic day of my climbing career," Chris said.

Then I felt the air stir. It was only a breath, but even that stung the exposed skin on my face. It calmed a moment, then puffed again. This time the puff did not die, and soon gusts were hitting us at twenty, thirty, then forty miles per hour. We hunched over into the head wind, glancing up only to verify our course. We had only a few hundred yards to reach a notch at the base of a ridge leading to the summit. But then what? There we would be exposed to the full force of the wind and might be forced back. I glanced around at the others and saw their figures blurred through the spindrift now scudding across the hard surface.

I stopped to fasten the chin strap on my parka hood. I couldn't seem to get the two parts to match, and I motioned to Chris to give me a hand. By the time he had it secured the others had caught up, and for a moment we rested. It was too cold to sit, so we walked in little circles, stamping our feet and swinging our arms to force blood into our numbed fingertips.

Frank lowered his face mask to clean his goggles.

"Let me look at your nose," Chris yelled above the wind.

"What's it look like?"

"Completely white. First-stage frostbite. You've got to go down."

Frank digested this news. If he went down, and the others continued and made it, that left him without anyone to go with for another attempt. On the other hand, Dick would make it, so at least one of them would be successful. And obviously it wasn't worth losing his nose.

"Okay, I'll go back."

"Someone has to go with you."

Our cameraman said he would go back, too. Frank realized he had a chance for another attempt.

"If they're going back, I'm going, too," Dick yelled.

"What do you mean?" Chris asked.

"I'm in this with Frank."

"You've got to go up," Frank yelled. "We may not get another chance."

"He who fights . . . and runs away," Dick yelled between breaths, quoting Falstaff, "lives to fight . . . another day . . . but he who in the battle is slain . . . will never rise to fight again."

"Dick, don't be so flippant," Frank yelled back.

"Hell's bells . . . you're the one always saying . . . you have more than one chance on these climbs."

"I'll go down, too," I yelled.

"Don't be silly," Frank yelled back. "You're going with Bonington, and that's it."

No one said anything. Frank spoke with such final authority things seemed settled. The others turned downwind, and Chris and I lowered our heads and continued toward the summit. An hour later we reached the col and felt the full blast of the wind. I made the mistake of lifting my goggles to clean them, and the sudden temperature difference caused by holding the goggles away from my face made the plastic lens buckle. Worse, a layer of ice then sheeted the lens so thoroughly I was forced to stay on Chris's heels, following the fuzzy form of his boots making one step, then another, as we angled up the slope. Every time I stopped to clean the ice it re-formed a few seconds later. Since it was impossible to stop and take the time to set up a rope belay, we had agreed to untie, and there was an unspoken understanding that each of us was on his own. Temperatures were probably thirty to forty below, and the gusts now approached sixty miles per hour. That made the windchill, what? A hundred below zero? Whatever it was, it was brutal.

I saw Chris's boots stop. He turned to face me.

"These have to be the worst conditions I've ever climbed in," he said.

Chris turned and pressed on, and I paused again to clean my goggles, then struggled to catch up. My head was swimming, and I was off balance. Was it the typhoid? I looked up, but Chris had disappeared. I took off the goggles again and saw him traversing what looked like a picket fence of short rock towers. It was steep on both sides. I decided to go without goggles. I climbed to the first rock tower, tested my boothold, then my handhold. I was still dizzy. I looked down. There was a several-hundred-foot drop on both sides. I hunkered down in the lee of a rock and tried to think.

If I continued, there was a good chance I might slip. In this cold, even a short fall could be fatal. I thought of my wife, and then I had an image of our baby daughter as I carried her around the backyard and watched her eyes follow the branches in the trees. I shivered against the cold, reminding myself I had to move soon, whether it be up or down. I rubbed my eyes and shook my head, but the dizziness remained. I looked up and saw Chris past the last rock tower, and heading up the summit slope. I tried to think. I reminded myself I had returned to adventuring with a commitment to listen to my inner voice. Already I had nearly died from typhoid. This was no place to push things even further. I stood and waved to Chris, but he wasn't looking. Then I turned and started down.

At the col I stopped once more and looked back, toward the summit block. Where was Chris? Then I saw him, a lone red dot. He was on the summit, perched on top of the highest mountain in Antarctica. I smiled, content I had made the right decision.

Chris looked exhausted when he got back to camp. We fixed him tea, but there was so much ice in his beard he couldn't get the cup to his mouth. Remembering Lou on K2 and how I had yanked off the ice with beard attached, I took more care and cut the chunks out with Dick's Swiss Army knife. With the brew in him, Chris perked up.

"Fabulous view up there," he said, "but I was also able to see off toward the Weddell Sea. There are some very sinister-looking clouds moving our way. I think we have no choice but to pack up and get out of here immediately. Down to the bolt-hole."

"What about our next attempt?" Frank asked. "We'll have to come all the way back?"

"Better that than risk getting caught up here in a blow. A fierce wind could tear these tents apart."

There was silence. Chris could see the disagreement in Frank's face. "Frank," he said, "mountaineering is a serious game. Believe me, I know."

"I think Chris is right," I said. "We shouldn't risk it."

"I don't agree," Frank said. "But I suppose I'll have to defer."

"Well, I'll just go along with our leaders," Dick said. "I'm sure we'll still get our chance."

We broke camp, carried the tents down, and set them up again next to the bolt-hole. Though we had now been on Vinson for a week, it still felt odd to go to sleep with light and wake up with light. We could see the windstorm continue higher on the peak, and we passed the next twelve hours sitting in the tent swapping stories until finally, about midnight, we got drowsy enough to sleep.

It was past noon the next day when we awoke. The clouds were thinning, and up higher it looked like the wind was dying.

"Let's wait awhile and make sure it's a solid spell," Frank said.

"We might as well wait until about three A.M.," Dick added. "That way we would do most of the climb during the highest sun."

Even with twenty-four-hour daylight we had noticed that it was warmer during the "daytime," and everyone agreed with Dick we should make the climb then. We also decided to go directly from our present camp to the summit, bypassing our intermediate camp to take full advantage of any break in the weather.

We went back to sleep and woke again at three A.M., but once again clouds were scudding over the ridge above camp. By six the clouds started to ease, and we decided to take the chance. I was better acclimatized now, and I felt much stronger than I had on the previous attempt. Then once more the clouds began to build. We climbed steadily, but by the time we reached the site of the high camp, another storm was on the way. Once more we retreated.

As the storm continued for another day and a half, we slept, ate, and sat in Frank and Dick's tent listening to Dick read aloud from his photocopied sheets of Kipling and Tennyson poems and recite from memory those of Robert Service. We still hoped to climb directly from this lower camp to the summit—a vertical gain of more than five thousand feet—until Frank questioned if he was strong enough to go all the way in one push. He asked if it might make more sense to once again establish an intermediate camp.

"But it will take longer," I argued. "And the window of good weather may be short."

"What if you and Dick go straight to the top, and Marts (the cameraman) and I go slower and set up Camp 2?" Frank said.

We agreed that this would improve our chance of success if good weather were brief, and give Frank a better chance to reach the top. By four that afternoon the weather was again improving, and Dick and I loaded our backpacks and left. We realized that we would be climbing on the upper mountain during the coldest part of the twenty-four-hour cycle. For the first several hours we were in sun, and comfortable. We made good time back to the site of our high camp, where we stopped to unload some gear we were carrying for Frank and his party. Then the sun moved in its crabwise crawl behind Vinson, and we were climbing in shadow. The temperature dropped to forty below, then fifty below. We climbed for six hours without stopping, until Dick motioned that he had to rest, and he pulled his water bottle from his pack. Even though he had filled it with hot water, and placed it inside a foam pouch, it was frozen solid. My candy bar was also frozen, and I felt as though I were biting into a bar of steel.

"My toes are goin' on me," Dick said. "Fingers too."

"Mine too."

We walked in circles, swinging our arms, stamping our feet.

"'Talk of your cold, through the parka's fold, it stabbed like a driven nail.'"

"Dan McGrew?" I asked, as Dick and I continued to walk in a tight circle, swinging our arms.

"No, Sam McGee. You know, I always enjoyed *reading* it, but *living* it is something else."

"I think I'm getting worn out from this rest stop," I said. "Let's keep climbing."

It was now midnight. We had been climbing, with only two brief stops, for eight hours. Yet Dick stayed right behind me, and I thought, If only I can match that when I'm fifty-three. At the col I looked up at the picket fence of rock towers where I had turned around on my attempt with Chris. Now, with better visibility and clear goggles, I could see an easier route traversing into a basin that led to the summit. Dick was a few feet behind me, climbing steadily. A half hour later I crested the ridge, looked to my right, then to my left, where Dick was close behind.

"Dick, you've got maybe thirty feet before you're standing on the highest point on the coldest continent."

"Rico, are you pullin' my leg?"

"No, Dick, we've got it."

Dick crested the ridge, and arm in arm we marched the last steps to the top, then bear-hugged. It was a solid, long-lasting hug, and I wasn't sure whether it was for joy or because we were freezing to death. I decided it must be joy because I had tears in my eyes. That presented a new problem when they quickly froze and glued my eyelashes together.

"'When our eyes we'd close, then the lashes froze, 'til sometimes we couldn't see.'"

"Dan McGrew?"

"Still Sam McGee."

The sky was a clear, cold blue, and we could see the length of the Ellsworth range as though the view were held in a vacuum. I looked at the horizon line, a distant but fine distinction between ice and sky. The air was so clear you could see that it curved. Someday I will tell my children about this, I thought. Tell them that if somehow the ancients could have stood here, where I now stand, and seen the view that I now beheld, they could have *seen* that the Earth was round.

"Rick, wake up," Asia says. "Wake up."

"What is it?"

"A bear," she whispers. "Outside the tent. I heard it."

"Heard what?"

"This deep exhale sound. It was like very deep, and whatever made it was big. I heard it twice."

We are still in our tent high in the basin at the base of the mountain. I slip out of my bag, and on bare feet go outside. By the stars it looks to be about three in the morning. A sickle moon, combined with starlight, allows me to see several hundred feet. I climb to the crest of the ridge above our tent before I pause to ask myself what I will do if I do see a bear. I decide that I will hold ground, and if he charges, act submissive, but then at the last second curl up and protect my head and neck. I don't see anything, however, so I return to the tent.

"I wasn't imagining it," Asia says.

"I'm sure you weren't."

Neither of us sleeps much, and two hours later, just before first light, I start the stove to make tea.

"I feel awful," Asia says.

"What's wrong?"

"My head aches, and I'm nauseous."

"That's normal at this altitude. I've got a headache too, so don't worry. How are your blisters?"

"Okay, I guess. But I didn't sleep much. I was claustrophobic."

"Are you going to be able to do this?"

"I'm going to try."

The water is boiling, and I make tea for both of us. I tell her it will make her feel better, and she thanks me. Asia waits for her tea to cool, and I put more snow in the cook pot to make water for oatmeal. It takes another half hour, and light is beginning to reveal the ranges to the south. Asia manages a few spoonfuls of cereal, and I'm hoping that is enough to give her sustenance for the morning's climb. We finish our tea, then dress. I pull on my climbing boots, noting as I do that they are an old pair that, because they fit perfectly, I have kept around for ascents like this where you don't need the extra insulation required in Antarctica or on the higher peaks of the Himalayas. Then I realize I bought these boots in the spring of 1980, which means I would have taken them later that year to Minya Konka.

I lace them slowly, noticing from the side of my vision Asia as she also pulls on and laces her boots. She has a new pair she has purchased for this trip, slightly too large. We both think this is the reason her feet have blistered.

"You wearing two pairs of socks?" I ask.

"Yep. That seems to keep my feet from slipping."

I'm thinking of telling her that when you find a pair of boots that fit it's worth keeping them, thinking of telling her that I've had my boots for a long time, and, in fact, I was wearing them in the avalanche, and had them on when I was holding her father when he died. Then I could tell her about this strange sense I have at the moment that time is losing its attachment to reality, that it's no longer the mechanism that separates events, but rather in its absence events are overlapping, even coexisting. It's similar to the feeling I had over a month ago when I stopped by the small creek and saw the white-capped river chat, and remembered how Jonathan had come along on the trail and squatted next to me to watch the same bird, just as his daughter then did twenty years later. But I decide not to tell her about that moment, or about this one, because I don't want to break it, to bring it back into time.

We leave just as the direct sun breaks over the ridge, and the slanting light reveals the wind texture on the snow. Our boots have sufficient grip that we can hike without crampons, and the only sound is the crunch of our footsteps in the crusty snow. When the slope steepens, I stop to show Asia how to use the ice axe to arrest herself should she slip and begin to slide. She has never used an ice axe or crampons, but I have selected this peak in large part because it has a long ridge that leads directly to the summit. Staying on the ridge will not only reduce avalanche potential, but also allow me to climb directly above Asia so that I can easily stop her with the rope if she should slip.

I don't think there is much likelihood that will happen, however, because she is a very quick study. I have her slide down the slope twice, rolling over once she has momentum and plowing the tip of her axe into the snow until she stops.

"If you do slip make sure you hang on to your ice axe no matter what."

"I got it."

We continue, and a half hour later arrive at the col. As the sun has risen the wind has started to blow, but conditions are still comfortable. We fasten our crampons to our boots, then I show her how to walk to avoid hooking the sharp points on the inside of her gaiters. We tie in to the rope, and as I lead I pause to call down to her and demonstrate the various combinations of boot placements she can use depending on the angle of the slope. When the slack in the rope is taken, she follows me. I try to set a steady pace, and I am mindful when the rope goes taut not to force her to climb too quickly. That concern evaporates when my feet start to break through the crust and I sink to my calves, then to my knees. I have to lift each leg out of its hole, move it upslope and set it again, knowing when I weight the leg my boot will again break through. The effort makes me slow to a pace that Asia has no trouble matching.

"Look up," Asia calls.

I turn to see that the griffon has returned and is hovering above the summit, stabilized on the wind that starts to blow against our backs. The day before the avalanche on Minya Konka, as I lay in the door of the tent I shared with Yvon and Jonathan, I spotted a falcon hovering far above our camp. We were ourselves perched on a small snow platform at about 19,000 feet, and none of us could guess what the falcon was looking for at such an altitude. The next morning, as Kim, Yvon, Jonathan, and I roped up to begin the ascent to locate Camp 2, I noticed the falcon was there again, high above, hovering and watching.

As I did earlier in the morning when we were preparing to leave camp, I remind myself to focus on what I am doing. I have a rhythm: My body's movements are timed to my breathing. I am at a pace I feel I can maintain until we reach the top. The ridge is longer than I estimated from below, and already we are at an altitude that makes us even with the tops of the peaks I can see emerging to our left. The mountain we are climbing appears to be one of the higher peaks in the range, which means we are somewhere between twenty and twenty-one thousand feet. I consider again that we are in a place that, in the passage of our species' time on Earth, has never been visited by humans. But that is a vain consideration, I think, and one that Jonathan would be quick to purge from his thoughts.

I continue to move steadily, breathing deeply but feeling strong. Then I stop for a moment, not to rest but to pause. I look to the north, to the snow summits that march down the ridgeline. To the west, to the sere expanse of the Chang Tang. To Asia in a bright red jacket, her eyes through the lens of her goggles looking at me and beaming. To my own body, in its black-and-yellow suit, my legs, my hands, my arms, my left one still with the big knot in the muscle from my injury on Minya Konka. But everything still functioning, still able to do this after all these years. Then back to Asia, the daughter of my good friend, my friend who no longer can do this. I breathe deeply, give thanks to whatever strange confluence of events has allowed me to be here, at this moment, on this mountain, in this far corner of the world, in company with this young woman. Then I ask myself again—as I used to frequently after the avalanche—why did he die while I lived? I watch Asia move up, and I realize again there is no answer, and I repeat to myself, Be thankful, be thankful, be thankful.

"The summit . . . right above . . . tight rope . . . could be corniced." I'm looking down, yelling to Asia over the wind. She nods that she understands, and I look up to where, no more than twenty feet away, the slope rounds off, scribing a white line across the cobalt sky. The wind from the west is strong at my back, and since that is the prevailing direction I know that means there could be a cornice formed over the summit hidden from my view. I begin to crawl upward on my belly, looking down to make sure Asia is keeping the rope tight. I reach forward with my axe and drive it into the snow all the way to the adze. It feels firm underneath so I belly-crawl another three feet, then once more plunge in the axe, alert to the possibility I could at any second break through and find myself dropping into space. In another ten feet I raise my head like a snake, and I can see over the crest that the opposite slope merges with the summit, which is only a few feet away. No cornice. I stand and take a few steps to the top, then coil the rope as Asia climbs to join me.

On the summit she plops down on a rock that has been scoured of snow by wind. I am standing, but it is a trick to stay upright against the increasingly strong gusts.

"Aren't we even going to shake hands?" I yell.

She has her head down and motions me with her hand to wait. I worry for a moment she may be spent, or scared, or both. She doesn't move. Then she raises one leg, forces herself up on the other, and lifts her head. She has a big smile, and her eyes through the orange lens of her ski goggles are twinkling. We each take an unsteady step toward the other, and she gives me a hug.

"Let's go down there a few feet," I yell, motioning toward the lee slope. "Have some lunch."

We find protection behind a small rock outcrop and each take from our packs an energy bar. In front of us we can see the full expanse of the Aru Basin: the turquoise expanse of Aru Co and to the north its sister lake, Memar Co.

"That's where we were the other day," I say, pointing to the section of lakeshore that Asia and I followed on our walk.

Beyond the lakes and away to the east the alpine steppe of the Chang Tang stretches to a horizon that, at this altitude and through air this clear, must be two hundred or more miles away. Glaciated mountains 20,000 feet high rise like islands out of the grass plain. In the far, far distance I can see the tip of one summit peeking above the edge of the Earth.

Asia clicks a picture, and I pan the range with the small video camera I have brought along. We each take a swallow of water. Then I say, "I want to get some video of you on the summit. Let's go back, grab a quick shot, then get out of here."

We climb back to the summit, and as soon as we rise above the lee the wind hits us. It has continued to strengthen, and I estimate it's blowing sixty or seventy miles per hour, maybe more. It's difficult to stand, and both Asia and I are knocked to our knees by the gusts. The spindrift gravel is so abrasive we are forced to look sideways, shielding with our gloved hands the windward side of our faces.

"Go down . . . over the edge . . . then come back up."

I want her to descend a few feet the way we climbed, then return to the summit. "Okay, I'll try," she says, jockeying herself to the lip. She starts over but then just stands in place peering over the edge.

"Go down," I yell.

She yells something in return, but her words are carried away by the wind.

"Go down," I yell again, motioning with my hand. She turns and shakes her head and waves her hand in reply, and I realize she is trying to tell me she can't go down because the wind is so strong upslope and over the lip that she cannot force her body against it. I secure the camera in my pack, weight it with a rock, then walk to her, bracing my legs with each step. At the lip I motion her to turn around and face downslope, and I push on her back, but even with that the wind is too strong to get her over the edge. I signal to her to wait, and I step to the edge and push with all my leg strength until finally I get past the lip and downslope a few feet. There I brace my legs, take the rope and pull in slack until I have her like a fish on a line. Then I pull hard until I am able to reel her in next to me. As I climb back up, I tap her shoulder and she looks at me: her eyes are still twinkling, so I know she's okay. I work my way back into position on the summit, retrieve the camera and start it, then lean over the edge and wave to her to come up. She climbs back to the lip, steps onto the summit and is blown down as the wind sends her skidding across the ice. She struggles back to her feet and waves her ice axe over her head, then gets knocked down again. When she's back on her feet, I can see her eyes are still beaming.

"Looked great . . ." I yell. "Now . . . let's . . . go home."

Back at the tent I start the stove to make tea.

"I wasn't afraid," Asia says. "I thought it was all a normal part of climbing mountains."

"It doesn't always blow that hard."

"One of those times when it pays not to know better."

"So, you going to become a mountaineer?"

"Ask me tomorrow."

She sits in the door of the tent and takes the crampons off her boots, then lies on top of her sleeping bag. I start the stove and drop a hunk of snow in the pot, and when the water is boiling I make two cups of tea, putting a small piece of snow back in Asia's cup before handing it to her.

"You know, Asia, I just realized something."

"What's that?"

"All the things we've done that are physically challenging—the hike around Kailas, skiing back up to the col, now climbing this peak—they all had their moments when you didn't think you could make it. But each time you have made it, so I think I see a pattern developing."

"About thinking I can't make it, or making it?"

I laugh and say, "About telling yourself you're not sure you can make it, but making it anyway."

9

_____

Just before we reach the truck camp, I spot Jon and the L.O. sitting on a rock waiting for us. Jon explains that they found a clutch and fixed the truck, but now have driven it and the Land Cruiser out of the narrow canyon for fear the creek, swollen by warming weather, will trap us. Asia and I follow them down the canyon, and in a mile we see the vehicles parked on the gravel alluvium next to the rushing creek. We take a moment to have lunch, and as Asia and I eat, Jon shows me on our chart the route he and the Tibetans took to find the gold mine where they purchased the clutch.

"We had to cross two streams that were already pretty swollen, and if the water gets any higher I'm not sure the truck or even the Land Cruiser can get out of here."

"Are you saying we should leave now?"

"It might be the smart thing to do."

"We worked ten days to get here, and we've been here ten minutes."

"I know," Jon replies empathetically, "we might be ten more days before we get out. Maybe even more."

Jon knows how much I have been looking forward not only to exploring the Aru, but even climbing another peak or two. I'm about to tell him we should just take the risk, but first I turn to Asia to ask what she thinks.

"I'll do whatever you guys want, but we should think seriously about the possibility of getting stuck here."

Jon tells me that in three or four days we'll pass another range of peaks on the southern margin of the Chang Tang that has at least one or two summits that have never been climbed. There's also a pretty good dirt road running along the base, so even if the weather turns bad, we wouldn't get stuck.

"Give me a second to think about it," I say.

I know that Jon and Asia's caution has merit, and I remind myself that on expeditions it is essential always to be flexible, and more, to be that way without regret. This range of peaks Jon has mentioned sounds good. We have had our two-day ski and hike across this south end of the Aru Basin, not to mention the climb Asia and I have just completed. And Jon has told us that the drive out is spectacular. Taken together, feeling badly that we can't spend more time here seems a bit silly.

"You guys have a good point," I say with a nod and smile. "So let's get moving."

An hour later I look back and see that the truck, a mile or more behind but marked by a contrail of dust, is keeping pace. We cross the second of two rivers we have to ford, and as rising water nears the bottom of the Land Cruiser's doors, it is clear that we are leaving none too soon.

"It's straightforward from here," Jon says when we are across the river.

As he promised, the country is spectacular. To the side, dark squalls occlude the glacial mountains that border the basin, and ahead more squalls march across the steppe. Between these clouds, shafts of light fall on the land, creating a patchwork of mineral hues; in the near distance the spring *stipa* grass tinges the steppe pale green; and at close hand blooming cinquefoil paints the desert pavement in swatches of wild-flower yellow.

For Asia and me it's been a long day since we woke in the predawn to start the stove and prepare for our climb, but now I feel the contentment that follows strong exertion in wild country. As we climb out of the basin, ascending a gently rising upland, the air has a clarity as though no air existed. In the distance a squall looses rain that falls with remarkable weight onto the steppe, and provides a backdrop curtain to a foreground hill that glows in yellow light. Jon tells us that in this same place two days ago he and the Tibetans flushed out a pack of eight wolves who ran alongside them for a mile or more. Now a pair of kiang pace our vehicle, dust rising in metronomic puffs from their hooves; a covey of sandgrouse take flight, the sound of their gull-like calls entering the open window; and a pair of white-rumped snow finches fly up, splitting so that we pass them one on each side. In all directions there are companies of chiru running like *lungpa,* the mythical flying lamas; and like the lamas the chiru also are not running, not even flying, but floating like phantoms as they speed over the plains.

The smell of rain rises out of the land, and I feel a joy so intense it spreads through me with a warm flush. We pass a mound of rocks sitting in curious isolation—their lava textures revealed in the slanting light—and they look as though they belong to a landscape other than that of this Earth. Above, I see a solitary upland hawk who, in a wheeling gyre, is surveying the steppe; below, a pika runs from our approach, saved by its burrow from us and—who knows—from the hawk. We drive out of the pillared light of late afternoon and into the afterglow of early evening. We stop on the featureless steppe at a location marked by nothing and set camp. Darkness encloses the plains. There is no moon, and the stars in the nightsky are electric.

On the afternoon of the second day after leaving Aru, we pass the small range of glacial mountains known as the Shar Kangsum. There are a half-dozen peaks, and the highest is about 22,000 feet. There is no wind, and for one of the few times on our journey the sky from one horizon to the other is without clouds. The dirt road parallels closely the base of the mountains, and some of the peaks have never been climbed. We have all the mountaineering gear in the back of the truck, and we have no fixed schedule.

"What do you think?" Asia asks.

"I don't know. They all involve approaches up glaciers, and they all have at least a few technical pitches."

I can see that ascending any of them would involve glacier travel, and Asia has no experience in rescue techniques should one of us fall into a crevasse. Even more, they all have steep pitches that would require setting anchors and belaying, all things that might test Asia further than would be prudent.

"One climb is all I need," Asia says, guessing what I am thinking. "You and Jon should go do one of these peaks."

"I guess, but . . ."

Now I admit to myself that citing Asia's limitations is really an excuse to cover the simple fact that my desire to climb isn't as strong as it was only two days ago.

". . . to tell you the truth, I just don't feel like climbing. I'm actually content standing here looking at these peaks."

"But the weather's perfect?"

"I know."

"And some of them have never been climbed?"

"I know."

"I just figured you would want to climb them," Asia says, "considering how you've been waiting for everything to line up with the weather and all."

"It's hard to explain, but I think it has something to do with getting closer to Minya Konka."

I turn to her and smile. "I guess that's it. Thinking about going back to Minya Konka, it's putting me in a different frame of mind. Like the way I felt after the avalanche, when I stopped climbing for a while so I could think about things."

That afternoon we camp in a narrow canyon near a stream of crystal water reflecting flashes of sunlight as it flows around black rocks. Asia and I wash and do our laundry, then have a rare moment to relax away from the group. Asia sits in the sun drying her hair, and I watch two mergansers eye us from their position in a downstream eddy. I catch movement out of the corner of my eye and turn to see a bird called the plumbeous redstart hunting insects in the riverine rocks. This thrush is about half the size of the American robin, and like its cousin it too is widespread, occurring from Thailand to Burma, over the Himalayas and across most of China. It's a scintillating little bird, with a blue-black body and a bright chestnut tail.

The sun drops behind the canyon rim and the temperature plummets as Asia and I gather our laundry off black lava rocks still warm when I place my palm on them. We head back to the tents just as Dawa calls out that dinner is ready. In the cook tent Dawa smiles widely as he hands us our plates and watches our enthused reaction. He has outdone himself again, baking a thin-crust pizza in his two-pot oven. After dinner Asia and I go to our tent, and we end the day—as we do most days—writing by headlamp in our journals. After a few minutes, though, Asia looks up from her writing and tells me she had a strange dream last night.

"About what?"

"You and I were walking across a wide snow plain. It was high up, kind of like the pass above Aru, and there were mountain ranges in the background. Ahead I could see something, like a form or shape lying in the snow. I knew immediately what it was. We started hiking toward it, through the snow, and as we got close I got so tense it woke me up. But I knew it was my dad's body."

I decide it may be time to bring up something I have been thinking about since she first asked me to take her to find her father's grave. I've been reluctant to discuss it, but I've known I would have to at some point before we reach Minya Konka.

"You know, Asia, there's something you need to consider."

"What's that?"

"The possibility that your father is not there."

"What do you mean?"

"I mean we buried him on this rock buttress next to the slope where the avalanche stopped. As I remember it's a very unstable area with lots of loose rock. What I'm saying is, a rockfall or another avalanche could have swept the grave away. Twenty years is a long time."

"No, he'll be there."

"I'm just saying you need to be open to the possibility he might not be."

"He'll be there. My whole life, I've known he'll be there."

I wake as a vague brightening of the walls of the tent telegraphs the first light of dawn spreading across the high steppe. I zip open my sleeping bag, then discreetly pull on my pants. I slept in my boxer shorts, and as I do each morning I manage to dress under the spread of my bag. When Asia needs to undress, she waits until I'm outside the tent. I've developed the habit of asking permission before I reenter. When we were planning the trip, I was uncertain whether it would be awkward for her tenting with me for two months, but we've both developed these little discretions that respect each other's space. And just as with my own daughters (now that they are teenagers), these are things neither of us even thinks about, but just does as a natural part of our daily round.

Asia wakes and gives me a cheerful "Good morning, Rick!" and we both stuff our sleeping bags, roll and truss our inflatable pads, and pack our duffels. Then we go to the cook tent, have tea with Dawa, go and disassemble and roll up our tent, return to the cook tent for breakfast, then help Dawa and the Tibetans strike the rest of camp and load it in the back of the truck.

As it does most mornings, the procedure takes a little over an hour, then we are under way. Asia, Jon, and I alternate each day between the front and backseat in the Land Cruiser, and today is my turn to be up front. We are traveling a dirt road that cuts in a generally north-to-south direction between the two main east-west arteries that cross the Chang Tang. As we've gained southing, we've begun to see a lavender bell-shaped flower growing out of the barren steppe, accompanied sometimes with a scant forb, sometimes with nothing more than the blossom itself rooted to the gravel floor. Now in places there are so many of these flowers the hills look like the wake of a wedding procession whose celebrants have tossed handfuls of blossoms around the countryside.

We are silent as we bump over the dirt road, and as I look across the gray expanse decorated with this scattering of flowers, I am thinking of my conversation last night with Asia, and a related story she told me a week ago. She said that beginning as a young child she had this ongoing fantasy that her father had gone away on a long walk into the mountains, and that someday he would simply return to town and she would meet him. Then, one night, the fantasy took a different shape in the form of a dream.

"My father had come home, just walked in," she told me, "and I met him. It wasn't like we actually talked to each other—it wasn't that concrete—but I definitely met him, and he was definitely alive. Then he was taken away from me again, and I saw him die and I woke up screaming."

I don't think Asia has an illusion that finding her father's grave will fill the gap she has lived with her whole life, but if it is there, we both realize she will at least have a tangible connection to him, something concrete to place next to this yearning she has had since she first became aware as a very young kid of the difference between herself and her friends who had fathers. And if the grave isn't there, I am confident she will find a way to accommodate that, too.

We pass two lakes, the first a saline turquoise, the second a sweetwater blue that apparently supports a population of fish, as there are large flocks of black-headed gulls sitting on its surface. Behind the lakes a cone-shaped peak is topped with snow that runs down the sides like candle wax. I ask the driver to stop so I can photograph this composition of steppe-lake-steppe-mountain-sky, the forms of which appear as though they have been colored with natural dyes.

When I've taken the photograph we wait for the truck to catch up, and when it doesn't arrive we backtrack to discover the driver replacing a flat tire. While we wait we decide to have a picnic on a swatch of grass next to one of the lakes. After I finish my sandwich I open my journal to work on the day's entry. I've kept journals every year since my first sailing voyage to the South Seas (I use those black hardbound sketchbooks with blank pages), and if my house were to catch fire, they would be the first items I would grab—along with the family albums, and Jonathan's signed photograph he took that morning on Everest when he, Chris, and I stopped to rest above the icefall. I start a new journal each year, and on New Year's Day I take a few hours to read the previous year's book, making resolutions to correct patterns that I decide need changing (although like most who make resolutions, I find mine too are usually short-lived).

I am already looking forward to rereading this journal in later years because not only will it include this journey but it will have been written during the year I turn fifty. I feel fortunate that this trip coincides with my fiftieth birthday because instead of taking one day to consider where I've been and where I'm going, I have more than two months. Everyone I've met who is over fifty likewise has taken at least some time at this milestone to pause and reflect. Many of my climbing friends have in addition chosen to go on adventures that are in essence rites of passage that have tested all their skills. Just before Yvon turned fifty, for example, he put together a trip (that I went on as well) climbing and sea-kayaking in the uninhabited canals north of the Straits of Magellan, and it took both of us as close to the edge as we had been since the avalanche.

The most quintessentially midlife rite of adventure was, of course, Frank and Dick's Seven Summits climbs. Dick was fond of telling people that he hoped his and Frank's example would inspire people over fifty to realize that "the second half can be and should be the best half." He also told friends that to get his own "batteries fully recharged," he needed somehow to get to the tops of all seven peaks.

The day after Dick and I reached the top of Vinson, Frank also reached the highest point in Antarctica. Three weeks later the two of them hiked to the top of Kosciusko, the highest point in Australia. Most people in Frank and Dick's position might have taken both solace and satisfaction knowing they had climbed six of the seven summits, but instead they set their sights on the one mountain that eluded them.

When Frank's wife learned he wanted to return to Everest, however, she drew the line. Frank realized that he had put his family through enough, so the next year Dick returned to Everest as part of an expedition to clean garbage off the mountain, taking Frank with him only in spirit. Once more Dick reached the South Col, but this time, instead of weak partners turning him back, the Nepalese government informed the team that their permit did not allow an attempt on the summit. Dick returned to the United States and arranged to join a European team going to the mountain the following year. This time there was no doubt the permit was in order. To cover the risk of getting strapped with weak partners, Dick brought David Breashears along. Once more he reached the South Col, but now David told Dick that he wanted to climb unroped. Because there was insufficient time on the summit day to set snow anchors, wearing one rope would mean two people getting killed if either of them were to slip.

Dick understood Breashears's concern and while it gave him pause, he convinced himself he could get up and down on his own, rope or no rope. They got an early start, leaving the South Col at two A.M. They climbed steadily, and when the first rays broke above the eastern horizon, they were already at the point where two years before Dick had been forced by his companions to turn back. Then the snow hardened, and the points of Dick's crampons seemed only to penetrate the ice surface a fraction of an inch. To his left he could see the glacier floor of the Western Cwm 7,000 feet below, and to his right, the glaciers snaking into

Tibet 18,000 feet below. He felt a gasping faintness, and decided it wiser not to look down or up, but instead to focus on each step.

They rested briefly on the South Summit, then ascended the Hillary Step on a short piece of line left in place by a previous party. It was the only roped protection Dick had the entire day. Once past that difficulty, they then faced the narrow summit ridge with a section of hard blue ice. Dick concentrated on each step, telling himself over and over, What the mind wills, the body follows.

It was one in the morning when I heard from Frank. He was phoning from New York, where he had gone on business—he had just become president of Disney. I knew in an instant something had happened.

"I just got news from Kathmandu."

His voice was two octaves above normal, and my stomach tightened.

"It's Dick . . . Dick's . . ."

Frank stammered, his voice now breaking. I held my breath, clinching the receiver of the phone, getting ready for the worst.

"Dick's . . . made it. He's climbed Everest."

There was another pause while he collected himself. In the two years that I had known him, in all the months we had spent together—through the storms, the bad food, the cramped tents, the freezing temperatures—it was the only time he'd come to tears. On the other end of the line, I heard him take a deep breath. Then, his voice still breaking, Frank finally said it.

"We've got the Seven Summits."

When our driver finishes changing the flat on the truck, we continue down the dirt road and every few minutes pass trucks coming the other way, presumably transporting freight to either Shiquanhe or to one of the two or three other towns that have sprouted along the one-thousand-mile length of the principal thoroughfare of western Tibet. As we travel farther from the heartland of wild Tibet, the yak-hair tents of the nomads are displaced by permanent dwellings of adobe brick. We pass one of these hutments just as a beer bottle flies out the door and breaks into pieces, becoming the most recent contribution to the thousands of glass shards that already surround the dwelling. The perimeter of every house we pass likewise glitters in the meridianal sun.

In the afternoon we see in the distance a long line of telephone poles that parallel a road that must be the one that cuts across the southern margin of the Chang Tang. This is the same road we merged into a month ago on our way to Kailas, which from here is about five days' travel to the west. On our map I can see that the junction of these two roads will mark the completion of a great loop we have scribed around and through the Chang Tang, first westward to Kailas, then northward to the turnoff to Aru, then eastward, and finally southward to this intersection.

When we arrive at the junction we can see, sitting in the dirt, two young soldiers from the P.L.A., each armed with a semiautomatic rifle. They stand and wave to us to stop, then lean in the window to speak to our driver in Chinese. I know Jon understands what they are saying, but he keeps quiet. Our driver answers, then shakes his head and drives away, leaving the two soldiers as we found them.

"What did they want?" I ask Jon.

"A ride."

"What did we tell them?"

"That we don't have any room."

We are at perhaps a hundred yards distance when suddenly I hear the pop-pop-pop of rapid rifle fire.

"Get down!' I yell to Asia, and we both duck in our seats.

I can see our driver looking in his rearview mirror, and he doesn't seem concerned, so I rise up and look back to see the two soldiers firing into the air, aiming at nothing more than the distant sienna hills. Our driver, still looking in the mirror, says something in Tibetan.

"What did he say?" I ask Jon.

"He said, 'Fucking Chinese.'"

. . .

We feel fortunate in late afternoon to ascend into a compact range of low hills and find a small pasture inhabited only by two yaks. We drive the truck off the road a hundred feet and set up our tents.

"This is our last camp," I tell Asia.

"What do you mean?"

"Tomorrow we'll spend the night in Shigatse, and the day after that, we reach Lhasa."

"I don't know if I'm ready for that. I mean, our last camp with Dawa and these other guys? That's too sad!"

When the water is boiling, Dawa calls us to the cook tent for tea. He hands me my mug and smiles when I thank him. He is rapidly alternating over his single propane burner two pots and a skillet, cooking simultaneously noodles, steamed greens, and a curry of julienned cabbage. When he is finished he raises his hands in a Sherpa version of "Voilà!" and hands each of us a filled plate. Then he turns to complete the lentil and rice *dal-bhat* he is cooking for the Tibetans.

"We're not going to eat until you join us," Asia says.

"No, you must eat now before it gets cold," Dawa answers.

"No. We wait."

I have my fork halfway to my mouth, but lower it back to my plate. I see Jon follow suit.

"No, you must eat," Dawa says again.

"No, you must eat with us," she repeats. "We'll help you finish cooking if we need to."

Dawa's smile turns to a pleading frown, but Asia holds her ground. The young Sherpa refuses our help as he works at madcap speed to finish the *dal-bhat*. After a few minutes he calls to the Tibetans to come and get it, then serves himself.

"That's better," Asia says, as Jon and I, following her lead, begin to eat. Dawa is looking down at his plate, but I can see that he has recovered his smile, which seems to have grown even a little larger than usual, engendered, I suspect, by the attention of a very pretty girl only two years younger than he is.

When we finish eating we have another cup of tea, thank Dawa, and step outside. The nightsky is cloudless. I drag my sleeping bag and pad from out of the tent and lay them atop a ground cloth.

"You sleeping outside?" Asia asks.

"It's a perfect night."

"That's a good idea."

She positions her bag a few feet from mine, and soon I am identifying for her the stars and constellations I first learned when I was her age, standing the night watch on my sailing voyage from Hawaii to French Polynesia. She bids me a good night's sleep, and I continue to gaze at the stars. My thoughts, however, are not with the stars, or even with past adventures, but with my own three children, who all of a sudden I am missing to the extent that I relive in my mind how it feels to hug each one of them, reviewing the different nuances of their embraces.

Then I consider that it is now the middle of June. That means we have been on our journey a month and a half, yet we still have nearly a month to go. It is not a long time measured against past trips. It took over four months to climb K2, including the trek in and out, and when I was twenty-one and I made my second voyage to the South Pacific, followed by the long windward passage to Central America, the stint in prison in Panama, the monthlong hitchhike to Peru, the job with the anthropologist in the Quechua village, and the full season climbing in the Andes, I was gone two years.

After that first full year of my marriage, when I went on three of the Seven Summits expeditions and fitted between them the crossing of Borneo, I tried to limit my outings to one or two a year, and then to trips that were only a month or so in length. It was during that period that Yvon Chouinard and I became close friends. We lived only a few houses apart, and we went on frequent surfing outings to the local beaches. By then my wife was also working with Yvon, as photography editor for his award-winning catalogs.

The two of us slowly returned to climbing, first on Frank and Dick's ascent of Aconcagua, and also on local outings, sometimes inviting our other friends so that each of us brought the other into our circle of acquaintances. One of these people was Tom Brokaw, whom I had met a few years before when I was flying home from the K2 climb. Brokaw had contacted Jim Whittaker, the expedition leader, to see if anyone from the team could appear on the *Today* show, which in those days Brokaw hosted. Other than Whittaker, I was the only one able to lay over in New York. We went from the airport to the NBC studio, and I was still wearing the only clothes I had following the climb: light cotton pajama pants I had picked up in the Rawalpindi bazaar, an aloha shirt, and flip-flops that I preferred over my holed sneakers because they didn't hurt my blistered feet. My hair was long and uncut, my lips were cracked and bleeding, and all my fingers, from the first joint to the tip, were black from frostbite.

"I've been doing this show for quite a while," Brokaw said when were introduced, "and I've never seen anyone come on looking like you."

When we finished, he invited me to come back once I had completed the book I was going to write about the expedition. So two years later I was on the show again, and following the interview, we had a few minutes to talk.

"I've always had a fantasy of learning to climb someday." Brokaw said.

"Let's do it then."

"You mean it?"

"Come on out to the Tetons this summer. I'll introduce you to my friend Yvon Chouinard, and we'll climb the Grand."

After we climbed the Grand Teton, Tom, Yvon, and I continued every year to go on hiking, climbing, and fishing trips. One of those was an ascent of Mount Rainier, up a less-frequented route called the Kautz Glacier. Yvon also invited his lifelong climbing partner Doug Tompkins. Both Yvon and Doug had dropped out of high school to pursue climbing. In the mid-sixties they loaded a Ford van with surfboards, skis, and climbing gear and painted on the back the words *"Puercos Deportivos,"* Spanish for "Fun Hogs." They drove from California to Argentina, surfed, skied, and climbed the entire distance, and, at the end of the trip, made the third ascent of a monumental tusk of granite in Patagonia called Fitzroy. By then Doug had started a small company in San Francisco manufacturing tents and sleeping bags he named The North Face, after the great north-wall climbs of Europe. Later he and his wife started Esprit clothing, which had grown to a billion-dollar-a-year company by the time I met him on Rainier.

Doug had a placard above his desk at Esprit that said "Commit And Then Figure It Out." It was a fitting epigram for the way we taught Tom Brokaw how to climb snow and ice. After a brief lesson walking in crampons and arresting practice falls with his ice axe, we started the climb. The first obstacle was an icefall—a miniature version of the one on Everest.

"The only way to reduce the risk is to climb fast," Yvon told Tom.

"Aren't we going to rope up?" Tom asked.

"We'll go faster unroped."

Tom stood quietly, digesting this news.

"It's just like catching a taxi in New York," Yvon said, sensing Tom's thoughts.

"How's that?"

"Nice guys finish last."

We laughed, and then took off, scampering through the icefall, leaving Tom on his own. Once he was through the icefall and caught back up to us, however, the slope started to steepen so we tied the rope to his harness and belayed him. Then he began to slow.

"Sorry, guys. My television career is catching up with me."

"New York money and Park Avenue legs don't get you far up here," Yvon said.

We laughed again, and Tom smiled and shook his head. He had been with us enough by then to know our teasing had a serious side. Tom was committed to taking the most he could from these climbs, and we knew

the best way to do that was not to pamper him with mock encouragement and false compliments, but rather to give him the basic tools and
then let him figure it out. As we approached the crater rim at the top of
the mountain, however, Tom got the last laugh. We climbed into an
enveloping cloud, and visibility dropped to a few feet. When we reached
a point where, groping in one direction and then the other, we couldn't
find any higher ground, we concluded that we must be on the summit.
Our plan, however, was to traverse the mountain and descend in the
opposite direction by the regular route.

"It's going to be tough to find the trail," I said. "Did anybody bring a
compass?"

"No," Doug said.

"Me neither," Yvon admitted.

"Allow me, gentlemen," Tom said, unzipping the top flap of his pack
and producing a small Boy Scout compass. Once we established the right
direction, we soon sighted a bamboo marker wand, and then the
stamped-in trail that led out of the cloud and down the mountain, where
we arrived at the visitors' center an hour before midnight. Tom called
the nearest restaurant and talked them into staying open. When we finished our meal, the restaurant's owner, who also ran an adjacent motel,
invited us to use the Jacuzzi.

"Ah, no thanks," Yvon said. Tom looked at him imploringly, but Yvon
only chuckled and said, "We wouldn't want you getting too soft."

That same year, 1985, I received an invitation from the Explorer's Club
to join a mountaineering group traveling to Bhutan to attempt a peak
called Gangkar Punsum, the highest mountain in the country. No American mountaineering team had ever been allowed into Bhutan, and no
team from any country had been allowed to attempt Gangkar Punsum.
The expedition needed more climbers, so I mentioned it to Yvon, and
he mentioned it to Doug. We were all excited about the possibility of traveling to an area of the Himalayas few outsiders had ever seen. Some of my

old friends were already on the team, including John Roskelley. The only problem was the mountain. At about 25,000 feet, Gangkar Punsum was close to the same altitude as Minya Konka. It was close enough to the same end of the Himalayas that we knew it would have the same wet-snow conditions that had triggered the avalanche five years before.

I was certain Yvon had the same reservations. After the Minya Konka expedition we had seldom talked about Jonathan's death, or our own near deaths. Yvon was circumspect that way, keeping his most intimate thoughts close to his chest. One day about a year after the tragedy we were driving to the beach to go surfing, and I told him I thought about the avalanche at least once a day, and he nodded and said, "Yeah, me too."

Now, however, it was something we had to discuss. "Gangkar Punsum will have the same wet-snow conditions as Minya Konka," I told him.

"I know," he replied.

"I get the willies just thinking about it."

"Me too."

"If we'd never been in the avalanche, we wouldn't hesitate," I said. "Jonathan would still be alive, and he'd probably be going with us. Bhutan is supposed to be the last stronghold of pure Himalayan Buddhism."

"That's the thing," Yvon said. "The chance to see a place like that, before it's spoiled."

The expedition was set to leave in the fall, still many months away, so we had a little time before we had to make a decision. Then I received a phone call from a friend who knew my old climbing partner, Chris Chandler. By then it had been seven years since the K2 expedition, but I had kept track of Chris through the climbers' grapevine. I heard that he had built a boat, and that he and Cherie had sailed to Hawaii, and then tried to get from there to Alaska but had been caught in a series of difficult gales, and after nearly sinking had limped into California. Then I heard that just the two of them were planning to return to the Himalayas, to try to make the first winter ascent of Kanchenjunga, the third highest peak in the world, and to do it without oxygen. When I heard about his plan, I smiled; it sounded like the Chris I knew, always pushing things as far as he could take them.

"Apparently they were in a snow cave high on the mountain when Chris got both pulmonary and cerebral edema," my friend told me over the phone. "Cherie and a Sherpa who was with them tried to get him down, but he died the next day, and Cherie had no choice but to leave him there."

Later Cherie published her memoir, and I learned more of the story. During the ascent Chris had been moody, sometimes bursting into angry tirades. Retreating to their Base Camp in the middle of a storm, Cherie had been moving slowly when Chris became so frustrated he threw his pack and ice axe at her. Although Cherie was circumspect about it, I suspect that Chris's anger was rooted in the increasingly frustrating dilemma he faced trying to maintain his responsibility to his ex-wife and children, and still have the freedom to follow his adventures.

At 26,000 feet Cherie and Chris, and the Sherpa accompanying them, dug a cave into the side of a snow slope and started their stoves to make enough water to rehydrate after an arduous day of climbing. They had only a little more than 2,000 vertical feet to gain the summit, and felt they could reach it the next day. They knew the night would be difficult, however: The snow cave was so cramped their feet stuck out the entrance, and it was the middle of January and extremely cold.

In the morning the weather was favorable, and Cherie was confident they were going for the summit. They started the stoves to make more water. Cherie put on her crampons, then crawled out of the snow cave to check the weather. When she returned, she discovered both stoves had gone out and Chris was sitting inside breathing the gas fumes that were still hissing out. She asked him what had happened, and he just smiled. She dragged him outside, and after a moment he said he felt better but he wanted to go back in and lie down. Then he started to gag and spit up green phlegm. Cherie realized he was in trouble and knew his only hope was to get down as fast as possible.

Chris was unable to put on either his crampons or his harness, and Cherie had to take off her mittens to help him. In only moments her fingers felt like they had turned to wood. She tied Chris into the rope and talked him onto his feet, but as they began the descent he kept collapsing.

Cherie stopped to discuss with the Sherpa what to do, and when she turned back she saw Chris had untied the rope. She scolded him, but he smiled again and said he was just trying to help.

The day ended, and they continued in the darkness. Finally Cherie realized they had to bivouac. The Sherpa cut a platform in the slope, and they placed Chris in a nylon bivouac sack. During the night Chris began rolling and lurching, and Cherie planted her ice axe in the snow and tied it to the bivouac sack so he wouldn't slide off the platform. Then she saw his hand fall out of the sack. It was limp. She looked at his face and saw that the tension that had been there through the day was gone. He was dead.

In the morning the Sherpa stood looking out over the Himalayas in their winter blueness, letting out a high keening wail. Cherie had no choice but to leave Chris where he lay. It took four days to descend to Base Camp. By then her hands and feet were severely frostbitten, and by the time she got home and to a hospital all her fingers and toes had to be either partially or completely amputated.

After I received the news of Chris's death, I went for a walk on the beach and recalled the early-morning departures from Base Camp on Everest, when Chris and I scouted part of the route through the icefall. I remembered the contention and arguments on K2, the split in our friendship.

I pictured Chris's sculpted cheeks, his long blond hair held in a bandanna. I imagined his enthusiasm planning the expedition to Kanchenjunga, telling Cherie that because the slopes of the mountain were moderate they wouldn't need fixed ropes, and other than perhaps a Sherpa or two, they could climb with just the two of them. No crowds, no jockeying for position, no arguments, no fights. And why not try to climb it in the winter? No one had ever done that. Sometimes in the winter there were spells of calm and clear weather. Short days and cold—very cold—but they could handle it. And besides, it was the kind of cold that held its own beauty, when through the day in the low light the snow was gold and in the shadows it was blue, and through the night the stars blazed as though you had already left the Earth and were seeing them from the deep of space.

To climb with only two people and no oxygen the third-highest mountain in the world, in winter? Chris once drove by himself the thousand miles to my house from Seattle, averaging eighty-five miles an hour, while at the same time he read *Sometimes a Great Notion* cover to cover, the novel propped on top of the steering wheel. Chris never wanted to recognize limits. But had he died on Kanchenjunga because he exceeded them? Cerebral and pulmonary edema can hit anyone, from novice to the most experienced mountaineer, with no warning and no previous history of susceptibility. Still, I had a strong intuition that Chris's own susceptibility was linked to the stress and tension he carried up the mountain; that his headlong path through life had incubated and hatched its demons, and on Kanchenjunga they had loosed inside him.

I had learned mountaineering in Peru under the wing of Ron Fear and Chris Chandler. Together, the three of us were going to climb the highest unclimbed peaks in the ranges of the world, from Peru to Alaska to the Himalayas. Now I was the only one of our trio still alive. I had long since recognized that Ron was dead because of the willful way he had courted danger. Now Chris was gone, perhaps in part for the same reason. But what about Jonathan? Wasn't he innately cautious, willing to step beyond the bounds of his experience and skill only if he was in the company of companions more experienced? But Yvon, Kim, and I, despite our experience, had still misread the snow conditions, and if the trajectory of avalanching snow had shifted slightly, the three of us would now be buried next to Jonathan.

As I faced the decision to go to Bhutan, I had just lost another friend. Moreover, my wife was pregnant with our second child. In the end, I decided to go anyway, knowing I would probably encounter wet-snow conditions, but drawn by the prospect of exploring an unexplored land. I told myself, however, that this time there would be no heady, free-form glissade down a loaded slope. That innocence was lost. In avalanche country, I would have to study every step I took.

10

Driving toward Shigatse, we cross the first fence line we have seen in three weeks. By late afternoon we crest a rise and see on the other side a wide valley with barley fields bordered by rows of poplars and willows, the first trees since we entered the Chang Tang. In an hour we transit the village of Namring overlooking a large and very blue lake of the same name. In the four days since we left Aru, traveling first entirely off-road, then following faint tracks that have led to these dirt roads, we have gone from wildland to rangeland to farmland; in two more days we will be in Lhasa. As I look out the window at the barley fields, I consider how our horizontal journey mirrors the vertical time of our species' social evolution from hunter-gatherers to pastoralists to agriculturists to urbanites.

We pass a group of houses nestled snugly between two ridges, sides marked with a black and orange sash that indicates the inhabitants belong to the Sakiya sect of Tibetan Buddhism. On the roofs, at each of the cardinal corners, there is a bundling of willow wands that hold prayer flags. Mature poplars border the neighboring fields where men, women, and children pause from their work to wave as we pass.

"It's so wonderful," Asia says, "to finally see houses that are well built and taken care of, that look lived in, to see real villages."

I share Asia's sentiments about these houses compared to the hovels we have seen in the frontier towns of western Tibet. I know, however, that years from now, when I recall this journey, it won't be this quaint village with its hospitable farmers that I will remember. It certainly won't be the shoddy gold-rush cities like Shiquanhe, or the mud hutments surrounded by broken beer bottles of former nomads beginning their poverty-level entry into the national economy. Rather it will be the nomads still living in their yak-hair tents, and even more, the wildlands and the wildlife of the high steppe: the horizontal bands of blue sky, turquoise lakes, and sienna plateaus; the lines of kiang and chiru galloping to the horizon; the background glaciers descending from the Crystal Mountains.

By temperament I would have fit in better in another age when by camel I could have traveled between caravansaries, watching the next oasis appear on the distant horizon and then grow slowly with the advance of each day's stage. If I return to the Chang Tang, I already know it will be to push north and east beyond the Aru, in search of the secret calving grounds of the chiru. If I do that, I also know it will be a journey I will make on foot, in the company of a few domesticated yaks packing supplies. I know this because these days it is only the few remaining wild places on our Earth that motivate me to travel.

The best journeys are to lands that have few familiar signposts, because it is on such journeys you find yourself answering questions that at the outset you may never have thought to ask. In the 1970s my journeys to Everest and to K2 held for me a sense of mystery, but more because I was young than because these areas were off the map. By 1980, I would find Minya Konka appealing not just as a climb but because it was in the land of Kham, a region that had not been visited by outsiders since the early 1930s. And by 1985 the opportunity to see one of the most remote corners of the kingdom of Bhutan was something I couldn't let pass, and neither could Yvon.

"We'll just be real conservative when it comes to snow conditions," I told him.

"We even get a whiff of an avalanche," he agreed, "and we're out of there."

In those days the only flight to Bhutan was on a small plane that departed once a week from Calcutta. John Roskelley and I arrived in the city two days early, and waited downtown in an old colonial hotel with a group of German trekkers also waiting to fly to Paro, Bhutan's only airport. They were led by that venerable mountaineer I had for so long esteemed because he wrote one of my favorite adventure books, *Seven Years in Tibet*. John and I invited Heinrich Harrer to have a beer with us in the hotel bar. He was then seventy-three years old, but clearly fit. He had a wide, square face, and thin lips and thin eyes, like someone who has squinted in the sun for many years. He seemed interested in our climbing project, and even more interested in the trek we would take to get there.

"I returned to Lhasa and Tibet three years ago," he told us, "and I have no desire to go back. The Chinese have changed everything. It is no longer the place I knew. Ah, but Bhutan! They have taken care of things, as you will see."

The next day the rest of our team arrived, including a few trekkers from the Explorer's Club which, along with Rolex, was sponsoring the expedition. We caught a flight to Paro, then took the two-hour bus ride to the capital, Thimphu.

"Nineteen expeditions to the Himalayas and I've finally found Shangri-la," John said when we arrived.

At seventy-six hundred feet, the temperature was moderate, the people well dressed and prosperous, and the buildings well constructed in the Tibetan style of hand-cut stone-block walls, hand-painted sash windows, and slate roofs. Many had been built for the 1974 coronation of the Dragon King, who was then twenty-nine years old and the youngest monarch in the world. We saw him the afternoon of our arrival when he descended from the palace to play the townfolk in a game of basketball. Every time the king got the ball, the other players waited for him to shoot. His team won.

It was a three-day ride by minibus to the trailhead. We loaded our gear on yaks, then followed a river of clear water flowing from mountains still covered with old-growth blue pine, silver fir, and live oak. Yvon and Doug had their fly rods, and they caught and released dozens of trout up to three pounds. There was no map of the region. All we had to guide us was a Landsat photograph that must have been taken in winter because most of the terrain was an overexposed white that revealed no features. We navigated using directions given us by our Bhutanese hosts in Thimphu, who had sent a reconnaissance team a few months earlier to scout the approach route.

Two of our team left in advance of the rest of us to verify that we were going the right way, and when we caught up with them their report was not the one we had hoped to hear.

"It's good news, bad news," one of them said. "The good news is we're heading up a valley that probably no westerners have ever been in, surrounded by a number of beautiful Himalayan peaks. The bad news is, none of them is Gangkar Punsum."

"Where is it?"

"It looks like it's one major drainage to the west."

"But the Bhutanese sent a reconnaissance up here."

"We've found out from the local yak herders they call all the mountains around here Gangkar Punsum. The reccy guys probably pointed up this valley and said, 'Gangkar Punsum?' and the locals said, 'Yes.'"

"So do we go back and try to find the right valley?"

Our permit was valid for only another six weeks, however, and that didn't leave enough time to go down, back up another valley, and still have time to climb the mountain. Even if we could get the permit extended, by that time winter would be approaching.

"On the bright side," Yvon said, "it's pretty amazing to be in a place so remote the people in the capital don't even know how to find the highest mountain in their own country."

"When I was younger," John said, "I made nearly all the summits I tried. Then as I got older I missed a few. Now I can't even find them."

"So what do we do?"

"Let's keep going up this valley and climb these mountains," Yvon suggested. "Who cares whether or not they're the highest ones."

We all realized Yvon's idea had merit, all except one of the trekkers who represented the Explorer's Club.

"I understand your position, but all of you need to remember we have an obligation to Rolex to at least *try* to climb Gangkar Punsum."

He had a point. We decided that once we arrived at the head of the valley we would see if there was any way to access the neighboring drainage, thereby gaining the east flank of Gangkar Punsum. If we could do that, then we might be able to connect to the summit, or at least to a subsidiary summit. We continued upvalley, walking a trail the yak herders followed to their seasonal pastures. The forest was prime and uncut, and we all recognized this was what Nepal must have looked like years ago. The trees measured our climb: silver fir, 10,000 feet; oak and rhododendron, 12,000 feet; juniper, 14,000 feet. We set our Base Camp near the snout of a glacier. We knew there were big peaks nearby, but any view we might have from our tents was veiled by a curtain of clouds. The next day we left camp and walked up a lateral moraine, hoping to get a glimpse of the peaks. Finally, through a few holes in the clouds, we glimpsed the surrounding walls of fluted snow and ice. To no one's surprise, we could also see evidence of avalanches. Nevertheless, there were two smaller peaks on the east side that appeared to have safe approaches to ridges with more secure conditions. The west side, however, which we would have to climb to get to Gangkar Punsum, was dangerous.

"Remember our vow," Yvon said to me.

"Nothing that even smells like it has avalanche potential," I replied.

The trekker from the Explorer's Club was disappointed, but he realized we weren't about to compromise our judgment to satisfy a sponsor. By then he was also realizing that some of us weren't the kind of "explorers" Rolex was looking for, anyway. Yvon who prided himself on being what he called a dirtbag climber, had never worn a watch in his life. Neither had Doug. I wore one only infrequently. Rolex had given each of us one of their stainless steel models with our names engraved on the back, but even before we left Yvon and Doug had donated theirs to an auction to support a grassroots group trying to save a white-water river in Idaho from damming, and I had traded mine to a photographer for a telescopic lens for my camera.

We may not have been Rolex explorers, but we were in high spirits. The morning revealed a cloudless sky with a gibbous moon setting over the western peaks, and a cold, dry wind from the north blowing tendrils off the high snow ridges. We had a lazy breakfast, then moved camp to a high meadow that was like an island of green surrounded by a moonscape of gray rock and glacial ice. At 17,000 feet, we called it Camp Shangri-la. For our own reference we also gave names to the mountains we hoped to climb: Rolex Peak, Explorer Peak, Mount Oyster Perpetual.

We spent one more day reconnoitering the peaks to make absolutely certain there wasn't even a whiff of avalanche potential. Satisfied, we went to bed early and woke before dawn to start the stoves. We stood outside our tents, fingers wrapped around warm mugs of tea, watching the dawn paint the peaks in pastels. It was clear and calm. We shouldered our packs and left camp. At the steep foot of the glacier, Doug went first, climbing up the hard snow on the front points of his crampons. He was unroped, as he usually was when he knew he was within his limits.

"Just like Styrofoam," he called down, giving a smile and a thumbs-up. Climbing conditions were perfect.

By midmorning we had crossed the glacier to the beginning of a snow gully that led to the crest of the ridge, where we roped up. It was sharp and narrow. We wove around cornices, balanced on knife-edges, and maneuvered on crampons up rock gendarmes. Doug and Yvon were in the lead. I stopped to photograph them as they made the summit. Doug was first, waving his arms; then he reeled in the rope and traded places with Yvon. There was room for only one at a time on top, and after a few minutes Yvon came down to give me a turn.

I held out my arms as I balanced on the crest, and felt as if I could fly. I could see east along the border between Bhutan and Tibet to the Assam region of India. To the north, rising out of the dry Tibetan plain, was another massive, unclimbed 25,000-foot peak known as Kula Kangri, and in between an area that was the focus of a border dispute between Bhutan and China. It added to the sense of adventure that I was looking into territory so remote it was unclear which country owned it.

We spent another week exploring the valley and climbing the smaller peaks that had safe routes. One of our team took careful altimeter and compass measurements on each summit, then drew a detailed ridgeline map of the complete cirque. When it was time to leave, everyone agreed the expedition had turned out for the best: even if we had found Gangkar Punsum, the snow conditions would likely have been too unstable to risk an ascent.

"There's just one thing that bothers me," Yvon said.

"What's that?"

"The map. I'm not sure we should publish it."

"Why not?"

"The same reason I stopped reporting new climbs I do in the Tetons. So the place stays unknown as much as possible. Then the next guys who come here can get as much out of this place as we have, because they won't know any more about it than we did."

"What should we do with the map, then?"

"Burn it."

"Burn it?"

"Yeah, torch the sucker. It would be the perfect ending to our trip."

Yvon the iconoclast. It took a few moments to consider it, but we soon got the idea. Our teammate who had drawn the map pulled out his Bic lighter and set it on fire. The rest of us stood around in a circle and cheered.

When I told Asia the story about the Bhutan expedition, I also told her that in the years since, burning the map has become one of the more important lessons I've learned from Yvon.

"How so?" she asked.

"It started me thinking about how the process of doing something is more important than the goal. That sounds simple, but not many people really pay attention to it. Yvon is always telling his employees to run the business the same way a Zen archer shoots an arrow. You concentrate on pulling the bowstring in time to your breathing, you clear your mind of extraneous thoughts, then you let the arrow go and it hits the bull's-eye on its own."

"You think Yvon learned that from climbing?" Asia asked.

"I know he did. He's never been a peak bagger. The route on a mountain has always been the only thing that mattered to him. The quality of the route, not the summit."

Asia had been around Yvon enough to know that the way he climbs mountains has translated into other aspects of the way he lives his life. He drives an old Toyota station wagon, for example, that is full of sand, damp wetsuits, fishing gear, and soggy towels. He wears his clothes until they are holed and ragged. He's been going to the same barber for forty years, and he's always had the same short haircut. When he climbs, he secures himself to the rope as climbers did fifty years ago, wrapping the cord around his waist a few times and tying a bowline. He's never once watched the Super Bowl. He's an excellent cook, washes his own dishes happily without a dishwasher. He's never used a computer, and he drives within the speed limit.

"The other thing to learn from Yvon," I told Asia, "is that he knows how to move quickly, but he's never in a hurry."

We arrive in Shigatse, the second largest city in Tibet, in midafternoon, and check into a guest house owned and run by Tibetans who have designed it to appeal to the Lonely Planet crowd: patio bar, walls painted in the bright foundation colors sacred to Buddhists, rooms with benches lining the walls covered with Tibetan carpets that double as beds. A young Tibetan woman with a wide smile brings us each a bottle of cold beer and, to share, a plate of fried potatoes. From the window we have a view across the street of the open-air market, the old Tibetan quarter of the city, and, rising from the top of a steep hill as though it has grown organically out of the slopes, the ruins of the ancient *dzong*, the fortress of Shigatse. A sudden hailstorm falling on our metal roof raises a thunderous din, and we watch out the window as merchants in the market scramble to shift their wares under the plastic tarps covering each stall. The hail continues to fall with such intensity the street is soon flooded curb to curb in water that rushes downhill in brown, standing waves.

"It's going to be a tough monsoon," I say. "Even if the political situation has eased, we may still have trouble just getting to Minya Konka."

"I read that Buddhists believe that when you are on a pilgrimage," Asia says, "the more hardships you have, the more merit you gain."

We hear some English speakers in the hallway, and invite them in to share beer and potatoes. There is one Dutchman, a German woman, and an American who says he's from Queens. They all appear to be in their late twenties or early thirties, and they wear loose-fitting cotton clothes picked up inexpensively in Kathmandu or Bangkok or Bali. They explain there are five in their party, traveling together so they can enter Tibet on a less expensive group visa.

"Where are the other two?"

"In our room, making love."

That stops the conversation for a few beats. Finally I ask if they've heard any news about the war in Yugoslavia.

"All we've heard is that it's supposed to be winding down."

That's good news, I think, if it's accurate. But we'll have more reliable information tomorrow, when we arrive in Lhasa.

"Where are you going?" Asia asks.

"Everest," the American replies. "We're climbing to Camp 3."

"In those shoes?" Asia says, pointing to his trekking sneakers.

"Why not? But we need one of those small camping stoves, you know, to melt snow to make water. You guys wouldn't have one for sale?"

"Afraid not," I say.

"That's okay. We can just hire a Sherpa to carry water for us."

I look at Asia and give her a conspiratorial wink. "That might not work," I say.

"Why not?"

"It would freeze at night."

"Oh," the American says. "I hadn't thought of that."

Next day, under a sullen sky, we leave Shigatse. The "Friendship Highway" to Lhasa is paved, and by early afternoon we are on the outskirts of the city. This is the first time I have been to the Place of the Gods: "Lha" for gods and "sa" for place. In 1980, Jonathan and I were as excited about the possibility of getting to Lhasa as we were about climbing Minya Konka. We weren't the only ones on the team to share that ambition. While traveling by minibus to the trailhead, we had passed the junction where the road split, one way going upvalley to Minya Konka, the other way going eventually to Lhasa. One of our team called the driver to stop. He ripped a piece of cardboard off a storage box, wrote across it, in block letters, "Lhasa," then walked to the junction and stuck out his thumb.

In those days Lhasa was still a forbidden city. In 1980, only about twelve hundred Westerners had ever been there, and 623 of those were with Francis Younghusband's military excursion of 1904. But in 1980 the avalanche intervened, and we did not make it to Lhasa. By 1985, when I met Heinrich Harrer on my way to Bhutan, my desire to see the place was starting to wane. I had heard from climbing friends passing through on their way to the mountains that large parts of the city looked like any other place in China that was growing quickly. I had seen enough of Chinese modernization to know it was not always a pretty sight.

I'm not surprised, then, to enter Lhasa on a wide boulevard modeled after the ones in Beijing. Or to see that what Heinrich Harrer said used to be a lively residential district opposite the Potala is now an enormous open square made to look like a smaller version of Tiananmen. Or that the monopoly on Lhasa's skyline no longer belongs to the Potala alone, which now competes with the megalithic twenty-story blue glass headquarters of China Telecom.

Every block has a new building under construction. It is common knowledge that the Chinese are pouring money into Tibet to buy Tibetan loyalty. By the river, this wealth has purchased two city blocks of karaoke bars and brothels. Along a cross street we pass shops wedged cheek by jowl: a beauty salon, shoe store, a Sichuan restaurant, jewelry store, a shop selling only floor safes, another only floor linoleum, another just beds, another just pillows. A drugstore specializing in cures for sexually transmitted diseases has a large sign in the window that says, in Chinese characters, "Sex."

A quick census of the sidewalk passersby reveals about as many Han Chinese as Tibetans. Now I pause to consider the ease with which I am condemning this transformation of Lhasa. Those who have studied the region closely report that the great majority of these Han Chinese view their country's investment in Tibet as magnanimous aid to an impoverished "autonomous zone." These experts also say the opinions of the Tibetans themselves are mixed. If I am really to see things as they are, I must recognize that even the majority of these Tibetans prefer the conveniences of modern life under the Chinese over the medieval lives they led under the lamaistic theocracy, lives that are within the direct memories of all the older Tibetans I see on the street.

My musings bring to mind the memory of a Sherpa woman from Khumjung, the village near Everest, who once came to our house for dinner. She had been living in the United States for seven years, and she did not want to go home.

"It is much harder than you know when you have no electricity, no washing machine, no gas, no cars," she said. "You have to walk up and down steep hills every day. Then you dig in the fields to grow potatoes, and haul the night soil on your backs. You just don't know."

I might not know, but I had spent enough time in other villages beyond the end of the road that I felt I could come close to imagining her life. Close enough that I knew better than to suggest to her that village life in the Khumbu was the answer, and that we should all return to it. Yet I also knew there was no way I could convince her that her new life, unsustainable as it is in its overuse of the world's resources, is not the answer, either. If there is any truth in this issue it is that no one has the answer, at least no one I have talked to or read.

We check into the Yak Hotel, and I see on the courtyard lawn a large stuffed yak that looks like a frozen relic from the Pleistocene. Asia has an upset stomach and wants only to take a bath and go to bed. Since she's been such a good sport putting up with me as her tent mate for a month, I've sprung for her own private room. Dawa and I help her with her backpack and duffel.

"I hope you feel better in the morning," I tell her when we get to her room.

"Don't worry," she says before she closes her door. "I don't want to miss anything."

We plan to stay in Lhasa for two days, so we can see the sights, then fly to Chengdu, where Jon has arranged for a local mountain guide to pick us up at the airport and take us to Minya Konka. But that's only if the political situation in Sichuan has cooled. Jon says he's going out to try to call his wife back in the States. He had asked her before we departed Kathmandu to gather as much information as she could, so we're hopeful she now has enough news to help us make an informed decision whether or not to continue the journey. I unpack and lie on my bed, trying, by my own form of homegrown meditation, to stay calm, repeating to myself as though it were a mantra the words of Molière that "men spend their lives worrying about things that never happen."

In an hour Jon is back, and Asia gets up and joins us, to hear the news.

"The United States still hasn't given what the Chinese consider a credible explanation," Jon says. "It sounds like the people in the street are still pissed. But things in Chengdu are calm. It's harder to get a read on conditions in the countryside."

I'm not sure what to do, and I remind myself again that I cannot place Asia in jeopardy, even when we are this close to completing the goals of our journey.

"This trip has been one obstacle after another," Asia says in an encouraging tone, "and so far we've got over all of them. We'll figure this one out."

I have an idea. What if we spend the night in Chengdu, then leave very early and try to drive straight through, to avoid possible confrontations in small villages? In 1980 it took us three days to drive from Chengdu to the trailhead, but Jon says the roads are now so improved he thinks it can be done in a day.

"Then that's the plan," I say. "We drive it in one day."

"One more thing," Jon says. "I've got a number of trips in development after this one, and my wife says if at all possible it would help to get home early to organize them. I called Meng in Chengdu [the guide who will take us to Minya Konka], and everything there is ready. So if it's all the same, I'd like to go back to Kathmandu with Dawa day after tomorrow, then fly back to the States."

I tell him that shouldn't be a problem. In the morning Asia says that although she is still queasy, she thinks she's up to a day of sight-seeing.

We drive north of town to the Sera Monastery, one of the great monastic cities of Tibet. In the days before the Cultural Revolution, Sera housed over thirty-five hundred monks and acolytes. It was one of the few institutions to survive the revolution relatively intact, and today it is still a vital college for about four hundred monks from all corners of Tibet.

We see at least a hundred of them in the Debating Courtyard, gathered mostly in pairs under the broad-leafed shade trees, arguing and gesticulating with their hands as they try to reveal weaknesses in their opponent's philosophical position.

"Do you think they would mind if I photograph them?" I ask Jon.

"Not at all. They see tourists here every day."

I have brought both the video and still cameras, and now I try to decide which one to use.

"Asia, if I get some video, could you get a few stills?"

"I'm not really comfortable doing that."

"Jon says it's okay."

"I know. But it still feels intrusive."

I tell Asia I understand. Then I take the video camera, set up the tripod, and tape the monks who pay me no heed; as Jon said, they probably see tourists doing this every day. I was sincere, however, when I told Asia I understand her reluctance. Not only do I understand it, I know where it comes from. I finish with the video camera, then put a zoom lens on the still camera, and expose a roll. The light is filtering through the trees, and I know the images will be good. I look over to see Asia sitting alone, watching the monks. What would her father be doing, I wonder, if he were here? But I know the answer. Like her, he would have been very conscious of intruding on the monks' privacy. But unlike her, he would have watched the monks until he had made eye contact with a few of them. Then he would have smiled at them, and when they smiled back, he would have lifted his camera slightly, mouthed an "Okay?" and when they nodded approvingly, he would have started taking pictures.

I am coming to understand that photography may not be the thing Asia should be pursuing. Maybe if I get a good opportunity, I'll talk to her about it. It wouldn't be the end of the world, either, if she were to pursue something else. Photography is a difficult way to make a living, to say the least. Not to mention that there have been occasions too numerous to count when I wished I could be on a journey without a camera hanging around my neck like an albatross, or a heavy film or video camera in my pack, or even a notepad and journal that I felt obligated to fill every day.

Over the past ten years I have made it a point to get away once in a while on an adventure with no film contract, no photography assignment, no book or magazine deal. To go on a trip only for the sake of the trip, to capture again the purity of purpose I used to feel when I first started high-altitude mountaineering.

One of the best trips I ever had that I paid for out of my own pocket began in 1988 when Yvon, sitting in his living room thumbing through the environmental journal *Earthwatch,* saw a photograph of a cluster of rime-coated rock spires rising from the back of a deep channel. The caption said "From the fiords of N.W. Tierra del Fuego." No doubt thousands of people saw the same photograph. A few perhaps even thought the spires looked like interesting climbs. There was only one reader, however, who decided to do something about it.

I lived a few doors from Yvon, and he called and asked me to come over. "We could get those collapsible kayaks you carry on planes as checked baggage," he said. "Paddle in there and climb one of these things. What do think?"

This was the trip we made only a week after Yvon turned fifty. On his birthday he had said it was important to do the trips he had been thinking about. He had tendinitis in his wrists and elbows, a chronically sore neck from a break he had suffered years before while diving headfirst into a muddy stream in Colombia, and he figured he had perhaps ten good years left. At the time, fifty didn't sound that old to me, but *Raiders of the Lost Ark* had come out a few years earlier, and I remembered Indiana Jones saying, "It's not the years, it's the mileage."

This adventure promised to add more miles to our bodies. Further research revealed the *Earthwatch* photograph wasn't from Tierra del Fuego but the labyrinth of canals, fiords, and islands just north of the Straits of Magellan known as the Magellanic Archipelago. Only one climber had ever been in the area.

"I think I know which peak you're interested in—it's like a miniature Fitzroy," the climber told us. "If you're really going to kayak in there, watch out for the williwaws—they're strong enough to flip you. The tidal currents are bad, too—up to twelve knots through the narrows, so fast they make standing waves. And then there's the weather. It's the worst in the world. I was there two weeks and never saw a thing but wind and sleet. And it's always that way. In a typical year there's maybe one clear week out of fifty-two."

We decided to ask two more friends to join us, Doug Tompkins and Jim Donini, a Patagonia clothing rep and a well-known alpine climber who had made some very difficult technical ascents in Patagonia, Alaska, and the Karakoram. We spread the maps over Yvon's dining table and realized that the most hazardous part of the adventure might be a ten-mile-wide bay we would have to cross, against the prevailing westerlies and exposed to williwaws, the tornado-like gusts that blow out of the fiords. We convinced ourselves that rather than make the entire round trip by kayak, it might be smart to charter a small boat in the fishing village of Puerto Natales for the seventy-mile upwind passage to the outer canals. There we would have the boat drop us off as close as possible to the peak we wanted to climb. After we made the ascent we could then assemble our kayaks and return with the wind at our backs.

In Puerto Natales we loaded our gear in the hold of a boat that smelled of aged crab juice, and cast off. Under a sullen sky we nosed into the wide bay, and the forty-five-knot westerlies blew spindrift in sheets over the decks. We huddled in the tiny forecabin galley, heating tea water on a cast-iron woodstove as the boat pounded into the short, steep seas.

"Hey, Fig, feels like we're onto something," Doug said to Yvon, using the nickname he'd given him during their climb of Fitzroy, in 1968, when they drove from California to Patagonia in the old Ford van. It had taken them two months to climb Fitzroy by a new route, and for Yvon the low point came when he slipped and drove an ice axe into his knee and had to lie on his back for fourteen days in a wet down bag inside a dim snow cave with a low ceiling. That ordeal had marked what he thought of as one of the key passages in his life, his thirtieth birthday. Now, exactly twenty years later, he and Doug were back in their old playground. And although Yvon didn't realize it yet, he had set himself up for a reminder that just as adventure is the elixir of youth, it can also be the harsh mistress of age.

Two days later, as we motored up a narrow fiord under a heavy blanket of gray cloud, we had to estimate from a dead-reckoned position where we thought the rock tower rose above the peninsula. We indicated to the fishermen to let us off on a forlorn toehold of land along the otherwise sheer-sided fiord. They rowed us ashore one at a time in a waterlogged skiff with barely two inches of freeboard. The fishermen then weighed anchor and waved to us as they disappeared into a squall line that marched down the fiord with such force it blew a wall of spindrift a hundred feet high.

"Well, boys," Yvon said when the fishing boat was gone. "We've cut the cord."

The nearest human habitation was seventy miles away over wind-raked water. We had made no arrangements for the fishermen to return, and they were the only people in the world who had more than a vague idea where we were.

We only hoped we were in the right place. We pitched our tents among the Antarctic beech trees and stretched a tarp over our outdoor kitchen. The next day the rain let up, but clouds still obscured the peak, or at least what we hoped was the peak. Then we noticed to windward a single hole in the clouds speeding in our direction.

"It might open for a few seconds," I said as I ran to the streambed near camp that allowed an open view. We waited as the hole passed overhead and then sped toward the peninsula. A few seconds later, through a thinning in the clouds, we glimpsed a vertical wall of rock. In another second the sky opened further to reveal a stunning rock spire, covered in fresh rime ice, directly above our camp.

"That's an improvement over our record in Bhutan," I told Yvon and Doug.

We returned to our kitchen and decided in the morning to carry and then cache our climbing equipment at the base of the peak. The beech forests of the west coast of Patagonia are notoriously famous as some of the thickest in the world, and it took four hours of crawling under and over knotted roots and branches to get above the tree line. Then we entered the zone of the even more notorious Patagonian winds. At the latitudes between fifty and sixty degrees south, prevailing westerlies blow across the great southern ocean without interruption until they slam into the Patagonian Andes. There they race up, down, and around the fiords and peaks in shrieking williwaw gusts that hit so quick and so hard they feel like hammer blows.

With the wind at our backs each step required a braking action with our legs to keep from being blown down. We found a secure cache for our gear and then faced the job of the return hike. We lowered our heads into the wind and pushed forward. Each step was like leg-pressing a hundred pounds. It was blowing sufficiently hard to pick rocks off the ground and hurl them through the air.

"This wind," Yvon yelled, "is the kind . . . you bite into . . . and chew."

Back in camp, we watched the rain sheet off our kitchen tarp. Three days passed, then four, then five. Between williwaws we jogged back and forth on the short cobblestone shoreline next to camp to stay warm. At low tide we gathered mussels and steamed them by the potful for lunch and dinner. Six days, seven, eight. Next to our kitchen the midden of accumulating mussel shells grew higher. Twice the altimeter showed a three-hundred-foot drop in altitude—the biggest barometric change any of us had ever witnessed—and the only visible shift in the weather was a drop in the wind speed, judging by its sound, to perhaps only fifty miles an hour.

Nine days, ten. Doug had to be back to work at Esprit in another couple of weeks. We knew we would need a week for our return kayak passage. We resolved to scramble to the base of the peak and come rain, wind, or snow, climb as high as we could. Getting an early start, we returned to our cache, loaded our packs, and ascended a glacier to the base of the rock wall. We were on the lee side of the spire, and as I looked up the rock the madcap winds spun in vortexes that drove the icy rain straight up. Where the spire disappeared into the clouds, occasional thinnings revealed the higher rock was covered in fresh rime. Even at the base of the spire, standing only three feet apart, the wind was so strong it forced us to yell to be heard.

"It looks grim," I shouted.

Doug agreed. Yvon didn't say anything one way or the other.

"I've come here to climb," Jim yelled. "Let's get in at least a couple of pitches."

He started to uncoil the rope. "Anyone going with me?"

"Yeah, I'll go," Yvon yelled.

Jim started climbing. The wind was so strong the rope arced off his waist and down to Yvon's belay without touching the rock, suspended in the air as though bewitched by a snake charmer; I could tell from Jim's effort that the pull on the rope alone was making the climbing difficult, notwithstanding the driving sleet and near-vertical angle of the spire. Jim finished the first pitch, then belayed Yvon who led the next pitch over a bulge that looked difficult. Ice water sheeted down the rock and then blew back up in the gusts, soaking them both. The climbing was so slow it didn't make sense for Doug and me to follow, so we stood at the base, stamping our feet in the snow and waving our arms to stay warm; neither of us thought they would keep going. Then Jim and Yvon completed two more pitches. It was five in the afternoon, and it would be dark by nine. They were perhaps one-third of the way, maybe less, and they had no bivouac gear. Finally they disappeared into the clouds.

"Let's climb around the other side," Doug yelled. "Maybe there's a better route."

By the time we were around the other side of the spire and up a few hundred feet, it was seven o'clock. The rock was steep and loose, and on the windward side we could only move one foot or one hand at a time for fear a gust might tear us off the rock. We gave up and descended. It was dark when we got back to the col, and there was no sign of Jim and Yvon.

"Maybe they rappelled down the other side," Doug said.

"I hope so. It'd be a grim bivouac."

"Let's go back to camp. I bet they're there."

The speed of the wind had increased, and we had to lean head down and push hard to make each step. In the beech thickets we crawled through boot-sucking bogs and cut our hands on sharp-edged leaves.

"I'm sure those guys are in camp, drinking tea," Doug said.

It was just after midnight when we found camp. As we approached we could see there was no light from either candles or flashlights.

"They're asleep," Doug said as we approached the tents. "Hey, Fig. Wake up. Fig?"

There was no reply. Both tents were empty. We slumped under the plastic trap and picked at some food, then went to bed. Doug crawled into his tent and I heard him say to himself, as though Yvon were there next to him, "You'll be okay, Fig."

I crawled into my sleeping bag. Alone in the tent, I went to sleep recalling the image of Jonathan dying in my arms. By then it had been eight years since the avalanche, and the image of Jonathan came back to me only infrequently. Now it was as real as the day he died.

I fell asleep, and when I opened my eyes I could see that the yellow fabric of the tent had a faint amber glow. It was getting light. For a second I thought Yvon was in the tent, but I looked over and saw only the limp form of his empty sleeping bag. Then I had an image of Yvon's and Jim's bodies at the base of the tower, crumpled in the rocks like rag dolls. I tried to exorcise it, but it kept coming back. Outside I could hear Doug in the cooking area clanking a pot, getting ready to make tea.

"Doug, any sign of them?"

"No, it's me."

"Yvon?"

"Yeah."

"Oh, man, I'm glad to hear your voice."

"Fig, you made it!" Doug called from his tent.

As I crawled out of my tent I could see Jim arriving in camp. There was just enough light to see his pants and jackets ripped and torn, his wet hair pasted above his sunken cheeks and eyes. Yvon looked just as bad.

"There were some tough pitches," Jim said. "Five-nine, five-ten, freezing wet. We topped out about nine, then had these miserable rappels all night. We had to keep moving."

"Bivouacking would have been suicide," Yvon added.

Once they completed their rappels and were safe at the base of the spire, the wind was so strong they had to crawl down the scree on their knees. Then they had mucked through the beech forest the rest of the night.

"Oh man, I'm wiped out," Yvon said. He crawled into the tent, and in a few minutes I could hear the slow, steady breathing of his deep sleep.

The next day Yvon and Jim woke at midmorning. Jim nursed a mass of water blisters on his hands. Yvon massaged his wrists, arms, and elbows.

"I just went up there thinking I would clean his pitch," Yvon said. "By the fifth pitch I knew we were going all the way."

"How's the tendinitis?" I asked.

"If it doesn't get any worse I should be able to paddle," he said, staring blankly at the rain dripping off the plastic sheet. "Man, that was the most strung out I've been in a long time."

The next morning we assembled our kayaks and disassembled our camp. Our plan was to paddle five miles up the fiord, then into the back of a side bay. Here we would break down the boats to portage them over a pass that led to another fiord that in turn led to the wide bay that would get us back to Puerto Natales. We knew it would be safest if we could cross this bay in a following wind, and making this portage to the opposite fiord would allow us to gain an upwind position on the bay. The trade-off was that we would have to make an initial paddle up the fiord, directly into the wind. At least we could stay close to the shore, and if a williwaw flipped any of us we could crawl onto the rocks. With icebergs from tidewater glaciers sailing down the fiord, we estimated the water temperature to be in the high thirties, which in turn meant we could tread water only five to ten minutes before passing out.

We pushed off and paddled into the fiord, trying to stay close together. Jim and Doug, however, sharing a double boat, made slightly better headway than did either Yvon or I in our single kayaks. Soon the first williwaw marched down the fiord toward us, and when it hit, it pinned me against the shoreline cliff, the surge bashing my boat against the rocks until it blew by. Twenty minutes later another one hit, and I fought to stay upright. We pulled into the shelter of a tiny cove to catch our breath.

"We've got to stay on our toes," Yvon said. "This is serious stuff."

Doug and Jim left in their double kayak and disappeared around the near corner. Yvon followed perhaps two minutes later, and I was a minute behind him. As I paddled out and the full channel came into view, I could see the next williwaw had already hit Yvon, and that he had capsized. I paddled as hard as I could to reach him, but against the williwaw I could only make the slightest headway. I glanced up and saw that he was straddled across his overturned boat, working to paddle it back to the cove. I managed to turn without capsizing, and we both regained the shelter of the small cove. Yvon dragged his boat across the low-tide stones. He was already shaking, and his face had a pinched expression I had never seen before.

"We've got to be careful," he repeated in a mutter to himself.

During the last williwaw Doug and Jim, concentrating on keeping their boat into the wind, had been unable to look back. I assumed that they had found shelter in the next cove. I hiked up the cliff and along the coast until I found them not far away. They hiked back with me, and we agreed we had to camp until the williwaws subsided. Yvon was by then hypothermic, so we built a fire to warm him, then set up the tents.

Next day the wind eased a little, and we once more ventured into the fiord. By noon we gained the side bay. There we collapsed the boats to carry them to the next bay. That took two fourteen-hour days. It rained even more than usual. The boats broke down into loads of sixty pounds each, and the beech forest was so thick that in places visibility through the tangle of roots and branches was ten feet or less. Still, for the moment, anyway, we were out of danger, and in the way peculiar to expeditions, we enjoyed the miserable work.

On the other side of the portage we reassembled the kayaks, and with the wind at our backs, flew like banshees down the fiord. Then the final gauntlet came into view, the ten-mile-wide bay. We could see a lineup of williwaws marching across the open water. We decided to paddle upwind along the edge of the bay, hugging the cliffs and rocks as closely as possible, until we gained a more windward advantage. Then we would camp and, in the morning, when the wind usually abated a little, paddle into open water, raft together by seizing the grab loops on one another's boats, and let the williwaws blow us home.

We turned and paddled directly into the wind. The shoreline was a continuous cliff with no landing. Dusk was approaching. We lowered our heads and paddled with all the strength we could muster. We didn't dare miss a stroke, or let up for a second. A half hour passed. There was no landing. My hands were cramped, and I knew the others were in the same shape. Doug and Jim were ahead, and Yvon was behind. I estimated it was blowing forty or fifty knots. I didn't dare even turn my head to check on Yvon. Was his tendinitis allowing him to keep up? There was still no landing. If it got dark we would have to keep paddling. If anyone flipped, he would likely die. Then I realized I had to force such thoughts out of my mind. I concentrated on paddling, on ignoring my cramped hands, my burning arm and stomach muscles. Ahead I could see Doug and Jim disappear around the corner of the cliff. In a few minutes I was around, and I saw them beached on a tiny sandbar. In three minutes I felt the gravel rocks skid under my boat, and I turned around. Yvon was no more than fifty feet behind.

Months later, Yvon confessed that in the final fifteen minutes of that paddle he began to doubt if he could make it. He said the climbing on the trip was hard, and on the ascent of the rock spire he had pushed to the edge. But in the last minutes of our paddle he had pushed to the edge and then made one or two steps beyond. It was as close to looking into the abyss as he had been since the avalanche.

We were out of drinking water, and there was none available on the tiny toehold of gravel where we spent that night. Next morning we found a small spring, and after satisfying our thirst, we paddled into the bay and rafted together as we had planned. Yvon was on one side of the double kayak and I was on the other, so that the three boats made a kind of kayak trimaran. When the williwaws hit we charged along at six or seven knots, surfing down the wind waves and steering with our rudders. When we arrived at Puerto Natales, the only people to greet us were two kids curious to see our boats. We showed one of the kids how to push the button on our camera, then stood next to our boats for a group portrait.

"Good trip," Doug said after the picture was snapped.

"Yeah, we pulled it off," Yvon agreed.

"How's the wrist and elbow?" I asked him.

"Holding up fine. In fact, I feel great."

Yvon looked past the fishing boats tied to the pier, to the bay beyond. He was quiet, in the way he is when he's thinking. Then he grinned slightly, in the way he does when he's content.

"You know," he said, "this trip was just what I needed."

In the predawn of our last full day in Lhasa, Asia and I say farewell to Jon and Dawa. Asia gives the young Sherpa a hug, and Dawa puts a *kata* scarf around her neck.

"This is my address," he says, handing her a piece of paper. "So you please write me."

"I will," Asia says.

"And next time you come to Nepal, I will cook for you."

"I would love that," she replies.

I shake Dawa's hand, then Jon's, and they climb into the Land Cruiser with our Tibetan driver at the wheel, and leave for the airport.

"He worked so hard," Asia says after Dawa left, "getting up early and staying up late and the whole time so cheerful. What a great guy."

After breakfast Asia and I take a bicycle rickshaw through the city to the Potala, then slowly climb the wide stairs that ascend in a single switchback up the great south facade of the palace. We walk through room after room of gilded statues of Buddhas, bodhisattvas, and high lamas, most of them housed behind glass. We are in the company of tourists from Europe and America and China. The only monk we see offers to escort us, for a fee. We climb the long steps to the roof and look over the city.

"This is where Heinrich Harrer used to sit with the Dalai Lama when he was a little boy," I tell Asia. "They had a telescope, and the two of them would gaze down on the city."

"Can you imagine being here then," Asia says. "What an adventure."

I then tell Asia how Harrer was the Dalai Lama's tutor, teaching him about the outside world. But Harrer also had a partner named Peter Aufschnaiter who was with him when they escaped from the POW camp in India and walked across Tibet. In some ways I think Aufschnaiter was the more pure adventurer. Like Harrer, he was also a bold climber, and twice had nearly reached the summit of Kanchenjunga. That was in the 1920s, long before anyone had scaled an eight-thousand-meter peak. But he didn't get famous making the first ascent of the North Face of the Eiger, like Harrer did, and he didn't stay here on this rooftop with the Dalai Lama, gathering the material that would make him even more famous when he published *Seven Years in Tibet*. That's not to say Harrer didn't take every opportunity to give Aufschnaiter credit for his part in their adventure. Harrer also complimented Aufschnaiter as being a quiet man who hated small talk, and someone you could always count on when the going got tough.

"Harrer once said something that I think reveals how much he respected Aufschnaiter," I tell Asia. "In fact, I think Harrer envied Aufschnaiter a little, for the kind of self-honesty he possessed. He said that Aufschnaiter lived by a personal motto he had adopted as a young man. It was the Latin phrase *Esse Quam Videri,* and it means "To Be Rather Than to Seem.""

That evening, back at our hotel, I bid Asia a good night, then go to my room to complete my journal entry for the day. My mind returns to the roof of the Potala, to Harrer and Aufschnaiter, the one musing about the great story he is going to write, the other focused on living it. Then I question whether the difference between these two men was real. I never knew Harrer beyond his books and the few conversations we had waiting in Calcutta for the flight to Bhutan, and now I pause to consider if perhaps my take on this difference in their motivations is more a reflection of my own history.

For several years after the Everest climb in 1976, every expedition I was on became the subject of either a book or a television show. I began to gain a public reputation as a mountaineer and adventurer, and while I enjoyed the recognition, I also knew that the accomplishments of others went unsung: the climbers scaling peaks more difficult than the ones I had ascended; the adventure travelers making journeys more daring than the ones I had undertaken.

After the Minya Konka expedition in 1980, I didn't know if I would climb again at high altitude, but I did know I was going to continue to write magazine articles and books, and to produce and direct television shows. But I began to document other people's adventures rather than my own. I still took an occasional trip, such as the crossing of Borneo, where I was in front of the camera, but whenever possible I stayed behind it. After the avalanche, I resolved that whatever public recognition I received should reflect accurately what I had done, and who I was. That resolution in turn was connected to another I made following Jonathan's death, to fold into the way I lived my own life his code of exorcising from his conduct anything connected to egoism.

Still, I found it hard to live consistently by Jonathan's code, and as the years passed, I sometimes slipped. In the mid-eighties, for example, *Rolling Stone* published a profile in which they labeled me "The Real Indiana Jones." The photographer assigned to shoot the lead-in had me dress in an aloha shirt and surf trunks, then climb with crampons and an ice axe up a palm tree. I knew it was a bullshit image, but I went along with it.

Now, fifteen years later, in my hotel room in Lhasa, as I reach from my bed to the nightstand to turn out the light, I redraw the parallel between Peter Aufschnaiter and Jonathan Wright, their understanding of what Ernest Hemingway once called the importance of owning a built-in, shock-proof bullshit detector. I can't help also wondering whether Heinrich Harrer would sometimes pause to remind himself what his friend had to teach him, just as I now pause to remind myself what Jonathan gave me.

Esse Quam Videri.

Part 3

Kham
July 1999

11

Twenty years ago the only hotel in Chengdu, the largest city in Sichuan, was a seven-story concrete block of proletarian functionalism called the Jin Jiang. Today there is a huge Holiday Inn elegant in everything but name; there is the Dynasty, the Min Shan, the Chengdu, all four- and five-star hotels.

To help invoke memories of my first visit, Asia and I check into the Jin Jiang. Sometime in the intervening twenty years it has undergone a remake as startling as the modernization of the city itself. The uniformed doorman salutes as we enter a lobby with a marble floor and crystal chandelier perhaps fifteen feet in diameter. In 1980, four years after the end of the Cultural Revolution, the floor was concrete and the walls painted in the pale institutional green then favored by both Chinese and Russian communists. There was a ten-foot sign at the entrance to the dining hall that had a portrait of a young woman with a wan face looking at three plates of food, and above her, in English, "Welcome You! Good Service, Rich Supply." At the desk our liaison officer had given us registration forms, and under "Occupation" Yvon had entered "Capitalist."

"Finally I'm in a place that can appreciate what I really am," he said.

The liaison officer read the form and nodded toward Yvon. "Ah, Mr. Chouinard, you are a capitalist. Very good! This means you also are very rich?"

"Yes," Yvon said, looking amused. "Very rich."

In the morning Asia and I have breakfast in the former dining hall of Good Service and Rich Supply, now renamed the Louvre Garden. We are escorted by a hostess in a French country dress with puffed sleeves to a table covered with a crisp, white cloth, surrounded by large, potted ficus. Behind the table, framed by the ficus plants, is a five-foot Eiffel Tower. The extensive buffet is presented on a series of ersatz carts, each with four polished brass poles supporting awnings striped in the blue, red, and white tricolor. In 1980 the walls of this same room were painted the same green as the rest of the hotel, and for breakfast we were served a grisly meat covered in reddish oil and green thousand-year-old eggs suspended in yellow suet.

"Oh, boy," one of our teammates had said when he sat down, "my favorite: bacon and eggs."

By that point of our earlier expedition we had been in China over a week, and each day had been an encapsulated adventure. On arrival our plane had stopped in Shanghai, then the largest municipality in the world, and as we made the nighttime approach there was hardly a light to be seen over the city. In Peking, as it was still called in English in those days, the wide streets were filled with tens of thousands of bicycles, and the cacophony of honking horns had yet to eclipse the ring-ring-ringing of thousands of noisemakers on bicycle handlebars.

We departed Peking in a train pulled by a steam locomotive. I shared an elegant prerevolution stateroom with Jonathan and Peter Pilafian. Our stateroom was made of hardwood aged to a deep, rich red, the dinette table was covered with a white cloth crocheted with delicate patterns, and on top of it a small porcelain bowl, hand-painted with a Chinese landscape, held a miniature juniper tree. Sipping jasmine tea, we watched the sunset as we crossed the Huang, the Yellow River. We entered northern Sichuan at dawn, and the pretty stewardess who attended our staterooms told us we would arrive in Chengdu by nightfall. The train climbed into the mountains and entered a narrow canyon. Our window was open, and although the warm air carried specks of coal dust from the billowing locomotive, it felt good blowing through the thin fabric of my shirt.

We read books and told stories from our past adventures. I related my first voyage to the South Seas, telling them about the paradise island with the barrier reef that had no passage, and the clouds in the sky that picked up turquoise off the lagoon.

"Every once in a while I think about that trip," I said, "and the image of that island comes back, like a little poem I had memorized when I was a kid."

"Do you remember it?" Jonathan asked.

I recited my childhood rhyme, and when I finished Jonathan and Peter sat back in their cushioned benches and watched the countryside roll by for a few moments, until our stewardess, wearing her official railway cap cocked at a coquettish angle, brought us another thermos of hot tea.

"Can you say that poem again?" Jonathan asked.

Again I recited my rhyme:

> "I should like to rise and go,
> Where the golden apples grow,
> Where below another sky,
> Parrot islands anchored lie,
> And watched by cockatoos and goats,
> Lonely Crusoes build their boats."

Jonathan smiled as he looked out the window. We were following a slow-moving river reflecting in jade green the trees at water's edge. I spotted an osprey in a cottonwood. We passed a lone fisherman in a wide straw hat working his punt pole from the boat's stern while in the bow his fishing cormorant stood alert and ready.

"That's what we're looking for, isn't it?" Jonathan said, still smiling, still looking out the window. "An island below another sky."

After breakfast Mr. Meng, our new guide, arrives in a late-model, four-wheel-drive Nissan. With him is our interpreter, a middle-aged woman who is a geology professor at the local university. A small delivery truck, loaded with food and camp supplies, pulls up behind, and we are introduced to its driver, and also to a young man in his late teens who will be our cook. Although now handicapped with bad knees, Meng was once an active mountaineer—he has scaled Minya Konka, or Gonggha Shan, as the Chinese call the peak. Meng is about five foot four, and has a compact build, similar to Yvon's. Meng's hands, also like Yvon's, are oversize and scarred from a lifetime of climbing. He has a smile that won't go away, and Asia and I take an immediate liking to him. Through the interpreter, he tells us he remembers meeting me here at the Jin Jiang Hotel in 1980, and he also remembers Jonathan, adding that he and the other climbers in Chengdu were saddened when they learned of his death. Asia and I both thank him for that consideration, load in the Nissan, and leave.

Meng, who drives the Nissan, tells us not to worry about the political situation.

"Mr. Meng says there will be no problems," the interpreter tells us.

"If it is possible," I say, "I would still like to drive all the way to Luba in one day."

Luba is close to the end of the road and the start of the trail to Minya Konka. The interpreter passes this to Meng, who nods.

"Mr. Meng says, 'No problem.'"

It takes two minutes, perhaps less, to regret my request. Meng grips the wheel with his powerful hands, and we race through traffic, honking our horn every ten to fifteen seconds. Out of habit imbued during our month driving across the Chang Tang, I look back to check on the small truck, and see that it is racing to keep up. Meng's smile widens to an amused grin as pedestrians run and cars swerve to avoid our approach. The truck, still trying to keep pace, is stopped by the police for speeding, and Meng, seeing this in his rearview mirror, pulls over and waits. When the police leave, the truck pulls up behind us, and the driver walks to Meng's window, where they have a short exchange. Meng starts laughing, and the truck driver, sullen and apparently angry, returns to his vehicle. Meng starts the Nissan's engine, and as we leave, he is still shaking his head in mirth.

"What's so funny?" I ask the interpreter.

"The truck driver says the fine he has to pay the police is more money than he will make from this job. Mr. Meng thinks this is very funny."

After an hour driving at high speed, we are still within the light-industrial zone of the city's perimeter. It is hard to imagine that Chengdu has expanded to these dimensions in only twenty years. In 1980, we were outside the city in half an hour (and at half the speed). We merge onto an expressway complete with toll booths, and in two hours arrive in Yaan, a passage that in 1980 had taken a complete day. There are high-rise office buildings in the city center, and nothing looks familiar. I recall twenty years ago we spent the night in an old government building converted to a guest house, freshly painted for our arrival. I had the beginning of a flu, and had asked Jonathan if we could share a room. He carried my pack upstairs. Our room had a high ceiling with floral designs molded in the overhead plaster, two night pots, a hall tree with clothes hangers made of steam-bent bamboo, and two four-poster beds, each with an ornately carved canopy that supported mosquito netting.

"Early Boxer Rebellion," Jonathan said.

I swallowed two tablets of aspirin against a growing fever, and lay down. It was an hour before dark, and Jonathan left with his cameras. I awoke when he returned.

"I don't think they've seen many foreigners here," he reported. "I was the Pied Piper followed by three hundred kids, maybe four hundred; I don't know, but it was a pack over two blocks long. I got some good shots."

He left again to join the others for dinner. When he came back, I awoke but didn't speak to him. My fever had reached a point where my vision was starting to distort. Thinking I was asleep, Jonathan quietly undressed, lifted the mosquito netting, and crawled into his bed. Soon I could hear him breathing steadily, making a slight sigh with each exhale. I turned and looked at him. His head, arched over the pillow and framed by the blanket folded back under his chin, was illuminated by the pale light through the room's one window. He was sleeping with his mouth open, and his breathing stopped, started again, stopped, started. This image of him, diffused by the gossamer veil of the mosquito netting, looked funereal, and I found it so disconcerting I looked away.

A few weeks later, on our way home, we stayed again in the same guest house, and I stayed again in the same room. This time, however, I was with Yvon, and he moaned from the pain of his broken ribs as he lay down. I told him about my previous fever, about my distorted vision, about Jonathan's face.

"He looked different, in a way I'd never seen him before," I said to Yvon. "I realize now it was how he looked just after he died."

Mr. Meng speeds through Yaan, and outside town the floodplains of Sichuan give way to the first hills that precede the high ranges that include Minya Konka. While these mountains lie past the eastern terminus of the Himalayas, they nevertheless share the same orogeny and similar vegetation: thickly forested slopes of pine, fir, hemlock, and spruce; and at higher elevations, oak and rhododendron. Minya Konka is also among the first mountains to lie in the path of the continental monsoon. It is unfortunate that we have to make our ascent after the monsoon's onset. I'm still hoping this year it might be mild, but the rain, snow, and hail we have encountered this last month and a half suggest just the opposite.

Past Yaan we are forced to take a long detour that checkmates any hope of reaching the trailhead in one day. But I am no longer concerned about anti-American sentiments among the villagers. Just as Meng predicted, on the few occasions we have stopped to stretch our legs, the locals have paid us no heed. I've promised myself on this last leg of our journey not to worry about things that may not happen, yet I can't clear my mind of the latest concern, and that is Meng. Is he alert? As we drive into the rainy night, I lean forward from the backseat every ten minutes or so to ask him if he's okay. Each time he nods and says, "Okay." Then I ask myself if once again I am fretting too much. No, I'm responsible for Asia, and I also recall two friends I have lost in two different car crashes in remote places just trying to get to the mountains.

"Okay?"

"Yes, okay!"

If I'm irritating him, at least that may help keep him awake. I'm relieved when finally, at midnight, we stop in a nondescript town and check into a nondescript hotel. I carry my pack to my room, set the alarm for five, and get into bed. It is firm, thank God, but the pillow is a cylinder about twelve inches in diameter and so hard it would make an effective weapon. I get up, pull my fleece pullover out of my pack, get back in bed and fold the garment under my head. I'm drifting to sleep when I hear a knock on the door.

"Yeah?"

"It's me, Asia."

"What's up?"

"There's a spider in my bathroom."

I get dressed and open the door.

"I'm sorry," she says.

"That's okay," I say, and I mean it. Asia follows me across the hall and stays in her bedroom while I go into the bathroom.

"Holy shit!"

"Do you see it?"

"This sucker's as big as a plate."

It's not quite that big, but its long legs would span my hand if stretched out, and it crabs across the floor as I take it out with a whip-snap of Asia's bath towel. I go back in the bedroom and ask her if she's okay. She assures me she is, but she looks shaken.

"You want to stay in my room?" I ask, remembering her bug phobia. "I can sleep on the floor."

"No, I'm okay now that it's dead."

"Well, just come over if you get uncomfortable."

I go to the door, and I'm just out the room when Asia asks what time it is.

"Something like twelve-thirty or one."

"Then it's my birthday."

I walk back in the room and give her a hug. "Happy twenty years old."

"Thanks."

"You sure you're okay?"

"Yeah, I am, really. Don't worry."

Next morning we leave before dawn. We are quiet in the vehicle, and as soon as there is enough light to see the hills and the river we are following, I once again wish Asia a happy birthday.

"Thanks," she says. "I opened my card from Grandma last night. She sent me twenty bucks." Asia's grandmother had sent me the sealed card before we left, and I gave it to Asia a few days ago, telling her, as her grandmother requested, not to open it until today.

"We can have a party," I say, "if we get to Luba in time. It may be too late, though; we'll have to see."

"That's okay," Asia replies. "This is birthday enough. The whole trip has been birthday enough."

At noon we arrive in the small city of Kanding, and stop for lunch. This place, too, has grown beyond recognition. In former days it was famous across Asia as the trading gateway between China and Tibet.

"This town used to be called Tatsienlu," I tell our interpreter, who passes this information to Meng.

"Mr. Meng says he's never heard that name."

"Tell him it is the Tibetan name that was used before the revolution."

"Mr. Meng asks if you are sure of this," comes the reply.

"Yes. Tell him it is described in many books."

I am surprised Meng doesn't know this, considering he has been coming here for over thirty years. But his unfamiliarity with the history illustrates how thoroughly the region has changed since the revolution. In 1932, when four Harvard students, on their way to make the first ascent of Minya Konka, arrived in Tatsienlu, they saw long trains of yaks coming down from the Tibetan plateau with sacks of salt and stacks of animal hides, which then returned with bricks of pressed tea. This tea arrived from the lowlands carried by porters who bore loads that weighed as much as three hundred pounds.

Even in 1980, part of old Tatsienlu still remained. There was a fairy-tale tower on one end of town topped with a square roof with upturned gables, and many of the houses were the same two-story wood structures, with potted geraniums on the window ledges, that the Harvard students saw on their visit. Now, however, the river that rushes through the center of town is crowded on both banks with concrete apartment and office buildings ten to twenty stories high. I don't begrudge the Chinese the need to replace the old buildings—although I believe the townfolk would have been served better if the old tower had been restored instead of destroyed—but this conversion to modern architecture is difficult to accept when the new buildings are so ugly, and already so cracked and crumbling.

Kanding marks the beginning of the region of eastern Tibet known as Kham, and we see a few Khampas walking the streets among the throngs of Han Chinese. The men are easy to recognize by their unusual height—most of them are six feet or taller—and by the red yarn braided in their hair. In 1980, when we spent the night here, Yvon and I had walked into a shop selling sundries, to see what kind of clothes they offered. (Yvon was always on the hunt for design ideas for Patagonia.) Inside there were two Khampa men, the first we had seen. They wore full-length *chuba* robes made of sheepskin, ornately embroidered felt mucklucks, and wide cummerbunds that held large knives. They were tall and straight-backed, wore their hair in long braids, and their demeanor was evocative of the American Plains Indians in the Edward Curtis photographs. Unlike everybody else we had seen up to then, these two Khampas not only avoided staring at us, but didn't even give us the deference of a glance. They left the shop arms over each other's shoulders; we could hear them laughing as they disappeared down the road.

I would learn later they were typical. The Khampas are the fiercist warriors in Tibet, and their resistance to the Chinese is legion. "Khampas are braver than the inhabitants of Lhasa, who have a great respect for them," Heinrich Harrer wrote. "They are real daredevils, and their knives come out at the slightest provocation."

We leave Kanding on a paved road that zigzags up switchbacks out of the steep canyon. Above the tree line, the hills are covered with stunted rhododendron that hold small, purple flowers. We enter the clouds, and in an hour reach a pass marked by prayer flags and a stone altar, freshly whitewashed, that issues smoke from smoldering juniper boughs. None of this was here in 1980. Back then, only four years after the death of Mao and the arrest of the Gang of Four, the hinterlands of China, and nearly all of Tibet, had yet to receive word of the new regime's liberalizations, and there were few overt indications of Buddhist beliefs or practices.

We descend only a short distance before we are in a wide valley; its bordering hills are open and treeless. We are back in Tibet, and in a few minutes we pass the first Khampa houses. They are substantial structures, three stories high, built of finely chiseled slabs of stone fitted with a thin masonry into smooth walls that lean inward with a slight but pleasing trapezoidal slope. The upper floors have framed windows paneled with latticework colored in muted reds, greens, and yellows. Some of these houses are said to be two and three hundred years old, and not a single one appears in disrepair.

We pass a junction that looks familiar. Meng confirms it is the road to Lhasa, and I tell Asia I recognize it as the same place where in 1980 one of our teammates asked the driver to stop, made a cardboard sign that said "Lhasa," then walked to the junction and stuck out his thumb. We take the lesser fork that soon converts to dirt, and pass a compound of houses surrounded by a head-high wall of whitewashed stones that I also recognize.

"Asia, see that graffiti on that wall?" It is now too weathered to decipher, but I explain to her that twenty years ago it was still recognizable as a crudely drawn scene of airplanes dropping bombs on a village. We knew it had to represent the so-called Kanding rebellion, when the Khampas in this region rose with their knives and matchlocks against the Chinese, who responded by bombing the towns and villages.

"Our liaison officer back then also knew what the graffiti meant," I tell Asia, "and he was pissed when we photographed it."

"Is this true?" our interpreter asks.

"That he got mad at us?"

"No, that we dropped bombs on these villages?"

"Yes, it is true."

I can see that she considers my reply with the same skepticism Meng considered my statement about the old name for Kanding. The interpreter doesn't ask any more questions, and I let the subject drop. I am thinking, however, about another incident that must have happened very near here. We had stopped in front of one of these Khampa houses to stretch our legs, and as happened everywhere, a large crowd gathered. Jonathan happened to have in his hand his string of prayer beads—the same beads Asia now has with her. He was advancing them through his fingers, as Tibetan Buddhists do when they recite their mantras, when an old man noticed and cried out in surprise.

The entire crowd responded in a buzz of gossip, and it was clear to us they were both amazed at our outward display of their religion, and yet careful not to react with too much enthusiasm. Jonathan handed the beads to the old man, who at first wouldn't take them but was eventually persuaded. Then he slowly advanced them through his fingers, his lips moving silently in prayer. In the back of the crowd, a young and very tall Khampa watched us carefully; he had the same fierce look of self-confidence I had seen in the two Khampas in the store in Kanding. I knew he was a warrior. He caught me looking at him, and his eyes held mine as he removed his hand from the fold of his *chuba,* lifted his fist above the crowd, and raised his thumb directly in the air.

Jonathan wanted to give the beads to the old man, but Edgar, our other cameraman, knew how much they meant to him. Edgar took from his pack a book on Tibetan religion, cut from the inside cover a color plate of Buddha, and handed it to the old man who stared at it briefly, then tucked it inside his tattered coat and clasped Edgar's and then Jonathan's hands. By then he had tears in his eyes. That night Jonathan wrote in his journal: "The surface of the culture has been changed and even destroyed, but that which is in a man's heart can never be taken. I have seldom seen such deep joy as I saw on the face of that old man. If this trip ended tomorrow, it would be complete."

Asia and I look out the window as we track a river swollen with brown floodwater that widens as we continue downstream. The closing hills are covered with pine. We turn up a lateral canyon, and as we gain elevation fir replaces the pine. We pass a small village that I recognize as Luba.

"The first place that looks the same," I tell Asia. "We camped in that courtyard, and spent two days organizing our gear, then loaded it on about twenty horses and started the trek to Base Camp."

In 1980 this was as far as the road was plowed. Now we continue upvalley, and after about ten miles Meng indicates a side drainage we can see a half mile farther away.

"Mr. Meng says that is where the trail to Gonggha Shan begins."

Meng drives another hundred yards, then stops at a Khampa house whose owner is standing in front. Meng motions him over, and the Khampa leans in the window. He is fit-looking, maybe thirty years old, and he has intelligent but critical eyes. Meng speaks to him in Chinese, but the Khampa doesn't answer.

"What did Meng say to him?" I ask our interpreter.

"If we can spend the night, and then if he can rent us horses for the morning."

I have the feeling the Khampa is taking our measure before he decides how to respond to Meng's request. After a moment he takes his cigarette from his mouth, flicks the ash, then speaks to Meng.

"What did he say?" I ask our interpreter.

"He said, 'No problem.'"

We follow our host through a door that opens to an enclosure that during the day is the stable for the milking cows. At night the animals come inside; they occupy the ground level of the house; the people live on the upper two floors. (This is the same floor plan Sherpas use in their houses, which may be more than coincidence. The Sherpas' oral history speaks of a migration by their people five or six hundred years ago from Kham to their present-day homeland in the Khumbu, and "Sherpa" means "People of the East.") We cross the stable on planks bridging an ankle-deep mix of manure and mud, past a Tibetan mastiff that barks furiously as it lurches against a chain that stops it about two feet short of mauling us. This is a major test of Asia's equanimity, and even though I stay directly in front of her, she is nearly in tears when we get to the other side.

We enter the house and grope in the dark trying to follow our host. Our feet make sucking sounds with each step as we pull them out of the mud, and there is the ammonia smell of manure and urine. I bump into a cow that doesn't budge, so I run my hand along her back as I feel my way past, then take hold of her horns as I move by her head, to make sure she doesn't turn suddenly and impale me.

"Hold her horns as you move by," I say to Asia.

"You sure she's a she?"

"Yeah, don't worry. She's tame."

We locate the stairs, and in a moment we're up into the refuge of the second floor, the main living quarters. Our host motions us to sit on a low bench around an open hearth, and introduces himself. His name is Tashi, and he has a daughter who looks about five and a son who looks seven. Both kids have inherited their father's intelligent eyes. Tashi's wife, perhaps in her late twenties, has broad cheekbones and open, dark eyes, and is stunningly beautiful. She offers us black tea mixed with fresh milk and salt, and *tsampa*. Both items are personal favorites, and the taste and smell of each takes me back to 1980 in a way that is more poignant than any of the sights I have seen all day.

Tashi and Meng have a lengthy conversation, and at the end of it our interpreter translates: "Mr. Meng has told Tashi about your climbing expedition to Gonggha Shan many years ago, and about the avalanche that killed Asia's father. He then told him that Asia's father is buried on the side of Gonggha Shan, and that you are going there to find his grave. Tashi says that he is very honored to be able to help."

Asia and I look to Tashi and nod, and he nods to each of us in return. Meng and the other three Chinese with us—the interpreter, the cook, even the sullen driver of the delivery truck—have also told us they feel privileged to be part of our mission. In Meng's case, I am guessing this is, in part, because he himself is a climber. As for the others, their empathy may be rooted in their own culture's tradition of honoring ancestors. Each year, for example, on Chinese All-Souls Day, men and women make pilgrimages to their parents' graves, to tidy the sites as well as to pay homage, and what Asia and I have set out to do appears to resonate with this tradition.

Later in the evening we all spread our sleeping bags over the wood floor in front of the open hearth.

"Happy birthday," I say to Asia as I crawl into my bag. "I'm sorry we didn't have a party."

"That's okay because I've had a really good day. I've been figuring some things out."

"Like what?"

"Like what I'm going to do with the rest of my life."

"That's up there in the scale. And what did you figure?"

"I've decided I'm going to change my major to architecture and industrial design. Designing and making things, like the work I did for Yvon last summer—the snowboarding clothes."

"You're a natural there. You've also got a good intuition for the way things work," I tell her, remembering the time she reconfigured the guy lines on Dawa's tent. "But what about photography?"

"I'm thinking photography might not be the best way for me to go."

"That's one of the great things about a long trip. You start to see things in a new perspective."

"Yeah, maybe that's why the decision doesn't seem like that big a deal, where before it would have been a lot more agonizing. So maybe I've gotten that out of the trip. There's one thing I regret, though."

"What's that?"

"When we were back in the Aru, I wish I'd pushed myself to do another climb. I was scared at the time, but I should have tried harder.

"Asia, if you really want to climb more mountains, then that's just what you'll do. The wanting to is the hard part."

In the morning it takes Tashi and an in-law he has conscripted to come with us two hours to gather a half-dozen horses from the bordering hills, and another half hour to secure the loads to the wooden packsaddles. We leave, and in a half mile turn up the side drainage that leads to Minya Konka. A cuckoo bird sounds its woodwind *cuuk-koo*; we pass a solitary stand of larch, green in summer foliage, that marks the tree line, and soon the open hills are stippled with a variegation of alpine wildflowers.

I remember that this lateral valley leads to a 16,000-foot pass called the Tsumi La, and as we continue to climb our interpreter starts to slow, then calls to Tashi—she wants to ride one of the horses. I ask Asia about her asthma, because her breathing sounds more labored than usual, but she is confident she can make it.

I step up my pace so I can beat the others to the pass in order to get footage of everyone transiting this high point. As I near the top I see the tip of the prayer flagpole that marks the saddle. When I arrive, my memory tells me just where to position the tripod. I have the camera ready by the time I see Tashi approach, leading the horses, with Asia close behind. At the pass he circles the pole and prayer flags three times, the horses and Asia following, then continues downslope. Asia joins me as I break down and pack the equipment.

"Did you get the shot?"

"I got the same angle your father did when he filmed us crossing here. The shot he got was a keeper, but overall that day didn't turn out very well. At least not for me."

"What happened?"

"Jeff Foote, who was the director of the film, got sick with what sounded like the same flu bug I had earlier. In the morning he couldn't walk or even ride a horse, so we had to leave him with the locals. Since I was the producer, I thought it made sense to step in and do his job—and it was a job I really wanted to learn. I knew it wouldn't be easy, because I was also appearing on-camera. But I wanted to try. The problem was most everyone else saw it as a move on my part to horn in on Jeff and take advantage of his illness."

"Even Yvon?"

"No, I was good with Yvon, and also with your dad. But the problems started on this pass, right down there on that second switchback."

I then tell Asia that as we approached the pass with twenty horses carrying our food and equipment trudging through the snow, I saw that it was going to be a great shot. The horses were a hundred yards behind, so I stopped everybody and told them I wanted to send the camera team ahead. Then when the horses caught up I asked the climbers to step into line between the animals. I wanted a shot of both people and horses walking single file up the trail. Some of the climbers were concerned that the horses would be spooked by so many Westerners at close quarters, but I insisted, telling everybody it was just this one shot.

I huddled with Jonathan, Edgar, and Peter, who was the soundman, gave them their positions, and they left. When the Tibetan packers and their horses arrived, I let two animals pass, then stepped in line with Kim and started hiking so we had horses ahead and behind us. The others did the same. It looked like both cameras were rolling, and with the snow up to our knees I knew it was going to be an exciting shot.

"Yyeeaahhh! Yyeeaahhh! Yup! Yup!" the Tibetan packer behind us yelled.

The caravan turned the first switchback. The collar bells clanked; the horses breathed in short puffs; the packers yelped. We were fifty yards from the pass when, all of a sudden, we heard a quick neigh from a horse and a sharp whistle from one of the packers. I looked up and saw the pony in front of us sliding down the steep slope, helpless as its cargo of wooden crates scattered behind it.

"It's going to break a leg," Kim called out.

There was nothing we could do but watch. The horse struggled to regain its footing, but turned turtle, its legs pawing the air. Then, as quickly as it started, the horse stopped. It lay motionless as two of the packers plunged through the snow until they reached it. They bent over and examined it, but the horse didn't move.

"It's either dead, or hurt bad," Kim said.

Suddenly the horse rolled to its belly, worked up on its front legs, then stood on its back legs. We cheered as the Tibetans led the animal uphill. They retrieved the scattered cargo, and in a few minutes had the horse reloaded. We continued toward the pass. Kim and I arrived first and waited for the others. When they caught up, I asked them to wait so we could get a shot of the horses crossing.

"Film it without us," one of team said as he hiked past. "We're not going to be party to any horse injuries."

"They think our bright clothing spooked the horses," Yvon told me as he walked by.

I explain to Asia that that evening several of the others all but ostracized me, blaming me for creating the situation that spooked the horse. They were also upset by the way I took over the job from Jeff, then ordered them to stage the scene crossing the pass. I asked Jonathan what I should do, and he recommended a "criticism session" like the Chinese have, so I could hear how the others felt. I got an earful, but rather than showing contrition I just got pissed off. I reminded them that the film was paying for the expedition and that they had a moral obligation to cooperate. Then I remembered that they all worked for the same guide service in the Tetons, and I felt as though they were dumping on me as the outsider. When he was asked his opinion, Jonathan offered that we did need someone to take the director's place—to conduct interviews, make sure all the scenes were filmed properly, to verify we had all the pieces the editor would need—and that I was the logical choice. He said he was sure we would be able to make the film and climb the mountain without conflict, as long as we listened to one another.

"Looking back on it now," I tell Asia, "I can see part of my problem was just how much I wanted to be a successful filmmaker. On K2 I had learned that if I put my mind to a goal and just kept after it, I could get wherever I wanted to go. I had learned a lot about tenacity but still didn't know anything about diplomacy, or even more, about putting myself in others' positions. Looking back on it now, I can see I was acting like a total jerk."

"Well, you've changed a lot since then."

"I changed a lot after your father died."

12

Asia leaves to catch up with Tashi and the horses, and I stay for a moment on the pass, looking into the next drainage where I can see on the far side, disappearing into the clouds, the lower flank of Minya Konka. I'm not sure, but I may also see the bottom of the buttress where the avalanche stopped, and if I'm right, that means I can also see the place where Jonathan is buried. To refresh my memory I've brought photographs of the buttress that show the position of the grave, but they're in a duffel on the back of one of the horses. We'll have another view of the mountain when we reach the Konka Gompa—the monastery on a hillside above the terminus of the glacier descending off the peak— and from there, weather permitting, I should be able to cross-reference the photographs to the features on the mountain.

I wait a few minutes, then pick up my pack and leave. The trail descends in switchbacks into a blanket of monsoon clouds that has filled the valley. I'm in a reflective mood, and the mist secures my sense of solitude. The last time I walked this path I was coming uphill, my arm in a sling. Yvon was behind me, his breath shortened by the pain in his ribs, and Kim farther behind him. We had trussed his torso with two foam pads, reinforced his knees with elastic bandages, and had given him two ski poles to hike with. He moved in halting steps, and two people walked next to him to lend additional support. His lips were tight, and his blue eyes, clouded with morphine, seemed to focus on the middle distance, even when you talked to him.

By then I was coming out of the first shock of the avalanche and beginning to feel the pervasive sorrow that was to frame my days for many months to come. On the hike out, there was no thought of the film, or of my duties. The last footage had been exposed when Edgar tried to film Kim starting out, but when he saw how much pain he was in, he lowered the camera.

"I don't want to do this," he said.

"Then don't," I answered.

Once we were home, I assumed that the Minya Konka film would be canceled by the network. I was surprised when I learned they wanted to finish it, and relieved when it turned out to be a sensitive tribute to Jonathan. I received offers from the networks both to direct and produce more adventure films. Eight months after the avalanche I documented a team of handicapped kids climbing Mount Rainier, and it proved an inspirational story that was also welcome antidote to the pain I still felt from Jonathan's death. I remained hesitant to film more difficult ascents, however, until I accepted the offer to coproduce the film on Dick and Frank's attempt on Everest, and after that I continued to make adventure films for the next two decades.

In the eighties I directed one documentary of a rafting team descending a remote river in the Soviet Union before the breakup, and another team descending a river in Tajikistan after the breakup. I documented two extreme skiers descending Denali, in Alaska, and six extreme explorers dog-mushing across Antarctica. On all these jobs I was content staying behind the camera, and even though I wasn't part of the team, I was still having the experiences. In the nineties, as I continued to make these films, several experiences affected me deeply enough that I wanted to share them with Asia.

The first was a trip to film four climbers scaling a granite tusk in the Upper Orinoco in an even more remote corner of the Amazon Basin than my first expedition there with Mike Hoover. We journeyed upriver until we reached the last Yanomami village in an area that had been contacted for the first time by outsiders only ten years before. The entire village—perhaps fifty people—walked to river's edge as we pulled up in our canoes. All of them were naked except for a narrow crimson cloth covering their genitals.

We had several Yanomami we had brought with us from downriver villages to help porter our equipment to the base of the spire, including one who had worked a number of years with an anthropologist and knew how to speak Spanish. I calculated we needed one more porter to get all our equipment through the jungle to the mountain, so through the Spanish speaker I asked the chief of the village if there was anyone he could recommend to come with us.

"Tell the chief we will be gone about one month," I told the interpreter.

The chief nodded, then pointed to a young man standing in the semicircle naked save for his narrow loin cloth and the bow and arrows in his hands.

"The chief says that man can go with us," the interpreter said.

"Terrific. Now tell the chief we will wait here while this man goes back to his hut and gets his things."

The interpreter translated this to the chief, but the chief shook his head and spoke back to the interpreter.

"The chief says he already has his things."

Without even saying good-bye to anyone, our new porter stepped into one of the canoes, climbing over our dozen duffels full of dried food, extra clothing, camera gear, and about three hundred pounds of climbing equipment. When he found a place to sit, we left.

We still had another thirty miles or so to travel before we started overland, and that would be through a region completely uninhabited, so remote even the Yanomami considered it wild. We had been warned by an old jungle hand that because this area was certain to have good hunting, the Yanomami might at any time abandon their porter loads to run after game, but that was a risk we had to take.

Each day the tributaries narrowed. We lay in the boats watching the jungle squeeze out the open sky until finally the canopy closed over our heads. A huge anaconda crossed in front of our boat and then swam into a tangle of roots along the edge of the water. Our new porter sat in the same canoe I was in, and one day he leaned back and laid his head in my lap. I started to flinch, then told myself that was an acculturated reaction, so I relaxed. He nestled until his head was comfortable. His skin was lightly oiled and smelled sweet. I placed my hand on his head, and in a minute he was asleep.

Eventually the deadfall across the tributary was too thick to justify the work required to cut it with machetes, so we shored the boats and started over land through untracked primary forest. On the second day I was following one of the Yanomami when suddenly he dropped his pack and, with bow and arrows in hand, dashed into the jungle.

There goes the first one, I thought.

I dropped my own pack and followed, taking care not to make any noise that might alert whatever it was he was stalking. Then, through the understory of spindly tree trunks, I caught sight of him standing in a shaft of light with his bow poised. Then I heard them: a troop of monkeys perhaps a hundred yards distant. The Yanomami made a call that mimicked the monkeys. Then he dropped his shoulders and began a monkey pantomime. The curious animals started to approach. The Yanomami continued his monkey dance and monkey calls. The monkeys continued their approach. Suddenly in one motion the Yanomami straightened, drew the bow, and released the arrow. The howling monkeys went wild, but the shot missed and the troop leapt away safely through the canopy. Then in the next instant the Yanomami turned and looked directly at me. He had known all along I was standing there, watching him. Then he smiled and starting laughing.

A few days later we arrived at the base of the spire, and when we started the first pitches, the Yanomami, watching from the ground, pointed and laughed; our climbing was one of the silliest things they had ever seen. It took five days to climb the spire. On the last day we bivouacked on a ledge just below the summit. There was a growing moon, illuminating on the horizon towering cumulus that also lit internally every few minutes with bright flashes of lightning. The saber wings of the nightjars sliced the air above our heads as they hawked their insect prey. Below, the moonlit canopy spread like a textured carpet over an undulating floor. The clouds, the jungle, the mountain, they each and together were just as they had been through the millennia, just as they had been when the first men, pushing each generation farther south, arrived here nine or ten thousand years ago. Like the jungle and the mountains, those men looked then as they did now. They looked like the monkey dancer.

There was something in seeing that Yanomami luring the monkeys that stayed with me. Sitting that night on the bivouac ledge, the image of him came back, and it gave me a chill. It wasn't until I was returned to my own world, however, that I figured it out. In that shaft of light in the jungle I had watched the Yanomami embody the behavior of a wild animal and, for the first time in my life, I had seen the ancient, wild creature that lives within all of us.

Four years later I had another journey that allowed me to *feel* what it was like when the only thing that separated us and the other wild animals were the spears in our hands. A climbing friend who lives in East Africa proposed we make a traverse of Kilimanjaro, ascending the Tanzanian side and descending into Kenya. Because of political tensions between the countries, no one had been allowed to do that for many years, but the two governments had recently initiated a rapprochement, and my friend had won permission to make the traverse.

"But the top of the mountain is where the trip only starts," he said.

His idea was to descend the mountain and keep walking east, along the small rivulets that gather and grow and feed into the Tsavo River. We would follow hippo trails that border the water as it flows fast and straight through wild bush country. After the Tsavo joins the Athi, and the river conflows with the Galana, we would continue on animal trails until the river leaves the parklands and becomes known as the Sabaki. We would then follow trails between villages set on the banks of slow, bending oxbows, until finally the waters of Kilimanjaro empty into the Indian Ocean.

"I calculate it to be about a five-hundred-kilometer walk, and much of it would be through the Tsavo parks," my friend said. "That bush country down there is uninhabited, and much of it is still without roads. You'll find that it's still quite pristine, looking pretty much as it's always looked."

I made a deal with a cable company to videotape the foot safari. It took about a month to climb the mountain and complete the walk. In Tsavo we were every day in the close company of animals that placed us a link or two down the food chain. We were every day, all day long, cautious of every step we made, receptive to every noise we heard. Three times we were charged by elephants, once to within fifty feet. We forded rivers only in the shallows where we could see the bow wakes of crocodiles. By night we listened to lions roaring outside the perimeters of our camps; by day we crept past hippos sleeping under the bush, knowing if they awoke they would charge.

I walked with an alert connection to who I was and where I was in a way I had never experienced. My first night home in California, I woke up in the middle of the night to a branch breaking outside the bedroom window, and my body tensed in response to my jet-lagged brain issuing the warning, "Lion!" It took a moment to realize where I was. By then a return to sleep was impossible. I took a bedside flashlight and went outside to see a raccoon crossing the leaves under the oak tree.

The small valley where I live a dozen miles inland from the Southern California coast used to be one of the prime grizzly habitats in North America. A Spanish rancher early in the nineteenth century counted just under one hundred bears in one day. Even as late as 1882, another Spanish rancher ten miles from where I now live counted nine in one sighting. The last one in my valley was gunned down in 1905. After I got home from the Africa walk, I was able to see in my mind's eye the grizzly bears walking the Ventura River on their way to the beach to forage for clams. More important, when I went hiking I was able to connect to what it was like to have been an Indian two hundred years ago, walking these hills in the close company of the big humpbacked bears. There was a certain terror to my imaginings, to be sure, but there was also an awareness, a connection to the land that all of us are designed as a species to have, that few of us living have ever felt.

A half hour after leaving Tsumi Pass I am still hiking alone in thick monsoon mist, and I am still enjoying the solitude. The only sounds are my footfalls on the trail, and even those are quickly absorbed by the fog. Then through the mist I see a red blotch that gels into Asia's rain jacket. She is sitting in a small meadow at the edge of a forest, and just beyond her I see the others. When I arrive Tashi motions me over and offers a small round of barley bread and a hunk of yak cheese. I walk back and share both with Asia.

"Hmmm," she says. "This stuff is *really* good."

Indeed it is. We eat the bread and cheese while the horses graze on the rain-season grass. A suckling colt, along on the trek because his mother has been pressed into service carrying our duffels, is so tired he lies with his legs splayed and his chin resting on the ground like a little dog. When it's time to continue, the colt struggles to stand and reluctantly follows his mother. We enter the forest of mixed live oak and rhododendron, and the misting fog darkens the trail enclosed by branches that drip with Spanish moss. The forest opens to allow just enough light to trigger a bloom of rhododendron blossoms—large swatches of red and pink flowers in bright contrast against the dark of the trees. Tashi and his assistant stop to adjust the loads on the horses, and I use the delay to pass everyone so I might continue to walk alone in this forest.

I follow the trail as it ascends the opposite side of the drainage, toward the famed Konka Gompa Monastery. Originally constructed nearly one thousand years ago, in 1980, after destruction at the hands of the Red Guards, it consisted of only a few broken walls enclosing a pile of rubble. Meng has told us that in the interim the monastery has been rebuilt, and today houses an active community of monks; further, he said, we will arrive there by nightfall.

I walk as quietly as I can, glancing down to avoid twigs and leaves, but otherwise keeping my eye on the trail ahead, or into the forest on the sides. In 1980 one of my companions chased a black bear close to where I am now, but I realize these animals were rare and elusive back then, and the chance of seeing one this time is even more improbable. I would be excited, however, if I could even glimpse *Crossoptilon crossoptilon,* the majestic white-eared pheasant. It used to be common in these mountains, but for decades it has been hunted for its ostrichlike tail feathers. In 1980 there was a sizable flock of these birds that frequented the forests around the Konka Gompa, but I have been told that even though they are now protected under recently enacted Chinese conservation laws, white-eared pheasants are still hunted to a degree they may be facing extirpation in the region; and if they are no longer here, they may no longer be anywhere.

When I was ten years old, my family moved to a two-acre parcel in southern California surrounded by large groves of orange trees. We started a business rearing the common Chinese ring-necked pheasant to sell for release on properties owned or leased by shooting clubs. First as a way to gain additional money, and later as a need to satisfy a growing passion, I began to raise more exotic species of pheasants that I sold or traded. I raised fifteen species in all, and I worked hard to earn the money to buy a pair of white-eared pheasants that, even in 1962, cost $150. When other fanciers visited my backyard zoo to consider a trade or purchase, I could tell them the geographic home of each of the species I kept. In my mind's eye I would imagine what those places were like: the rain forests of Sumatra and Borneo, the lowland *terai* of Nepal, the higher forested slopes of the Himalayas.

The canopied trail opens to a small clearing with a waist-high wall of *mani* stones, each carved with mantric inscriptions, that I pass on my right. I glimpse movement ahead, and focus my vision in time to see a diminutive musk deer scurry rabbitlike into the trees. Regaining the forest, I go only another fifty feet when I'm startled by a gooselike cackling, and in my next heartbeat I feel a swelling joy as I realize the white-eared pheasant still survives in these mountains. I have flushed a flock of maybe twenty of these birds, and they have split, one-half fleeing to my left and the other to my right. I drop my pack and quickly take my binoculars from my top flap pocket, and go after the group on my left. I run fast, dodging the undergrowth, paying no heed to the steep slope, or to the fact I'm at about 14,000 feet. I slow when I hear more cackling just ahead. Then I see one of the birds, and I freeze. I am guessing he's a cock (unlike nearly all other pheasants, male and female white-eared pheasants are almost indistinguishable) because, through the trees, I can hear a high-frequency chirping that indicates the hens are with chicks; this one is by himself, and appears to be protecting the flock. He is the size of a barnyard rooster, his back- and neck- and breast-feathers white, and his large draping tail greenish blue. He creeps ahead while I focus my binoculars. There is a bright red wattle around his eye, and he cranes his head to watch me. He takes two more cautious steps, then disappears into the trees. I decide not to stalk him further as he and his flock no doubt have suffered enough harassment from hunters. In any case, he has allowed me a good look.

I walk back to the trail and pick up my pack. Through the forest I hear the wind-chime tinkle of the neck bells of our approaching horses, and I decide to wait a few minutes for the others to catch up to me. I stand motionless, taking one more moment to look into the forests of the pheasant mountains of my youth.

When we made the long approach march to Everest Base Camp in 1976, one day I saw the iridescent purple, green, and gold Impeyan pheasant perched on a rock just off the trail. Behind it was the white summit of Ama Dablam, and I stood looking at it mesmerized not so much by the bird's beauty but by the realization that the scene was identical to a painting of this bird depicted in the book on pheasants I had owned as a boy. In the years that followed, as my interest moved beyond the big-name peaks to explorations in the remaining unknown corners of the world, there were other places—Borneo, Bhutan, Kham—where I saw pheasants that connected me to the imaginings of my youth.

As I ventured into more remote areas, I began to assemble a better idea of what much of the world looked like in the near past, when most of it was still wild. Then a year after the Africa walk I had a chance to see a corner of the world that allowed me to see what the Earth was like in the distant past. This time my job was to film a team attempting the first big wall climb in Antarctica. It had an all-star cast. Alex Lowe and Conrad Anker would do the lead climbing; Jon Krakauer would write about it; Gordon Wiltsie would photograph it; Mike Graber and I would film it.

Gordon had learned of a large granite spire in Queen Maud Land, the remote "far side" of Antarctica south of South Africa, that towered above the ice cap. It was absolutely vertical to overhanging, but Alex and Conrad were perhaps the greatest alpine climbers in the world, and if anyone could do it, they were the ones to try. Jon was also an excellent climber, and although reserved and even shy, he agreed, with some reluctance, to my request to be in front of the camera. He had even been reluctant to come on the trip in the first place. Eight months earlier he had been part of one of the teams caught in the sudden storm on Everest that had so notoriously killed five people, and he wasn't certain he wanted to return to climbing so quickly. After considering it further, however, he decided "some real climbing" might exorcise the demons he carried home from Everest.

Alex and Conrad did the leading, while Jon belayed. Gordon, Mike, and I ascended the ropes they fixed in place, and worked to the sides, or climbed to the high point and had the boys redo a pitch, to get the angles we needed. For the first few days we would work ten or twelve hours, then rappel the lines, ski back to our tent, cook a meal, sleep a few hours, then ski back to the base of the spire and again ascend the ropes. When we were about fifteen hundred feet above the ice we were ready to "commit," to sleep on the wall in our three porta-ledges—small tents that suspend from a single anchor point. We also hauled up about three hundred pounds of ice to melt for water. The wall was so steep there wasn't a single ledge to hold snow. We all enjoyed the comic absurdity of working our butts off to haul ice in Antarctica.

The last few hundred feet of the wall started to overhang, and now if we dropped anything it landed fifty feet from the base. Just below the summit Jon got to lead a pitch that included a long free climb up a jam-crack. "Man, I'm stoked again to climb," he said when he finished the section.

When I think back to the climb, two images come to mind. One is a vertical band on one side that is gray—the granite wall—and a horizontal line on the other that is blue above and white below—the sky and the ice. Two lines, one vertical and one horizontal, in three blocks of color—gray, blue, and white. It is a Rothko of the Antarctic. The other image is from the summit looking across the ice cap, and in the distance granite spires rising from the ice like faraway lighthouses out of a frozen sea. It is a vision of the Earth before humans, even before life.

When we reached the summit Jon produced a small green burgee appliquéd with an orange gecko that his wife had given him to fly on top of Everest. In the hypoxic concern of getting down that mountain alive, however, he had forgotten it in his pocket. He figured this remote mountain in Antarctica that nobody had heard of was a much better place for it, anyway.

"Here's to never, ever returning to Everest," Alex said as Jon placed the burgee on the summit.

"The hell with that pig and everything it stands for," Jon said.

All of us on the Antarctic climb had been to Everest. Alex had even guided the New York socialite Sandy Pittman twice on her previous attempts to climb the peak. One of those trips had been sponsored by Vaseline, a combination that all of us teased Alex about mercilessly. Sometimes the subject of the Everest tragedy would come up in our conversations. Jon had completed his book *Into Thin Air* only as we left Cape Town on our flight to Antarctica, and it was still painful for him to talk about it.

"I'll be having a hard time with this twenty years from now," he confessed.

We were all unanimous in our condemnation of guided climbs on Everest although I limited my criticism to those who hire guides to help them ascend the fixed ropes and then brag about the experience as though it were an achievement that had involved some level of self-reliance. Jon of course knew that I had written *Seven Summits* with Frank and Dick. After its publication, dozens if not hundreds of people were inspired by their story to try to climb the highest peak on each continent, even though most of them, like Dick and Frank, knew very little about climbing. In response to the demand, more than enough climbers stepped forward to be guides, and Nepalese officials were more than willing to change the rules to allow several teams at a time on the peak once they realized how much money could be made.

Jon and I never talked about it, but I've often thought about the irony of Frank and Dick's story fueling the Everest craze (and the further irony of Jon's book actually generating a new surge in demand). No guided Everest climber since Dick has made it from the South Col to the summit and back without a rope. If the authenticity of an adventure is measured by your life depending on your own actions and skill, then Dick's climb, or at least the summit day of his climb, was the real thing.

It's true that Dick's money bought him a shortened learning curve. Even when he made the top—notwithstanding it was his fourth attempt—he didn't own the skills needed to climb the mountain bottom to top on his own, with or without a rope. That last day, however, had required a high quotient of self-reliance. And it revealed the part of Dick's effort that I found most valorous—his unflagging enthusiasm.

In the years after the Seven Summits expeditions, I stayed in touch with both Dick and Frank. Frank and Michael Eisner had turned Disney around and had become, counting stock options, the highest-paid executives in the world. Frank was comfortable letting Eisner take most of the public credit for their success. He also always had time for his "climbing buddies." He would show up sometimes late at night, exhausted from a sixteen-hour day, and we would feed him dinner. His favorite meal was mussels and sea snails that Yvon and I would forage at low tide, with bread that Yvon baked. He loved the idea that Yvon and I loved to cook. We would sit at a big table, other friends over, cracking mussels with our hands, drinking wine out of glasses with no stems, and in those times Frank would lean back in his chair, and I could see in his face he was back with us in the mountains, dirty, unshaven, unbathed. Back when he had worn the same long underwear for six weeks in a row, back when he had worked side by side with us, carrying the same weight on his back as the guy in front of him and the guy behind him. Back when the only thing he hadn't done was cook, but, what the hell, his pals liked to do that anyway.

On Easter Sunday in 1994 I took my family to my mother's house for the holiday. After the egg hunt I was in the living room with my wife. The television was turned on, but the volume was off and no one was watching. I walked by the set and out of the corner of my eye I saw a full-screen picture of Frank.

Frank's in the news, I thought. Maybe he's starting to take some of the publicity from Eisner.

Then, superimposed under his portrait, it said "President of Disney," and, at the same instant above his portrait, "1932–1994."

"Oh my God."

"What is it?" my wife said, turning.

"Frank is dead."

I turned up the volume, but the newscast was over. I called a mutual friend who said Frank had been heli-skiing in the Ruby Mountains in northern Nevada, and there had been a crash. Bev Johnson (who had told me years before that the way you eat an elephant is one bite at a time) was also dead, and her husband, my old filmmaking mentor Mike Hoover, was seriously injured. In the next few days we learned the details: The chopper had set down to wait a few minutes for a cloud to dissipate, and the pilot left the engine idling, not realizing it was also sucking powder snow into the intake filter. When they took off, they were airborne only a few seconds before the engine shut down.

Frank's eldest son, whom we had come to know, was also skiing with them that day, but he was in a different helicopter. In the morgue he had to claim his father's belongings, including Frank's wallet. He looked through the contents and found a fortune from a Chinese cookie. It was worn thin, and it appeared Frank had been carrying it for a long time. His son opened it, and it was barely legible, but he could see that it said, "Humility is the only true grace."

The Konka Gompa Monastery is perched on a small bench on an otherwise steep hillside overlooking the terminus of a large glacier that descends off the east side of Minya Konka. On a clear day there is a stunning view of the mountain, but this afternoon the peak is shrouded in monsoon clouds. The monastery has indeed been rebuilt from the ground up, and although the work was completed only a few years ago, the square two-story building with inward-sloping walls already has the ambience of a place well used and well loved. We enter the *gompa* through a door that leads to an open courtyard encircled by a second-story balcony with doors leading to kitchens, living quarters, the bathroom, and the prayer and meditation room. Asia and I are escorted to a sleeping room we will share with one of the monks. The young Chinese cook we have with us sets up kitchen in the adjoining room, and since we have more food than we can eat ourselves, we are able to offer tea and treats to our hosts.

In the last light of day Asia and I stand on the second-floor balcony, leaning on the rail, looking at the prayer flags that hang like bunting under the eaves, the altar in the courtyard center, the bough of juniper sending a curl of smoke skyward. From the prayer room we hear the chanting of the senior monk, who is old enough to have known the former monastery before it was destroyed, and may even have lived and meditated in it.

"You need to soak this in," I tell Asia, "because it may be the only chance in your life to spend a night in what is truly a medieval setting. No electricity, no roads, few artifacts from the outside world. Everyone smelling like smoke from their fires, and after it's dark only candles lighting their faces, and only sheepskins keeping them warm. This place would have looked familiar to Marco Polo."

Asia nods her head in understanding. She doesn't say anything, but she doesn't need to. I leave her to circle the balcony, then descend the steep stairs into the courtyard. The Tibetans in this area who pooled their resources have done an admirable job building this new monastery, but even then, I can see it doesn't match the standard of its predecessor. For one, there are no paintings on the walls. When we were here in 1980, we camped just below the ruins of the old monastery, and after we set up our tents, Yvon, Jonathan, and I investigated the debris. We were quiet as we stepped over the shards of roof slate and chunks of plaster and pieces of smashed doors. Yvon picked up a joist of two beam ends fastened by a hand-carved dovetail spline that had been executed with near-seamless joinery.

"Think of the generations of craftsmen it took to perfect the techniques and tools to make a joint like this," he said, tossing the piece back in the refuse. "All wasted."

Jonathan then called us over to the most intact section of what was left of the walls. We could see all of them had once been painted with frescoes depicting various Buddhas and bodhisattvas, and all had been smashed to pieces. All except the one we stood admiring. The Buddha was still intact, and his visage looked back at us from what otherwise was a scene of complete destruction.

"It's interesting," Jonathan said, "that this is the one Buddha to survive."

"Who is it?"

"Maitreya," he said. "The Buddha of Things to Come."

"You think there's a message?" I asked.

"Yes, there's a message," Jonathan said, turning to me with a faint smile, a smile of someone content with what he knows, a smile not unlike the smile of Maitreya. "It's to remember that the first fact of existence is impermanence."

I lie in bed propped against the headboard writing in my journal by the light of a candle positioned on the bedpost. The room is about thirty feet long and ten feet wide. There are two windows whose frames are both covered with parchment. My bed is along one end, Asia's bed is in the middle; she lies on her stomach in her sleeping bag, her chin cradled in her hands as she reads by headlamp one of her father's journals. The monk who is sharing his room with us lies in a third bed on the opposite end. Like me, he also has a candle on his bedpost, and he chants a sotto voce mantra as he arranges his belongings on his nightstand: prayer beads, a bell, and two portraits, each in hand-carved wood frames, of lamas.

I look up from my journal. The single flame from my candle shows dimly the outline of my bed, the plastered rock walls, the slate roof supported by a latticework of twined poles, the small table made of hand-hewn lumber, Asia's bed a few feet from mine, Asia's dark hair and the cone of light from her headlamp shining on the photocopied pages of her father's journal.

"Asia?"

"Yes?"

"What's the most important thing you're getting from your father's journals?"

"His ability to always improve himself, I think. And maybe to realize it's a job that never ends." Then she pauses for a moment before going on. "But to really be honest, I think you are taking more from these journals than I am, because you knew him. I'll never know him the same way."

"I guess I have a picture of him in my mind as I read along."

"I'm getting more out of seeing what *you* get from them, because you're real to me. Your stories, too, I'm learning from those in a way that's different than reading my father's."

I thank her and go back to my journal, where I am describing the events of the day. I pause in my writing when I recount sighting the white-eared pheasants, and think about the birds I kept as a boy and the birds I saw today. The two sets of birds feel like bookends framing my life. In my imagination I see myself as a boy standing outside a cage looking through the wire mesh at my pair of white-eared pheasants. Then, as I suspect we all do on occasion, I have a fantasy wondering how I might have reacted if somehow, at age eleven, I had been foretold what would happen in my life in the years ahead.

I think of the stories I have told Asia, the ones she now says have meaning for her. Sitting on top of K2, leaning against my summit partner, telling myself to try to remember what I am seeing because some day, years later, it will seem important. Sitting at the base of a nearly unknown massif of mountains in Bhutan and burning the map we had worked hard to create. Seeing the wild Yanomami in the clearing in the jungle doing his monkey dance.

"Good night, Rick," Asia says as she turns off her headlamp.

"Goodnight, Asia. Sleep well."

I blow out the candle, and in the darkness I hear the rush of the river in the valley below. I take off my parka, shift into the sanctum of my sleeping bag, and place the jacket under my head. I close my eyes, and before I go to sleep, I have one final thought: If I were caught in the avalanche now, at age fifty, would I own the wisdom to ride the cascading snow not in fear but in wonder? Like Alice falling down the hole, would I look to the sides, watching the world that I know and that I have known speed by, wondering not in panic but in awe about the other world into which I am about to enter?

13

Sometime during the night it begins to rain hard, and a drip develops over my bed that lands around and on my head. I get up and try to shift my bed, but it's made of hand-hewn lumber, and it's heavy. Asia is apparently still asleep, but the monk hears me, lights his candle, then gets up to help. He is apologetic, gesturing that he wants to switch beds, but I motion that I am fine, and point to my rain jacket, indicating that I can sleep in that if I need to. That makes him only more insistent, however, that we switch. With one of us on each end, we shift my bed, and he goes back to his only after he has verified that the water drops are no longer hitting mine.

"You okay?" Asia asks as I get back into bed.

"Just a little leak on the head."

"It's really raining hard."

"That it is."

"You think we'll be able to get to the grave?"

"We've come this far, we'll get there. Now go back to sleep. We've got a couple of big days ahead."

I only wish I believed it myself. Back in my sleeping bag, I listen to the beating of the rain on the roof, and in the distance, the roar of the river coming off the glacier. If it continues like this, I think, we might not even be able to cross the river to get to our old Base Camp.

I drift to sleep, and when I wake it is still dark in the room, but the parchment on the windows carries a faint glow. I listen, but I hear no rain. There is only the rush of the river, but even at this distance it is an undertone that leaves in me a disquieting sense of its power. I unzip my bag, swing my legs and feet to the floor, and dress. I pick up my binoculars and the photographs of Minya Konka. I take care opening the thick plank door of our room so the hand-forged hinges don't squeak and wake Asia. Then I descend the steep stairs to the courtyard and open the heavy twin doors that lead out of the monastery.

From a grassy bench in front of the *gompa* I look upvalley and see that a gray blanket of cloud obscures all but the lowest flanks of Minya Konka. The tips of the tongues of the glaciers that descend the peak are just visible, however, and one looks familiar. Could it mark the way of our old route, and if it does, the location of Jonathan's grave? I look through my binoculars and study the hanging seracs at the tip of the glacier, and the surrounding rock outcrops, but they are only vaguely familiar. I remove the photographs from their envelope and study the snow and rock features of the buttress where I know we buried Jonathan. Then I look back at the mountain, but the clouds have descended and the bottoms of the snowfields and the buttresses have disappeared.

I return to the monastery and, over a breakfast of pancakes our cook prepares one at a time in his wok, we form our plan. We will take a minimum of equipment and food on horseback up the lateral moraine alongside the main glacier, to a high alpine meadow where, in 1980, we established our Base Camp. If we can get that far, Meng and Tashi will then leave Asia and me, and tomorrow just the two of us will see if we can find our old route toward Camp 1. Somewhere along that route is the small rocky promontory, with a prospect of this valley and this monastery, where we buried Asia's father.

Before we leave, I have our interpreter ask one of the attendant monks if Asia and I might have an audience with the old monk who is in his meditation room chanting. We find him sitting cross-legged on a carpeted pad before a small knee-high table that holds his hand-printed book of chants. He nods to us, but continues chanting, and when he completes his prayer cycle, he picks up a baton off the table, strikes a drum suspended from the ceiling, then begins another cycle. The attendant offers Asia and me a can that contains rice that has been blessed. Asia follows my lead as I clasp a small scoop of rice in my palm, then hold my folded hand to my forehead as I make a silent prayer, or more accurately, a silent invocation of Jonathan's grave, creating a mental image of the stone bier. Then I release the rice, tossing it across the altar.

The old monk completes another chanting cycle, picks up a set of cymbals from his lap, and clashes them loudly. He is ready to receive us and the attendant motions us toward him. We clasp our hands and bow as he hands two *kata* scarves to the attendant, who drapes them around our necks. The old monk, returning to his prayer book, resumes his chant; Asia and I step outside to the balcony. I wonder if anyone has told him who we are and why we are here. The answer comes when the attendant tells us that the old monk has suggested we place the *kata* scarves on the grave of Asia's father. Asia then gives the attendant the twenty dollars her grandmother gave her for her birthday.

"Grandma will like the idea that the money is staying here," Asia says.

All the monks in the monastery, save for the old one who is still chanting, gather in front of the *gompa* and wish us good luck on our mission as we depart down a steep trail to the river. Tashi and his in-law escort the horse carrying our duffel. Meng, wearing a small day pack, steps down the muddy trail in cautious halts that reveal the pain in his worn-out knees. The young cook has also come along, to wish us farewell, I presume, further down the trail, although he does not have to; I appreciate the gesture, however, and interpret it as his way of showing his respect for our mission.

In a half mile we reach the bottom of the valley. The river is rushing over glacial boulders in standing waves and foaming holes, and it's too swollen to cross. Tashi secures the horse, and all of us scout upriver until we find a narrow channel with a single wet log spanning the white water. With some care we can step across the bridge, but it's clear that the horse cannot. We walk back to where the animal is tethered and discuss what to do. Since the interpreter has stayed at the monastery, Meng motions in hand gestures that Tashi and his in-law can take the two small duffels from the horse and carry them. I nod in agreement, and Meng then discusses the proposal with Tashi, who firmly shakes his head no. It's clear that Tashi does not want to carry the duffels, and Meng, sweeping the air with his arms, yells at him.

"We've got more stuff than we need," I say to Asia. "So let's leave some of it here. The horse can take it back."

Asia and I plan to spend only two nights in Base Camp, but because we had the horse I brought food for four or five nights, in case it takes longer than hoped to find the grave. I also have in my own backpack my large notebook, journal, tape recorder, video camera, back-up battery, still camera and lenses, and tripod. I am computing in my mind how I will pare these things down so Asia and I can carry everything ourselves when Meng tells me by hand gestures that he and our cook will help carry our gear. He points to Tashi and dismisses him with a condescending wave. Tashi looks contrite yet firm, and I realize that although he has refused to help he still feels badly, and I believe I know why: He is a Khampa, not a beast of burden, and therefore it is below his station to carry loads on his back. Yet I know he likes Asia and me, and sympathizes with our mission. It was probably a hard decision, and I am guessing one that required him to weigh his reputation back in his village. I don't begrudge him his choice, but I am also thankful to our young cook and especially to the irrepressible Meng who, bad knees and all, shoulders a duffel and indicates we should get going.

We step carefully across the slippery log only to discover, in another ten yards, that the increasing water level has created another channel of rushing water. It is only fifteen feet across, but knee- to thigh-deep. To avoid this, we continue upriver between the two channels, hopping boulder to boulder, but soon I can see that a short distance ahead the steep banks on both sides constrict the river into a single channel with no possible crossing.

"We have to go back," I yell to Asia.

"And then what?"

"Cross the small channel and climb up the moraine."

I scout downriver until I find the widest point in the subchannel, where the water has the least power.

"We have to be careful," I yell. "If you slip with these heavy packs you could get pinned under a boulder."

Since firm footing is more important than dry feet, I wade in with my boots on and slowly cross, taking care with each step to brace my leg against the water that rushes in places to my waist. On the other side I dump my pack and wade back to help the others cross. When it's Asia's turn she wades in, and I can see a wince on her face when the ice water fills her boots, but she makes it across without a misstep.

When all of us have safely crossed, we climb a steep slope thick with rhododendron and scrub oak that I hope will lead directly to the top of the moraine. The clouds have now descended, enclosing us in a dewy fog. We twist through branches and over roots, careful not to grab for support the thorn stems of wild rose that are thick in the undergrowth. With relief we exit onto the top of the moraine, only to find it rough going as we scamper up and down piles of boulders bulldozed by the moving ice into loose heaps. I see that Meng's face pinches with each step, and wanting to tell him he has my sympathy, I point to my own knees and grimace. But Meng only shrugs his shoulders—he won't allow that he's in pain.

In another hour we traverse the moraine back to the edge of the river where the bank is now wide enough to walk easily, and also to pitch a tent. I drop my pack and motion Meng to do the same. I'm not sure where we are, and I have a sense it is still some distance to our old campsite, but I know Meng has done enough. Asia and I give him and our cook a heartfelt hug. They indicate they wish us the best of luck, and they leave.

"It's just us now," I tell her.

No sooner are Meng and the cook out of sight than a rainsquall darkens the head of the valley. I look around for a tent site, and realize the only flat ground is disconcertingly close to the river. Still, it's the only option, so Asia and I snap together the poles and thread them through the sleeves. We no sooner have the tent up and our sleeping bags inside than the squall hits, pelting the rain fly. Through the nylon fabric we can see a flash of lightning, and a moment later the thunder rolls down the valley, bringing memory of the hours that followed the avalanche—when I was alone in Base Camp waiting for the others who had gone to help Yvon and Kim—and the thunder that seemed like it was sounding for the departure of Jonathan's soul.

"What do we do if it continues to rain," Asia asks. "I mean if we can't see where we have to go."

"We wait until it clears. We didn't get within a few miles of your father just to turn back."

I look out the door and note a small bush partially submerged in the river that I can use as a gauge to measure any rise in the water. The river, were it to jump bank, wouldn't place us in danger but would make for a miserable night. My larger concern is the one Asia has just voiced: whether in this weather we will be able to find the grave. I try to hide my anxiety from her, but she reads it in my tone of voice.

"I just want to find my dad," she says, "and go home."

I can't think of anything to say to encourage her, so I assemble the stove to make tea. I pour hot water into Asia's cup and then mine, holding the warm mug in my hands. Then the rain stops and I look out the vestibule door, but clouds still enshroud the mountain. I check the bush at river's edge, and Asia notices what I'm doing.

"Is it coming up?"

"It's holding steady. At least the rain's stopped."

The truth is the river has risen maybe an inch, and has perhaps three to go before it jumps the bank. Still I don't want to worry Asia; I want her mind clear to focus on the job ahead. We sip our tea, then she says, "I had a dream last night, about finding the grave. When we got there my father was exposed, but he was somehow perfectly preserved. I don't know, maybe by the cold."

"I've actually thought about that," I say. "What it would be like to find your father preserved, almost the same age as you are now. But I know that can't be possible because where he's buried the altitude is too low for him to have remained frozen."

Then I think, What if it *is* cold enough that he's remained frozen?

During the night I wake to the sound of rain hitting the tent fly. I locate my headlamp and shine it on the travel alarm I've positioned near my head: four A.M. I sit up to open the tent door and point the beam on the small bush at river's edge.

"Is it higher?" Asia asks.

"Staying the same. Try to get some more sleep; we don't have to get up quite yet."

A half hour later I sit up again and start the stove, then lie down while I wait for the water to boil. It's still raining, and although I don't tell Asia, the truth is the river has come up and is now within an inch of jumping its bank and flooding our tent, which is already leaking. I know in these conditions I won't be able to find the grave. If we don't find it today, though, we'll try again tomorrow. And the next day.

I go through my mental checklist: compass, headlamp, lunch, camera gear, film, reference photographs, binoculars. The water boils, and I make tea. I hand Asia her mug, and she sits up in her bag and thanks me. Then the rain stops. I look outside to see that there is enough filtered moonlight to reveal the tip of a glacier hanging like a tongue out of the mantle of clouds.

"The clouds are starting to thin," I say. "Maybe we *can* pull this off today."

"Please let us have just one good day," Asia says.

I heat more water to make porridge. The stove's jet keeps getting plugged, and preparing breakfast takes longer than I would like. It's six A.M. by the time we are out of the tent and on our way. We parallel the river, following an incipient-use trail made by herders leading their yaks to seasonal pastures. If my memory is accurate, we will follow this river as it bends around a corner, and continue along it until it leads to a high meadow where, in 1980, we located our Base Camp. I also remember that from the meadow, weather permitting, we should be able to see the buttress we have to ascend.

"Wait," Asia calls, and I stop until she catches up. "Did you bring the photographs?"

"They're in my pack. Thanks for asking."

I take it as a good sign that Asia is attending to the requirements of the day, and I turn and continue. Soon the moraine squeezes against the river, and we are forced to walk on the edge of the roaring water, hopping boulder to slippery boulder. The river channel is steep, and I find the roar of the cascading water both distracting and disorienting. There's a lower-angled gully that appears to lead to the top of the moraine, and I tell Asia I want to go that way, hoping at least to find a route away from the noise of the river. We climb the loose glacial till and on top we can see the moraine continues upvalley, but it drops away sharply on both sides. Along the crest, however, there is a faint trail that, judging by hoofprints in mats of damp dirt between rocks, has been made by the passage of blue sheep and perhaps tahr, a mountain goat I recall seeing in this area twenty years ago. I follow the trail, and after a few minutes turn to check on Asia. She is keeping up, but behind her I notice that a layer of clouds has formed in the valley below the monastery.

The faint trail continues along the crest of the moraine. To my left I can still hear the roar of the cascading water three hundred feet downslope; to my right the moraine drops to a floor of thick till that has been pushed and shoved by the underlying ice into a gray moon surface. Straight ahead in the near distance three parallel buttresses descend out of the upper layer of clouds. One of them is vaguely familiar. I stop to set my pack down and, looking through the binoculars, I compare what I see with the photographs. Asia catches up and looks over my shoulder.

"So which one do you think it is?" she asks.

"I think it's this one, but I'm not sure."

Then I look back at the mountain and realize what has happened.

"The glacier has receded," I say, pointing to the mountain and then to the photograph. "See, it was here in 1980, and now it's way up there."

"What would cause that?"

"Climate shift. Maybe global warming."

I continue to study the buttress through my binoculars, then the photograph, then look back to the buttress.

"That's it, for sure. I can see where the avalanche stopped, which means your father must be buried somewhere in those rocks to the left."

I put the photographs in my pack, and we continue. During the five minutes we have stopped, the lower layer of clouds has risen toward us, and I realize there is a good chance we will soon be in a whiteout. If that happens it will be very difficult to find the correct buttress, photograph or no photograph.

I tell myself, If we have to, we'll bivouac. We can find a cave or a rock overhang and build a fire, then be in better position tomorrow if once more we only have a narrow window of workable weather. But wait, we have no matches. That's okay, we'll huddle. Be good for Asia, to learn to push things. But is that pushing her too far? Maybe, but that's okay too, because if we don't make every effort to find him we'll regret it for the rest of our lives.

The crest of the moraine sharpens, and I have to walk with my arms out for balance, mindful of each footstep: It is a long way down on both sides. I turn and wait for Asia.

"Really be careful," I say, "and make sure each step is solid before you put weight on it."

"Okay."

"Are you all right?"

"I don't know."

"What's wrong?"

"I just don't know if I'm ready."

"What do you mean?"

"Ready to find him, now that it's *real*."

I don't say anything, and I'm not sure what to do. Asia is looking toward Minya Konka, toward the buttress. She doesn't say anything, either. Then she looks back to me.

"Okay," she says. "Let's keep going."

I can see ahead that the crest of this lateral moraine we're following hooks to the right and merges into the moonscape rubble on top of the glacier. Straight ahead is the meadow where we set Base Camp in 1980. We drop off the moraine, and soon we're walking through monsoon grass blooming with yellow cinquefoil. We pass a collection of large flat stones that have been arranged like a miniature Stonehenge, and I tell Asia it is likely the kitchen site of some expedition that followed ours. Then we reach another collection of stones that I recognize as our own campsite. Looking toward the mountain, I can see the route we took to gain the bottom of the buttress. In 1980 it took three days to scout the best route to Camp 1. I have a vague memory that we had to find a way through a complex of rock towers and ledges. From where we stand I can see the best way up the initial section is to follow a talus that leads to a series of cliffs. How we get through those I'm not certain, but the first part, at least, is obvious. I don't express any of these ambiguities to Asia, because she has enough to think about getting herself ready to meet her father.

We begin the slow climb up the talus. I set a steady pace, one slow foot after the other, and Asia maintains a twenty-yard distance behind. The layer of clouds that fills the lower valley has continued to rise toward us. I look back to my feet, careful to avoid loose sections in the scree that cause me to lose a half step backward for every step forward. In an hour I reach the top of the scree, take out my water bottle, and wait for Asia.

I remember a rest break that Kim, Yvon, Jonathan, and I took in a place that must have been very close to the spot where I now rest. As we sat looking at the view, we noticed above Minya Konka a single cloud caught in a circling vortex that caused it to disappear as the convection carried it downward, then reappear as it flew skyward; we watched as the morning light, angling through this swirling dew, refracted into a hundred opalescent hues.

"I make my living taking pictures," Jonathan had said, "but there's no way I could get that cloud on film. And whenever I see anything like that I can't photograph, it delights me to no end."

Asia catches up, and I offer her a drink of water. She is quiet and somber. After we rest a few moments, I get up and we continue. Soon I recognize another feature: the boulder field where I had stumbled and fell when I was running to get help for the others, when I told myself, "Slow down. You can't sprain your ankle. Kim needs your help." Another five hundred vertical feet above the boulder field is the slope where the avalanche came to a stop. I think, We must have buried Jonathan somewhere to the left of that.

I study the area with my binoculars, but if his grave is still there, it's hidden behind the foreground cliffs. I recognize the largest of these cliffs as the one I feared we might all plummet over if the avalanche renewed its slow slide toward the edge. Since the grave is somewhere above this barrier, I have to figure out how to get around it. There's a passage to the right, but it's under a huge serac that teeters at the end of a glacier, waiting for the next slight shift of ice to send it tumbling. To the left the cliff merges into a short gully that we might be able to climb, but then we would have to traverse back right, and that way looks blocked by a steep rock rib. I have no memory of it being this difficult, and my only encouragement is knowing that twenty years ago we did find a way around the cliff, and we did it without fixed ropes or technical climbing gear.

"What do you think?" Asia asks.

"The route goes this way, then up that little gully there, then back right. Don't worry, it's not as hard as it looks."

The only reasonably safe route—or what appears to be reasonably safe—is to stay to the left of the serac as much as possible. That forces us to hug a cliff of fractured rock that looms threateningly over our heads.

"Isn't there too much rockfall danger here?" Asia asks.

I have no choice but to tell her the truth.

"Yes, but I'm even more concerned about getting under that serac."

"I don't like this," she says.

"I don't either, but I'd rather be here than over there."

It's just an instinctive guess on my part that there is less danger from rockfall than from the serac, but I don't tell this to Asia. We arrive at the gully, which is really only a cleft in the rock wall, and I can see that the first thirty or forty feet has a few moves that will require concentration. I am remiss in not bringing a rope, but I didn't remember anything this difficult.

"Asia, I know this looks hard, but it's not that bad if you concentrate. You go first, and I'll climb right under you."

She doesn't say anything, and she doesn't move.

"We need to keep going. If it starts to rain, this rock will get slippery, and we still have to come down."

"I'm scared," she says.

She turns, and I can see she is crying. I put my hands on her shoulders.

"It only looks hard. I know you can do it."

She shakes her head and says, "It's not that." She continues to cry, then she says, "I'm scared of what we're going to find."

I don't answer for a few moments, then I say, "Do you still want to do this?"

"I think so."

"Then we really do need to get up there before it starts raining."

"Okay."

She nods her head and wipes her tears, then turns toward the rock. She still doesn't move.

"There's a foothold here, then two handholds right there. Go up a few feet, then left into that little dihedral. There's a good crack there."

"Okay."

"Remember, I'll be right behind you."

She places her boot on the first foothold, presses up carefully, and reaches for the handholds. I can only guess how strong her emotions must be, and that makes it even more impressive to watch her move with athletic grace. I make the same moves behind her, mindful to have my hands and feet locked on the holds as tightly as possible because if she slips I will need all my strength to block her fall without being knocked off myself.

"You're doing great. Now traverse left into that dihedral. There're good holds there."

We reach the dihedral that has a crack where we can jam our boots. We're about thirty or forty feet up, and I know if she falls and knocks me off, we'll both be hurt, and this is no place to get hurt. I also know it's going to be even trickier to down-climb this section, and if it starts to rain, we could be in trouble. Should we turn back? We're nearly at the top of this section, and she's still moving gracefully. I decide to keep going. At the top of the dihedral I go in the lead again, and we ascend another field of boulders that are disconcertingly loose. Above us a wall of broken black rock rears steeply. I stop and wait for Asia, who is twenty feet below me.

"You okay?" I ask.

"Yeah."

But I can see she is crying again. I put my hand on her shoulder. I know she needs more encouragement, but I can't think of anything to do or say.

"I'll keep a slow and steady pace," I finally tell her. "Stay right behind me. That way if I knock a rock loose you won't be so far down it could bean you."

"Okay."

I angle at an upward traverse, bearing right. The only chance of getting to the slope where the avalanche stopped is a possible ledge I may have seen from below that I hope leads around the rock rib. I traverse that direction, looking up again to see that the upper clouds have continued to descend, and rain seems imminent.

"I don't think this goes around," Asia says.

"Then what do you suggest?" I reply, not quite with a snap, but with enough of an edge that I immediately regret my tone.

"Maybe that next ledge higher," she says, and there's also a tone of exasperation in her voice. I take a deep breath and exhale slowly, telling myself to stay calm, not to lose patience, to be supportive.

"Asia, I don't think we can get to that one. The climbing is too steep, and it looks too dangerous. We have to go this way." She doesn't say anything, so I say, "Stay close, okay."

"Okay."

I remind myself again that twenty years ago we found a way around this rib, and this looks like the only possibility. I no sooner complete this thought, however, than I begin to doubt it, thinking that perhaps Asia is right, perhaps we did traverse higher. I pause and look up again. The alternative still looks too dangerous, however, and now I remember Asia's mother before we left, saying, "She's the only daughter I have." That leads to a thought I have been trying to keep out of my head for the last hour, but it crowds its way in anyway: If anything happens to Asia right here where her father died, it wouldn't matter whether or not I survive . . . because I *wouldn't* survive.

I turn to her and say, "If this doesn't work, that's it. We'll go down. Okay?"

"Okay."

I reach the ledge and follow it to the rock rib. We still can't see around the corner, but I know the slope where the avalanche stopped is on the other side, and I can only hope the ledge will continue around the corner and connect us to it. It has to, it has to, it has to, I tell myself, as though repeating this mantra will make it so. Asia stays right behind me, following the steps I kick in the loose talus.

"There's no sense both of us climbing to the corner," I tell her, "so why don't you stay here, and I'll check it out."

The ledge is less a walkway than a sloping band of gravel cutting across this steep rib. With each step I first kick the loose debris, then work my boot to dig a foothold so Asia has as well formed a path as possible. I turn to tell her that the footing is tricky, but I see that instead of waiting she is following me.

"Make sure you kick-in each step."

"I am."

When I see she is making her steps with the necessary caution, I turn and continue. The crest of the rib is now only ten feet away, and I say again to myself, It has to connect, it has to connect. I keep my eyes on my footing, make five more steps, then see from the turn of the slope that I'm at the crest. I stop, then slowly look up. Above and to the right I recognize immediately the slope where the avalanche slowed and came to a halt. On the left side is the place where I held Jonathan as he died.

"It's just above," I say to Asia. "Fifty, sixty more feet of easy climbing, and we're there."

The snow has receded, leaving a jumble of barren rocks, but my mind fills in the tableau. *I see the snow blocks and the red rope winding in and out of the avalanche debris like the intestine of a gutted animal. Kim is right up there twenty feet away, and he screams.* Then I'm back to the present, finding one more foothold to get over this boulder. *I look to the side and see Yvon wandering next to the edge of the cliff.* Back to where I am, and ten feet farther there is a flat where I can rest and wait for Asia and, my God, it's the place. *There is Jonathan, lying in the snow and I go to him and he looks at me and I say, "We're all still alive, buddy. We're all going to get out of this alive."*

I reach the small flat and remove my pack, look down and see Asia about fifty feet away. There is the rock where I crawled to the side, panting, saying over and over and over, alive, alive, alive. I look up to the top of the rock rib and, my God, there it is. Right where we left him. Jonathan's grave; it's right there. But how can it be so close? It was so far that morning we carried him on our shoulders. But there it is, the rock platform we made out of the flat stones. But something's different. It's not as high as we built it. What has happened? Has it collapsed? What's that sticking out the sides? Shreds of clothing? Faded nylon? Yes, it's blue and yellow nylon. And at the end of the platform, the leg of his climbing suit? Yes, it's the leg of his suit. Oh God, what kind of condition is he in?

I turn and look down. Asia is only a few feet away, but she is looking down as she focuses on her feet.

"Asia?"

She stops and looks up.

"I see your father's grave."

She looks around, but she doesn't see it.

"Please prepare yourself, because he is not intact."

She is looking up and left, and then she sees the grave and her eyes freeze on her father's broken stone bier. Then she looks away, and for a moment she doesn't say anything. Neither do I.

"I don't want to go up there," she finally says.

"Come to where I am, then. It's a good place to rest."

She climbs the last few feet and stands next to me. She is still looking away. Then she turns toward me and she starts to cry, and I hold her in my arms. Her shoulders rise and fall, and her tears come from deep within. I hold her head next to mine, and I look past her, to the place only a few feet away where I held her father's head on my lap as I breathed into his mouth. *Yes, Jonathan, that's it, breathe, yes, yes, keep breathing, that's it, another breath, yes, yes, no. No, don't stop, keep breathing. God, please keep breathing. I bend down and breathe again into his mouth, once, twice. Yes, that's it, do it on your own, yes, you're breathing, good, do it again, no, no, don't stop.*

I move my head so that I am looking at her, and, still holding her shoulders, I say, "Why don't you take off your pack and set it next to mine." She sets her pack down and wipes her tears.

"I'm going up there, to have a look. Are you okay here?"

"Yeah."

"You sure?"

She nods her head again, still wiping her tears.

The grave is about fifty feet above us. I make slow steps toward it, not looking up. My foot kicks loose a slate shingle that hits its neighbor with the sound of breaking pottery. I remember that is how the rocks sounded when we stacked them to make the grave. They smelled like earth when we pried them loose. It was just Edgar and me, making the platform. Then Bill and Al arrived, and when we had the platform ready, the four of us carried Jonathan there.

I make another step, still not looking up, but I am aware of each of my footsteps; I hear the slate shift under my boots; I feel the years somehow lose their sequence and overlap, past with present and present with past. *"Can you guys stop for a minute. I have to switch sides, this arm is too sore," and we set Jonathan down carefully and we switch sides and then pick him up again. So heavy, and so cold. I feel his cold on my shoulder and next to my head, and I feel the heat of the sun on the other side of my face. There is sweat that beads on my brow and runs down my cheek and tastes salty on my lips. When we're there we move sideways stepping carefully on the shingle-rock and then we lower him gently off our shoulders and we have him under our arms, and I do the best I can with my bad arm and we lower him onto the platform.*

I make two more steps still looking down but in the top of my vision I see I am there, at the edge of the grave. I look up. One leg of Jonathan's climbing suit is fully exposed. The nylon is old and brittle and holed. The other leg is covered here and there by the rocks we placed over him. My eyes move up to the rest of my friend and I see he is still mostly covered, but parts of his jacket show between rocks. I reach down to his exposed leg and move the fabric, and . . . he is not there.

Maybe a snow leopard, I think. It would have taken something big to move these rocks, but then the griffons would have finished the job. Yes, the griffons.

I go down on my knees next to the grave, not sure what to do. Then I lift one of the rocks we had placed near Jonathan's head and see his long underwear top and on it the old-style label—somehow after all these years as bright as the day it was made—that says "Patagonia." And through the underwear, where it is torn, I see that part of my friend is still there, his backbone and his ribs and his collarbone. I shift another rock and see his hair is still in good condition.

I reach down and hold the strands between my fingers, rubbing them slowly and gently. *I move my fingers through his hair and his lips change color and suddenly his face pales and something goes out of him and I know he has just died, just this instant, I know the second it happens, and then slowly I resume again, moving my fingers through his hair and I bend down and kiss him and fold his arms on his stomach so he can be comfortable.* And I'm there, and I'm here, I'm in the past and in the present at the same time, and now I'm crying and bent over the grave and I hear myself saying, "Jonathan, my old buddy."

Then I'm here again. I clear my tears, take a breath, and turn to check on Asia. I'm surprised to see that she is coming up. She's only thirty feet away. I stand, not sure she should see her father in this condition.

"Asia, your father's clothes are here. But some of his bones are gone. You sure you want to come up?"

"I'm coming."

She sits down a few feet from the foot of her father's grave and starts to cry. Her sobs are deep and come from her heart. I walk the few steps toward her, put my arm around her, and she leans against me.

"He was so young," she says as she cries. "And everybody liked him."

"He was a very good man."

"He was my father," she says in a mournful sob. I hold her for several minutes, and then she stops crying. She looks at the grave, and I know she can see that in his pant leg there are no bones. She straightens, takes a deep breath and wipes her eyes. "Can we rebuild the grave?" she asks.

"Of course."

We bend to our task, and for the second time in my life I smell the earth as I pry loose the stones and carry them to the bier and set them gently on top of my old friend. Now I am with his daughter, and we do this together, she and I, and it is good work. We build the sides first, placing the stones carefully, moving and shifting them to obtain the best foundation for the next layer. When the sides are complete we gently lay more stones over the pant legs now empty of her father's remains, then over the underwear top where Asia can see the parts of him that yet remain.

With the grave rebuilt, Asia takes out the *kata* scarf given her by the old monk at the Konka Gompa, and begins to arrange it at the head of her father's grave. I am thankful Asia has given her grandmother's twenty dollars to the monastery that supports the old monk and his brethren. Asia secures the two ends of the *kata* under stones, and watching her make the final arrangement of the scarf on her father's grave, I am again struck by the similarity of her twenty-year-old legs and arms and shoulders to those of her twenty-eight-year-old father.

All is *anicca*, I say to myself, as Jonathan would have said to himself, and now change has come back on itself to complete the circle.

I ask Asia if I can take her photograph next to the grave, as I know this is something her grandparents would want to have, and she says, "Yes." I take the picture, then give her the camera and ask her to take one of me. I kneel next to the grave, place my hand on one of the stones, and remember a passage from the *Bhagavad-Gita* that I read in Jonathan's journal, which he had written during his first visit to the Himalayas.

"In this world we are all creatures of time. We and the objects of our love are only like pieces of wood that drift together for a time on the ocean flood and then part forever."

I know that in these words there is truth that should be for me, at this moment, a source of strength, but my strength leaves me, and a grief that feels like that ocean flood wells into my eyes. Asia sets the camera on a rock, comes over, and holds me.

"I don't know," I say. "I don't know. He's there, and I'm here. I don't know why he died and I didn't. We were more experienced than he was, but he paid the price for our mistake."

"He was doing what he loved, just like you," she says. "He was where he wanted to be, where he dreamed to be. Here, in Tibet."

I stand and Asia still has her arm around me.

"He knows you're taking good care of me," she says.

"Thanks," I say.

"He knows that you've been a father for me too, and a good friend to him."

Asia turns and we hug each other. I clear my eyes, and over her shoulder I look downvalley, toward the glacier and the moraine we followed this morning. The lower cloud layer is still rising. I turn and look toward the mountain. The upper clouds have begun to descend. There is the feel of rain or snow in the air. I straighten my shoulders, take a deep breath, and say again to myself, See things as they are.

"We need to think about getting down," I tell Asia.

We turn to leave, but before we start I place both my hands on Asia's shoulders, look her in the eyes, and say, "We've just been through a lot. I know you're shook up, and so am I. But we've got some down-climbing to do, and we need to be focused. So get all of this out of your head. All of it. Focus on each step and each handhold, okay?"

"Okay."

My hope is that from this higher vantage looking down I will be able to see an alternate descent that will avoid the steep rock we encountered on the way up. We traverse the ledge around the rock rib, and on the far side I stop and study the terrain. I can see that if we continue traversing there is another rock rib a hundred yards farther with another rounding ledge that looks as if it is marked with a cairn. I take the binoculars out of my pack and focus them. Sure enough, there is a stack of stones placed at the point where the ledge disappears round the corner. Did we build that cairn twenty years ago? I don't remember, but I head toward it, with Asia following a few feet behind. When we reach the cairn, I crane around the other side, then look back to Asia.

"It's a walk off. No down-climbing. We've got it in the bag."

We step down the scree in wide, easy strides, and in another hour we're near the top of the meadow, above our old Base Camp.

"Look there," I say pointing to the opposite hillside.

"What?"

"Next to that scree. I think it's a blue sheep."

I take out my binoculars and focus on the animal as it trots up the steep slope, then stops.

"It's a big ram, by himself."

His gray-blue pelage blends into the rocks, but I can still clearly see his large horns. I hand the binoculars to Asia and keep my naked eye on the spot where the blue sheep remains motionless. Asia is unable to make him out, however, and when she hands the binoculars back to me I focus on the spot where he was standing. Even though I have kept my eyes on the spot where he stopped—he is gone, vanished like a phantom.

It takes a few more minutes to descend to the meadow where we stop to eat lunch. We lie on a clump of grass, and I open a can of tuna and a package of crackers, then cut slices from a block of cheese. I am surprised by my sudden hunger, but then realize we have gone all day without eating. It must be about three in the afternoon. I build a small tuna-and-cheese hors d'oeuvre, hand it to Asia, then make one for myself.

"Asia, can I ask you something?"

"Yeah?"

"You don't have to answer. But were you okay that all of your father wasn't there?"

"Yeah, but what do you think happened to him?"

"I think it was griffons. Himalayan griffons, like the one we saw in the Aru."

"That's how he would have liked it," she says. "A Tibetan burial."

We're quiet for a moment while we eat our crackers.

"There's something else I haven't told you yet, but when I was holding your father in my lap I knew the second he died. The split second. I don't know if it was his soul or some kind of life force, but it was clear something left him. I saw it."

"There've been times on this trip when I thought I could feel his presence," Asia says. "When we reached that pass on the Kailas *khora* and I left the prayer flag for him. Also when we were climbing the mountain in the Aru. But I don't know for sure. If he is there, that's great. But maybe he just died and his remains decayed and trickled through the rocks into the water and washed out down to the Yangtze. If that's what happened, that's okay too."

I smile and make another cheese-and-tuna cracker for each of us. Asia thanks me, and again we sit quietly. As I chew my cracker I recall that day I hiked up to bury Jonathan, when I stopped to eat a snack and considered, as I chewed and swallowed, one peanut and one raisin at a time, the sustenance that the food was supplying to my body. The next day I sat in this same meadow on a rock only a hundred yards from here. It was lunchtime, and the others had gathered in the cooking area, cups and spoons in hand. I listened to the water in the small creek that flowed through camp as it purled over the rocks, watching it catch glints of sunlight. I remember how the air still held the residual cool of the evening. Near my feet a bee buzzed from wildflower to wildflower, and each small leg was weighted with a clump of pollen. I leaned back and closed my eyes, and felt the sun on my face, and I remember thinking, The sun feels good on my skin. Exquisitely and boundlessly good.

Now I look around and see the five-petal blossoms of the yellow cinquefoil, and slowly chew and swallow my cracker and hear again in my mind the water purling over the rocks and feel the sun on my face.

"I will strive to treat every day as though it were my only one," Jonathan wrote. "I have wasted many days, and no doubt I will waste more. But by experiencing and accepting the reality of the present, I can learn not to regret the past, nor to fear the future."

Sitting on that rock twenty years ago, I felt as if I had died and been reborn, and my life was starting anew. Now, lying on the grass in the same meadow, I remember how I watched high on Minya Konka a tendril of snow blow off the summit ridge as the air stirred to the warming day. The ridge was so white it seemed to belong to a world just formed, a world still waiting for color to be added. I stared at the glint of the sun off the meadow stream, the starbursts of light filling my vision. Then I looked up again, this time to the sky. It was a different sky, another sky that was fathomless blue—like the blue of open ocean—and everything below it was new and fresh—like the island I saw when I was nineteen years old.

"I will strive to live each day as though it were my only one," my friend wrote.

Sitting on that rock twenty years ago, I knew the wisdom in those words, even though I had yet to read them in his journal. Then as time passed, as my life grew more complex, I sometimes forgot those words, even though I told myself I never would. Even though I knew I owed it to him to use his wisdom to improve my life, and that way to bring value to the fact he had died while I had lived. Now I vow never again to let his wisdom be crowded aside, and for this I thank him for saving his biggest lesson for his last.

Then I turn to his daughter and ask her if she is ready to keep going.

"Yep," she says with a confident nod. "I'm ready."

Acknowledgments

Foremost I wish to thank Vincent Stanley for helping me edit the book, and for providing toward the end of the project warm fellowship in what otherwise can be a dishearteningly solitary endeavor. Similarly, Susie Caldwell, my longtime associate, and David Sobel, my editor at Henry Holt, provided crucial guidance. My agent, Susan Golumb, provided encouragement from the start.

I additionally wish to thank Susie Caldwell for helping me organize the expedition before we departed, and Jon Meisler for his assistance once Asia and I were in the field. I thank George Schaller for graciously sharing his field experience in the Chang Tang Plateau and for directing Asia and me to the fabulous Aru Basin. I acknowledge with sincere appreciation our journey's sponsors: Canon Inc. for their cameras, Kodak film, Kelty Pack Inc. (for their tents, sleeping bags, and adventure travel luggage), Tua Ski, Montrail Boots, Black Diamond climbing gear, Chukar Cherries food products, and Magellan navigational systems.

Mickie Butterbaugh provided valuable assistance typing and retyping the manuscript. Edgar Boyles, John Roskelley, and Gordon Wiltsie once more confirmed their friendship by allowing me to reproduce their photographs. Geri Wright sent me the original of Jonathan's photograph that I so cherish, and she demonstrated once more her support and friendship by photocopying Jonathan's journals so that Asia and I could read them during our journey. I furthermore want to thank Geri for her larger support backing her daughter's desire to go with me on a journey that was not without attendant hazards. Thank you, Asia, for proposing that we go on the journey, for being there every time it counted, and for learning to take the uncertain road with the uncertain destination.

Gretel Erlich, by reminding me to see things as they are, was more significant than she probably realizes in helping me achieve my goal of taking from this journey what it had to offer. My three children, Connor, Cameron, and Carissa, once again supported my decision to be away from home for a long spell, and my wife, Jennifer, also backed the decision. In addition to dedicating this book to Jennifer, I want to thank her for her wisdom, helping me distinguish over the years what is and is not a "matter of consequence." My final acknowledgment goes to Jonathan for, as I said at the close of this story, saving his biggest lesson for his last.

About the Author

Rick Ridgeway, one of the world's foremost mountaineers and adventurers, is known to many through his writing, photography, and filmmaking. His articles have appeared in numerous magazines, including *Outside* and *National Geographic,* and he is the author of four previous books, including *Seven Summits* and *Shadow of Kilimanjaro.* He lives with his wife and three children in Ojai, California.